Foreword by Professor Sir Co

C000282752

JESUS

THE SOCIAL ENTREPRENEUR

Understanding both His Entrepreneur
Mindset and Nature 'Miracles'

Emeritus Professor L Murray Gillin AM

Jesus the Social Entrepreneur
Understanding both his Entrepreneur Mindset and Nature 'Miracles'
© L. Murray Gillin 2021

ISBN: 978-1-922532-57-2 (Paperback)

 A catalogue record for this book is available from the National Library of Australia

Edited by: Ocean Reeve Publishing
Cover Design: Ocean Reeve Publishing
Design and Typeset: Ocean Reeve Publishing
Printed in Australia by Ocean Reeve Publishing and Clark & Mackay Printers

Published by L. Murray Gillin and Ocean Reeve Publishing
www.oceanreevepublishing.com

About the Author

Laurence Murray Gillin AM, FTSE, HonFIEAust

- Professor Emeritus of Entrepreneurship & Innovation, Swinburne University of Technology,
- Adjunct Professor, ECIC, University of Adelaide,
- Adjunct Professor, AGSE, Swinburne University of Technology,
- Chairman, Ausentrepreneurs Sans Frontieres Pty Ltd,
- Chair, Tabor Institute, Adelaide,
- DBus (Honoris Causa) Swinburne University of Technology,
- DPed (Honoris Causa) North Eastern USA,
- PhD (Cantab.) UK, BMetE, MEd, MEngSc (Melb).

During a career spanning sixty years, Murray worked in the fields of defence science and technology, as Defence Research Attaché in the Australian Embassy in Washington, USA, and Head of Laboratory Programs DSTO, and in education until 1998 as Dean of Engineering, Professor of Innovation and Entrepreneurship, and Pro Vice-Chancellor at Swinburne University of Technology. In 'retirement', Murray co-founded the Australian Graduate School of Entrepreneurship and was Director to 2009, was a by-fellow at Churchill College Cambridge 2004, and since 2011 teaches entrepreneurship classes for Pitcher Partners to 2021.

Over the same period, Murray has been a faith-based leader in church and community-based ventures contributing an entrepreneur mindset. He is currently chair of Australia's leading non-denominational Christian tertiary college.

Murray's unique contribution to entrepreneurship education goes well beyond adding an elective or concentration to an MBA program. He and his team demonstrated convincingly that a totally opportunity-focused and integrated real-world program produced much better applied learning results. Indeed, entrepreneurship behaviour can be learned. Murray is a fellow of the Academy of Technological Sciences and Engineering, and in 1997, was made a Member of the Order of Australia.

Murray holds the award for Inaugural Best Entrepreneurial Educator of the Year, is a life fellow of the Babson Kauffman Entrepreneurship Research Conference, and received a Lifetime Achievement Award from AGSE Entrepreneurship Research Exchange. He also has honorary doctorates from Northeastern University (USA) and Swinburne University of Technology for contributions to entrepreneurship, AGSE, and community.

Dedications

Team Gillin—my incredible group of PhD scholars committed to understanding entrepreneur mindset:

Lois Hazelton PhD
Frank LaPira PhD
Stephen Spring PhD
Janusz Tanas PhD

With expert contributions by:

Science Contributors:
—Em Professor William Tiller, PhD (Stamford University, USA)
—Dr Ranjit Thuraisingham PhD (Cambridge UK)

Intuition Contributors:
—Dr Raymond Bradley PhD (Columbia University, USA and New Zealand)
—Em Professor John Hayes PhD (Leeds University, UK)
—Dr Frank LaPira PhD (Swinburne University, Australia)

Theological—Jesus as 'fully' Man and 'Servant' Leader:
—Professor Bruce Ware, PhD (Fuller University, USA)
—Pastor Robert R. McLaughlin (Ordained in Houston, Texas, USA)

Personality of Jesus:
—Gayle Weinraub, MBTI(R) Certified Practitioner (Texas, USA)

Social Entrepreneurship:
—Dr Loris Gillin PhD (Swinburne University, Australia)
—Dr Lois Hazelton PhD (Adelaide University, Australia)

Testimonials

It is no surprise that Murray Gillin used his stay-at-home time during COVID-19 to craft a scholarly book that is a creative blending of religion and entrepreneurship. Gillin's insights come from his long history and leadership in entrepreneurship education and his strong Christian values and beliefs. Entrepreneurship scholars and religious believers will gain a new appreciation of Jesus as one of history's earliest social entrepreneurs. If that is one good thing that comes out of the Covid pandemic, it is Gillin's book.

—Professor Patricia McDougall-Covin,

Associate Dean Emeritus,

Kelly School of Business, Indiana University, USA.

Written while we were all examining our contributions to science, our professions, faith and family, during the greatest pandemic of the century, Gillin provides an argument that entrepreneurial spirit and faith are compatible. After all, each entrepreneur is required, like Jesus, to provide a leadership team that continues work into the future, to work miracles with decision-making and forecasting, and often is expected to walk on water. This book could be entitled: Jesus the Greatest Entrepreneur; and might be beneficial reading with St. Thomas Aquinas, Dr Francis Collins, Sir Colin Humphreys, and Dr William Tiller. Christian colleges with business schools requiring students to examine biblical analyses related to business could also benefit from this book.

—Dr. Kathleen A. McCormick,

PhD, RN, FAAN, FACMI, FHIMSS,

SciMInd, LLC., Principal/Owner.

Could there be a better image of love in action than Jesus as a social entrepreneur? Jesus is the world's greatest exemplar of love. Entrepreneurship epitomizes the importance of taking action to bring about change in society. By showing us, in this compelling and scholarly book, how love and entrepreneurial action came together in the person of Jesus, Murray Gillin has revealed the sacred heart of social entrepreneurship and why it matters in the world today.

—Professor Tom Lumpkin,

Michael F. Price Chair and Professor of Entrepreneurship,

Price College of Business, University of Oklahoma, USA.

Jesus the Social Entrepreneur—Understanding the Entrepreneur Mindset is a unique, but brilliant scholarly narrative, arguing with conviction, and an engineer's mind, that Jesus might in fact best be described as a social entrepreneur if he lived in modern times. Anyone who has an interest in the life of Jesus as both a deity, and a man, will be intrigued as the transactional, transformational, and transcendent events and opportunities are shown through the lens of opportunity, science, and entrepreneurship. This book will appeal to the religious enthusiast, the academic scholar, the evangelical entrepreneur, as definitely as a source for reference, reflection and a thoughtful personal response. A book for every professional's library.

—Dr. John Reynolds,

President and CEO, Los Angles Pacific University, USA.

This book breaks new ground. It ventures the reader into emerging understandings of entrepreneurship as a force for good in a world crying out for meaningful change. It shows the path to becoming and being an 'innovative social entrepreneur'. It does so in what can only be described as a pioneering way by integrating well-percolated insights from the domains of faith, academic research, and the cutting edge of modern science. The crowning act of the book lies in using Jesus as the ultimate example of the above, in a way that begs the reader to follow suit. An innovative and ground-breaking 'must read' for the thoughtful person of today desiring to make a meaningful difference for good in our world.

—Dr. Johan Roux,
President and CEO, Tabor College, Adelaide, Australia.

Prof. Murray Gillin has written a well-researched book full of information and insight about the social entrepreneurial mindset of Jesus. It challenges one to think afresh about Jesus in the Bible and the relevance of his life and message today. The Spirit connection that is necessary in exhibiting a true entrepreneur mindset and delivering real effective action is expounded very well in this book. Religious sceptics, biblical literalists and everyone in between will have much to think about after reading this book.

—Dr Ranjit Thuraisingham, Hon,
Research Fellow at University of Sydney.

This is a fascinating book. Emeritus Professor Gillin's unique contribution to entrepreneurship education has enabled him to achieve an incredible personal vision to apply an entrepreneurial ecosystem concept model to express a holistic view of Jesus as a social entrepreneur. The book compels the reader's attention by establishing evidence from the literature for both the existence of and behaviour of Jesus the man and successfully integrates 'body', 'soul', and 'spirit.' The book is a must-read for a broad audience, particularly scholars and students of entrepreneurship and entrepreneurial mindset.

—Professor Milé Terziovski,

PhD (Melb), MBA, MEng(Hons),

BEng(Hons), Dip. Mgmt., GAICD,

FIML Director Australian Graduate School of Entrepreneurship (AGSE) Swinburne University of Technology.

It has been my privilege, honour and pleasure to read the draft of Laurence Murray Gillin's new book, Jesus the Social Entrepreneur. There is much meat here to feed the souls not only of entrepreneurs, but also of anyone interested in Christianity and/or personality type. I found the descriptions of Jesus's and His disciples' personalities, and the scientific analysis of four of His miracles, to be among the book's highlights.

I've seen a number of books about Jesus's leadership style and what we can learn from it. Professor Gillin's book appears to be unique in its presentation of a well-supported argument that goes beyond being a powerful leader - Jesus can also teach us much as an exemplary social entrepreneur.

—Gayle Weinraub,

Certified Practitioner, MBTI (R) Personality Assessments and Truity Psychometrics LLC.

As members of 'Team Gillin' we add our appreciation of Murray as a wonderful teacher of 'entrepreneurship'. As his PhD students we were challenged by his understanding of this topic as he was at times tested by our different explorations of the topic. Together we all examined different contexts of business, industry, government and private sectors. We understand that opportunity can exist anywhere - recognise the opportunity, identify the need and turn it into an outcome valued by the user—true innovation. This is the real entrepreneur mindset that defines entrepreneurship. Our congratulations on publishing this book, a new and different examination of Jesus as social entrepreneur - sent to deliver the innovation message demonstrated thru a life of faith, teaching and service.' Proud members of Team Gillin.

—Dr Lois Hazelton; Dr Frank LaPira;
Dr Stephen Spring; and Dr Janusz Tanas.

Jesus Christ has been called a 'superstar' in contemporary music and on stage but never has he been called a social entrepreneur until this book, Jesus the Social Entrepreneur, was created by Emeritus Professor Murray Gillin. Murray takes a deep dive into the life of Jesus, asking the right questions, framing arguments to support the notion and exposing tensions where they exist. Using insights from research, his in-depth spiritual knowledge and academic capabilities in entrepreneurship, he applies scientific rigour to come to some mind-blowing conclusions.

Congratulations Murray on taking up the opportunity presented during the COVID pandemic under lockdown to produce a book that helps us make meaning of the world today and educates us all on how to create value for the benefit of people living in the 21st century.

—Leanne K Raven, FAICD,
Adjunct Associate Professor,
University of Sunshine Coast 2014-2019,
CEO Crohn's & Colitis Australia.

Contents

Foreword

This is a highly original and thought-provoking book. It is essentially in two parts, linked together. The first part argues that Jesus was a social entrepreneur; the second asks and answers some fundamental questions about how Jesus may have performed some key miracles, such as turning water into wine and walking on water.

I suspect that most people have never thought of Jesus as a social entrepreneur. What does Murray Gillin mean by the term? Murray is an international expert on entrepreneurship, and he is the Professor Emeritus of Entrepreneurship and Innovation at Swinburne University of Technology in Australia. Murray writes about Jesus not only through the lens of his experience in entrepreneurship but also from his deep Christian faith. He notes that entrepreneurship is not just about creating start-up businesses. The focus of the first part of his book is on what he calls 'social entrepreneurship', the use of innovative ideas to fundamentally change people and society. He argues powerfully that Jesus had an entrepreneurial mindset which changed individuals and society through a new relationship with God and which continues to change people 2,000 years later. He emphasises the importance of the Holy Spirit in this mindset. He states: 'Jesus was the greatest social entrepreneur of all time.'

I suggest that looking at Jesus from this new viewpoint gives us important fresh insights into his life and work. Let me select one such insight from this book. Murray argues that Jesus, prior to his baptism, was essentially a man growing up and maturing. During this period, the Bible does not record him performing any miracles. It was only after he was filled with the Spirit at his baptism and during his subsequent desert experience that his entrepreneurial mindset was developed, and he was energised by the Spirit to perform miracles.

The second part of the book is devoted to case studies of four 'nature miracles': the transfiguration of Jesus, turning water into wine, walking on water, and stilling the storm. There is a linking chapter between the two parts in which Murray discusses some profound questions, such as the nature of reality. He argues that there are two levels of reality: physical reality, including our five senses and, on another level, consciousness, mind, prayer, etc. Murray writes: 'Clearly, man's physical body functions together with the five senses, enables us to observe the facts and gather the data necessary for living. But there is more, much more that complements our perception and reality of what it is to be a human being (body, soul, and spirit).'

Murray's approach to nature miracles is based on the words of Augustine of Hippo: 'Miracles are not contrary to nature, but only contrary to what we know about nature.' He argues that Jesus used his enhanced powers and close personal relationship with the Holy Spirit to effect the observed nature miracles using the natural mechanisms of physics and chemistry. Murray emphasises that such a science-based explanation does not destroy the wonder and awe of the event: the wonder and awe is in the extraordinary timing.

This book asks big questions: What happens when we pray? How does God act in our world? How did Jesus perform miracles? Murray invokes cutting-edge science to answer these questions. Some of his ideas are controversial, so prepare to be intellectually challenged.

Let me end by quoting from the final paragraph of this book.

In no way does the science explanation [of the nature miracles of Jesus] destroy the wonder and awe of the observed event. Indeed, the wonder and awe experienced by witnesses of the events were substantial, just as we today can stand back in awe at the wonder of created man having the capacity to deliver change through a practising spiritual means. Of particular significance is in the timing of the event so that the 'miraculous' observation occurs at exactly the time and place it is required.

Most books are read and then quickly forgotten. But not this one. It is a pleasure to commend this memorable book to you.

Colin Humphreys
Professor of Materials Science,
Queen Mary University of London
Distinguished Research Fellow, University of Cambridge Fellow, Selwyn College, Cambridge.

Acknowledgements

It may be ironic, but I first acknowledge the reality of the COVID-19 pandemic lockdown and its contribution to my continuing stay-at-home situation. With this uninterrupted and unique experience, I took the opportunity to review and share my thinking and conclusions concerning Jesus as a social entrepreneur. But without the encouragement of all those I acknowledge below, no manuscript would have evolved to a book edition. In seeking to develop this opportunity, and in the true spirit of entrepreneurship, I reached out to my colleagues as the 'team' in this exercise and sought their knowledge as the complimentary resources to complete the social opportunity process model for assessing *Jesus the Social Entrepreneur*.

It is a pleasure to acknowledge the many colleagues comprising the team, whose wide range of expertise and willing participation have helped me consider a wide-ranging canvas to the content of the book. The evidence-based approach used in this book derives from my respect and friendship with Professor Sir Colin Humphreys and his two published contributions, *The Miracles of the Exodus* and *The Mystery of the Last Supper,* in understanding the science and meaning of nature miracles.

As fellow materials scientists, we have regularly shared in his research during many visits to Cambridge, and I have valued his recent contributions to the subject of this book. I express my sense of honour by having Sir Colin write the outstanding foreword to the book.

Another materials scientist, Emeritus Professor Dr William Tiller, who I first met in 1968, has, over the years, shared his trailblazing research into the power of human intention and consciousness in understanding how intention can influence reality. Dr Tiller is now in his nineties, and I acknowledge his encouragement for me to apply his theories and experiments in interpreting the nature miracles of Jesus.[1]

Given my lack of credibility to interpret the concept of 'Jesus the man', I very much appreciate and acknowledge permission from Bruce A Ware, Coleman Professor of Christian Theology at the Southern Baptist Theological Seminary, to quote, at length, from his scholarly book *The Man Christ Jesus: Theological Reflections on the Humanity of Christ*. I am also indebted to Pastor Robert R McLaughlin to use his insights and leadership assessment of the Twelve Apostles in appendix 6.1.

Some outstanding scholars and practitioners have read draft chapters and helped me greatly. They include Prof Patricia McDougall-Covin, Associate Dean Emeritus, Kelly School of Business, Indiana University, and expert in social entrepreneurship; Dr Kathleen McCormick, a highly awarded senior practitioner, researcher, and policy executive in nursing, health informatics, bioinformatics, and gerontology with experience in dealing with 'wicked' problems; Dr Johan Roux, President and CEO of Tabor College with expertise in theology and teaching Kingdom principles; Dr John Reynolds, President and CEO of LAPU (Los Angles Pacific University) with expertise in online learning, academic entrepreneurship and innovation.

In addition, I have valued the professional experience and spiritual insights of: Gayle Weinraub, Certified Practitioner, MBTI (R) Personality Assessments and permission to include

1 Text and diagrams © Dr. William A. Tiller 2009. Used with permission throughout book.

her blog on 'human behaviour of Jesus and published by Truity Psychometrics LLC; Dr Ranjit A. Thuraisingham on quantum entanglement of prayer and his permission to include the article in appendix 7.4; Dr Ray Bradley for our many discussions on non-local intuition and permission to include his article on quantum coherence in appendix 7.5; and the important contribution made by Professors Christopher Allinson and John Hayes for developing the Cognitive Style Index (CSI) to better assess intuitive decision-making—the index is reproduced in appendix 4.1.[2]

My wife, Dr Loris Gillin, with experience in not-for-profit faith-based missions, has strongly encouraged me in this project. I both acknowledge her support and the provision of the 'social entrepreneurship index' instrument for use in this project, together with the 'enablement effectiveness model for social entrepreneurship ventures'.

Important to the completion of this project has been the involvement of the members of 'Team Gillin' comprising Dr Lois Hazelton, Dr Frank LaPira, Dr Stephen Spring, and Dr Janusz Tanas. This self-formed team of loyal and dedicated PhD graduates are all committed to enhancing and understanding entrepreneurial behaviour through integrating intellectual, emotional, and spiritual intelligence into a theory of entrepreneur mindset. I acknowledge their encouragement and commitment to this venture. In addition, their personal contributions to assessing the perceived entrepreneur behaviours of Jesus— in evaluating opportunities and in estimating His 'decision-making propensity' index and reviewing some chapters—was very professional and appreciated.

Also acknowledged are the agreements to use specific entrepreneur performance instruments in the book. Dr Lois

2 C.W. Allinson & J. Hayes 1996. All rights reserved.

Hazelton contributed to the 'entrepreneur mindset audit', Dr Frank LaPira the adaptation of the 'cognitive style index' to entrepreneur behaviour, and Dr Stephen Spring the 'dimensions of opportunity recognition'.

The colleagues I have acknowledged above may well not agree with all the contents (and some have probably been too polite to say!) I am extremely grateful to all of them for the time and effort they have spent in helping me to write this book.

Significantly, to the printed reality of this book, has been the creative, professional, and dedicated support of the editorial team at Ocean Reeve Publishing. I enthusiastically convey my deep gratitude to Sarah Hill, Kristy Martin, Jason Smith, Joshua Clifton, and Mikayla Harmon for their courtesy, encouragement, and inspiration to complete the process.

Finally, I honour the memory of my mother, Vi, who, single handedly, introduced me to the joy of learning and encouraged me to identify opportunities and go on to make them happen. This foundation is fully realised in this book.

THANK YOU

Preface

Entrepreneurship—a very 'in vogue' topic, especially at a time of seeking the way out of the COVID-19 crisis. Much emphasis has been placed on the health and economic factors impacting our recovery, including new vaccines and job-creating businesses. Significantly, it will be entrepreneurs who recognise these opportunities and deliver new and necessary products and services that are designed to add value and purpose to our way of life. Entrepreneurship infused with effective innovation will drive our recovery.

Another side of entrepreneurship, which is the focus of this book, is the concept and delivery of social entrepreneurship to meet the needs of the 'whole' person and with values raising both the personal and spiritual wellbeing of the community. In this paradigm, a social entrepreneur is a person who pursues novel applications (innovative ideas) that have the potential to solve community-based problems. These individuals are willing to take on the risk and effort to create positive changes in society through their initiatives.

Given the forced lockdown by governments as a result of the COVID-19, and severe restrictions on both domestic and international travel, a fresh opportunity presented itself to review and consider the possibility that Jesus the man, both in His thinking and His actions, could be described as an innovative social entrepreneur.

How so? It can be argued that the situation in first-century Judea and Palestine was similar to that of today. The social compact was strained to crisis point and characterised by exploitation, violence, poverty, and spiritual segregation. Jesus identified this crisis in human and spiritual values, recognised the downside of this condition and preached a new way to follow—one not based simply on the past, but rather by radically reinterpreting previous ideas as a way of reframing the future. Jesus identified several opportunities, delivered as innovations, so the followers could participate in a fuller and more meaningful life. His leadership demonstrated true innovation in practice. I have summarised Jesus' entrepreneurial opportunity as to *'change societal values and behaviours through a new relationship with God.'*

This reality lies close to my own heart. From a lifetime focus of seeking to recognise opportunities—in the world around me; in my careers; and with a passion and commitment to making opportunities happen—I now seek to apply an evaluation of the evidence for Jesus exhibiting an 'entrepreneur mindset' to deliver real change.

Being informed by my Christian faith, experience as a research materials engineer, an academic, entrepreneurship teacher, and innovation practitioner, I recognised that entrepreneurship was not simply about business creation. Successful entrepreneurs are characterised by a unique mindset. This is a human mindset that integrates intellectual, emotional, and spiritual (not religious) intelligence in seeking to deliver added value as perceived by the user of the innovation. So, again, the question arises: was Jesus, as he lived on this earth over two thousand years ago, a social entrepreneur, utilising all the principles we today consider foundational to an entrepreneur mindset?

Principally, I was convinced that Jesus did not act like a 'sorcerer' (to use the words of Josephus the Jewish historian) but in all respects as a 'man', albeit in a relationship with God the father. It is a bit like a marriage—we are in a relationship with a significant other, which affects our behaviour, but it does not take away from our personal and individual responsibilities for our behaviours.

To address the overall question—was Jesus a social entrepreneur who delivered valued outcomes for his followers?—this book seeks to evaluate five areas of thought:

In part 1:

1. An understanding of the life and times of first-century-CE Judea and Galilee.
2. The development of Jesus the man and His approach to fulfilling His mission by making opportunities happen.
3. Demonstrate how his entrepreneur mindset facilitated effective innovations both in the first century CE and over the centuries until now.

In part 2:

1. Consider new concepts and understandings of the created world (physical and spiritual) to explain selected 'miracles' attributed to Jesus.
2. Propose how Jesus used his entrepreneur mindset, non-linear intuition, and focused human intention to influence physical reality.

Chapter 1 introduces first-century-CE Judea and Galilee in terms of political, economic, and cultural factors that are relevant to our consideration of Jesus growing up and then leading a mission to the people of the area.

Significant to the premise that Jesus can be described as a social entrepreneur exhibiting an entrepreneur mindset is the acceptance Jesus was born a man—a human being—using all the holistic aspects of being human in body, soul, and spirit. Chapter 2 establishes and expands the fact that 'Jesus is fully man'.

Chapter 3 seeks to establish the relevance and linkages between social and commercial entrepreneurship using the concept and principles of entrepreneur mindset. Fundamentally, this concept involves reallocating resources to a new use (both/or material and social) that produces a preferred outcome in line with market and user needs/demands. Thus, entrepreneurship is a planned behaviour. It is not the product of unconscious and unintended antecedents, but rather is a 'conscious and intended act' that is 'aimed either at creating a new venture or creating new values in existing ventures.'[3]

Before considering Jesus' life and mission from an entrepreneurial perspective, the concept of an entrepreneurial ecosystem is explored to put into context Jesus' life experiences and the resulting world impact from His ministry. Using the definition for social entrepreneurship and a model of entrepreneur mindset, the chapter addresses the question as to whether Jesus and a social entrepreneur mindset are compatible concepts. It is concluded that Jesus the man and an entrepreneur mindset are interconnected realities in which to assess both the innovation outcomes encompassed within the ministry of Jesus and the identified opportunity—to 'change societal values and behaviours through a new relationship with God.'

---

3 Donald Kuratko and David Audretsch 2009, 'Strategic Entrepreneurship: Exploring Different Perspectives of an Emerging Concept', Entrepreneurship Theory and Practice, Vol 33, Issue 1.

Chapters 4 and 5 are designed to separate the importance of the period of Jesus' 'formation' (0–30 years of age) and His 'ministry' (30–33 years of age). This arrangement is founded on a personal belief that leading to the baptism of Jesus (end of formation years) and culminating with 'the Spirit of God descending like a dove and alighting on Him', and prior to His forty days in the wilderness communing with God, Jesus functioned and experienced what it was to live as a 'man', even though He knew inwardly where He came from.

The premise is that in the desert experience, Jesus fully comprehended the significance and power of access to the Holy Spirit and hence the purpose of ministry. Significantly, I am suggesting there is a 'spirit' connection between exhibiting a true entrepreneur mindset and delivering the actions necessary to effectively make the opportunity a reality. It will be shown that this connectivity within the conscious mind of the entrepreneur is the inner characteristic of 'spirit' which is identified within the dimension of 'awareness'. Furthermore, it will be argued through the expounding of four 'miracle' case studies and that it is this same 'spirit' that provided the energy for Jesus' reported behaviour.

Both Chapters 4 and 5 describe validated instruments designed to 'measure' cognitive style in entrepreneur decision-making, screening potential for mission opportunity, a social entrepreneur index, and an entrepreneur mindset audit. For each instrument, a number of practising entrepreneurs with awareness of the Jesus story answered the instrument's questions from their perceptions of Jesus' recorded behaviour style.

An important corollary to entrepreneurial behaviour is the performance of the mission team in relation to: (1) the entrepreneur/leader; (2) team development; and (3) team member commitment and attitudes. Chapter 6 provides an assessment of the leadership team using an understanding of current concepts and practices.

Having examined the contribution of 'entrepreneur mindset' to Jesus' leadership of the mission to the peoples of Judea and Galilee, Chapter 7 (opening part 2) changes the direction of the book by seeking to better understand the concept of 'being made in the image of God' and how such insight may impact the integration of intellectual intelligence (IQ), emotional intelligence (EI), and spiritual intelligence (SI) into a recognisable and practised entrepreneur mindset. Using the deep understanding of Professor William Tiller and his work on the possibility that human consciousness might meaningfully influence physical matter, Chapter 7 seeks to build a bridge between science and spirit. Consideration is given to Tiller's many experiments and applied mathematics in demonstrating the reality of human capacity to interact between what we know as physical space (emphasising the five senses) and that of reciprocal space (the mirror image emphasising the human consciousness). This ground-breaking research seeks to 'seamlessly join the foundations of traditional science on one end, and extend through the domains of psyche, emotion, and mind so it is firmly planted in the bedrock of Spirit at the other end.'[4] Tiller demonstrates the fundamental role of prayer, meditation, and commitment in reaching a spirit-directed state where the formalised human 'intention' can influence material change in physical space.

The final four chapters, 8 to 11, examine cases in Jesus' ministry associated with a miracle where the reported outcome would involve physical change to material properties of matter. The hypothesis examined in each case is that 'Jesus used His

---

4 William A. Tiller and Walter E. Dibble, 2001, 'Conscious Acts of Creation: The Emergence of a New Physics' Walnut Creek, CA, Pavior.

enhanced powers of human intention, interconnectedness, and close personal relationship with God the Holy Spirit to effect the observed "miracle" using the natural mechanisms of physics and science.' This description of a 'miracle' concords with Augustine (Bishop of Hippo) 354–430 who said, 'Miracles are not contrary to nature, but only contrary of what we know about nature.'

Based on the science theory developed by Tiller, his physical experiments to demonstrate the 'power' of 'intention'; the Gospel texts; and eyewitness accounts of the disciples, Catholic saints, and other recent confirmed observations; it is reasonable to consider (or believe) that 'spirit'-powered actions, such as human intentions, can influence the outcome results.

'Final Reflections' seeks to harmonise the social entrepreneurship behaviour of Jesus, as discussed in Chapters 1 to 6, with the observed spiritual characteristics identified in the 'nature' miracles described in Chapters 8 to 11 by using the principles identified and discussed in Chapter 7—'Bridging Science and Spirit.' These final reflections provide a rationale for claiming the observed behaviour of 'entrepreneur mindset' in social entrepreneurs relies on well-developed connectivity between the entrepreneur's body, soul, and spirit, or one's IQ, EI, and SI.

Part 1

Chapter 1: Introduction to the First Century CE

The destiny of mankind is not decided by material computation. When great causes are on the move in the world, stirring all men's souls, drawing them from their firesides, casting aside comfort, wealth, and the pursuit of happiness in response to impulses at once awe-striking and irresistible, we learn that we are spirits, not animals, and that something is going on in space and time, and beyond space and time, which, whether we like it or not, spells duty. [5]

—Winston Churchill

Introduction to the first century CE

Discussion in today's world is often focused on terrorism, climate change and, as of now, the COVID-19 pandemic. These can be characterised as times of crisis with no simple or single solution. They are what can be identified as 'wicked' problems—a situation in which no single or linear solution is the answer and where the perception of the actual problem is really the symptom of another multi-dimension problem or problems. As such, 'wicked problems are characterised as malign, vicious, tricky and aggressive.'[6]

---

5 Winston Churchill, 'Birth Throes of a Sublime Resolve,' broadcast 16 June 1941.
6 Jeff Conklin, 2005, 'Wicked Problems and Social Complexity' from Chapter 1 in the book *'Dialogue Mapping: Building Shared Understanding of Wicked Problems,'* John Wiley & Sons.

Indeed, such crises are closely associated with 'people' problems as experienced in national behaviours associated with human and societal culture, ideology, and personal self-interest. Usually, the media paints a very depressing prognosis but, to get to the other side, these 'wicked problems' provide a platform for recognising and evaluating opportunities to offset the debilitating downside. This reality was well-stated in *The Australian* newspaper on 4 April 2020:

> *The abnormal is Australia's new normal, but only for a while. What is more important is that the nation in the fullness of its social, economic, and spiritual life does not revert post-crisis to the old pre-2020 politics. The past cannot be fully restored and that creates a new opportunity—to reinvent and improve upon the past.*
>
> *This might sound a useless polemic. Except that what is now happening, day after day, is the most radical and fastest public policy revamp across the social and economic landscape Australia has seen since World War II. It is a real crisis, and that spells a golden opportunity.*
>
> *This emergency revamp is being done on the basis of a social compact. There is a new spirit of concord. The crisis has transformed awareness of our interdependence as a community. We realise, as never before, how much society and the economy need each other, rather than being enemies.*[7]

It can be argued that the situation in first-century Judea and Palestine showed that the social compact was strained to crisis

---

[7] Paul Kelly, 2020, 'Team Australia' our new normal, for now', The Weekend Australian 04/04/2020.

point and characterised by exploitation, violence, poverty, and spiritual segregation. Jesus identified this crisis in human and spiritual values, recognised the downside of this condition, and preached a new way to follow—one not based on the past, but rather radically reinterpreting previous ideas as a way of reframing into the future. Jesus identified a number of opportunities, delivered as innovations, so the followers could participate in a fuller and more meaningful life. Based on Jesus the 'man', His actions, His leadership, and inspiration, we will explore Jesus' ministry from the perspective of an entrepreneur.

Opportunity and Need in Meeting the 'Wicked' Problems of Aging

Back to the crisis of our times that begs for new ways forward. A good example of the conundrum is that of 'aging'. Indeed, the aging of the population and care of the elderly is an excellent example of a 'wicked' problem in which the personal reality of aging awaits us all and we will need both understanding and outside facilitation to get us through the experience. As with many such issues, this massive societal challenge represents a growing opportunity for alert social entrepreneurs who recognise opportunities to bring about change and solutions to problems that will be valued by potential users. Together with investors and colleagues committed to achieving such outcomes and minimising the destructive impact of crises on life and the environment, alert entrepreneurs support these new projects, products, and processes that demonstrate the human capacity for continual innovation.

Individuals, as they age, have always been concerned about the 'who, what, where, why and how' of their future. Families and significant others have become increasingly concerned with the quality of aged care services at all levels: decision-making, access to quality services, and bedside care are three such areas of concern. Elderly care is a major industry that consists of many components to make a functioning whole, and we will continue to face challenges as the baby boomers retire.

There are close to two million Australians over the age of seventy and the number is set to double in the next twenty years. Between 2010 and 2020 we will see, for the first time in history, people over sixty-five outnumbering children under five.[8]

Given advances in health care, specifically disease control, humans are living longer. In 1903 in the USA, for example, 15% of white women lived to the age of approximately eighty; but today close to 70% of white women live to be eighty years old.

In 2017, 15% of Australians (3.8 million) were aged 65 and over; more than half of older people (57%, or 2.2 million) were aged 65–74, one-third were aged 75–84 (30%, or 1.2 million), and 13% were aged 85 and over (497,000). By 2047, people aged 75–84 will account for 35% (2.6 million) of the population and 1 in 5 older people will be aged 85 and over (20%, or 1.5 million).[9]

This aging population creates significant challenges for society. Pensions and retirement incomes will need to last longer. Healthcare costs are likely to increase. The service economy will capture an increasing percentage of GDP as the elderly require more help from services as opposed to products. Also, consider that the workforce pays for many social benefits of the elderly. As the population ages, there are fewer taxpayers supporting

8 Hazelton and Gillin 2017, 'From Compliance Culture in Elder care to Resident Focus Innovation as Social Entrepreneurship – A Global Opportunity'. In Campbell C.L. (eds) The Customer is NOT Always Right? *Marketing Orientations in a Dynamic Business World. Developments in Marketing Science: Proceedings of the Academy of Marketing Science.* Springer.

9 Australian Institute of Health and Welfare, 2018, https://www.aihw.gov.au/reports/australias-health/australias-health-2018/.

the growing number of non-working retirees. But in addition to these tangible issues are the intangibles such as the emotional and physical sides of aging. The aging of the population creates challenges socially and economically, yet there are also issues related to human rights and the effectiveness of care. This crisis will not be solved by regulation or a linear approach to care processes or procedures; such change that brings innovative outcomes will depend on new and creative opportunities being recognised, developed, and implemented.

Jesus' Scenario

Now compare this example of aging with the situation in Jesus' time. This provides a fascinating insight into the way Jesus observed and experienced the dire need of the Judean-Palestinian peoples living in CE 29–33.[10] Palestine was under occupation from the Roman empire, subject to great restrictions on social interaction and life as a whole and produced a cultural experience amongst all levels of society of despair, fear, and hopelessness.

It was a problem that Jesus identified as a human crisis and, specifically, an opportunity to challenge the human condition with a solution of delivering a new personal relationship with, and a spiritual or life-changing connection to, God as a new covenant (Luke 22: 20), replacing the old legal covenant God established with Moses.

Jesus identified and characterised this crisis as a problem of both personal and societal 'sinfulness' requiring a new solution. Jesus identified this opportunity as the need to 'change societal values and behaviours through a new relationship with God. His pursuit, passion, leadership and delivery of the solution was

10 Colin Humphreys, 1995, 'Star of Bethlehem' Science and Christian Belief , Vol 5, (October): 83–101.

valued and implemented by his followers.' This example fully complies with the definition of entrepreneurial behaviour and entrepreneur mindset:

Entrepreneurship is essentially creating or identifying an opportunity in answer to an identified need, pursuing it with passion (i.e., 'make it happen') using tangible resources you do not currently control, and—critically—deliver an outcome valued by a real 'user'.[11]

Making possible a new personal relationship with, and a spiritual/life-changing connection to, God was the real innovation. It did not stop there because Jesus also brought a new way of life, making possible an alternate reality to living in a personal relationship with God. The fulfilment of this ministry provides a fascinating insight into the way Jesus observed and experienced the dire need of the Judean-Palestinian people living in CE 29–33 and delivered on these identified opportunities to be valued outcomes accepted by the people.

To better understand this first-century-CE Judaeo-Christian worldview, the activity of Jesus, the early Jesus movement in Galilee, and the potential opportunities for possible innovations, it is essential to know the social and economic context where He and His followers lived, worshipped, and worked. An ecosystem concept model, as shown in Figure 1.1, broadens our appreciation of the lifestyle, survival pressures, political, economic, social, cultural, and power structures and world forces present at the time of Jesus' life and ministry in Judea-Palestine.

By keeping a focus on the 'worship-centred living' perspective at the micro level and the 'power' perspective at the meso level,

---

11 Gillin, 1998, adapted from Howard Stevenson, 1983, 'A perspective on entrepreneurship', Harvard Business School Working Paper, 9-384-131.

it is possible to relate these levels holistically with the remaining macro and mega levels of the Judaeo-Christian ecosystem.

In later chapters, this introduction will provide a platform to enable the identification of a number of opportunities and practice innovations used by Jesus in His ministry between CE 29–33.

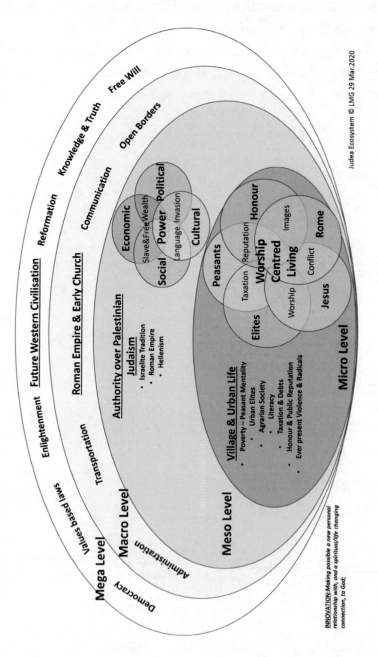

Figure 1.1 First-century-CE Judaeo-Christian Ecosystem

Consideration of the ecosystem in Fig. 1.1 provides a holistic view of the importance of the political, social, theological, and economic forces impacting our behaviours and awareness of reality. Such a reality emphasises the importance of access to available resources, both material and human, in achieving success and impact on our contribution to personal and community life. In this book, I will refer to such assessments as 'value-based' needs or outcomes. Such a framework will provide the scenario to better understand the society into which Jesus comes as a social entrepreneur.

In developing this ecosystem, I have reviewed literary and scholarly sources to assess the value-based propositions that inform the characteristics used to construct each of the four levels. One primary source is Flavius Josephus (Jewish historian), writing in the first century and essential for seeking to reconstruct the world of Judaism into which Jesus was born.

However, this reconstructive perspective is considered by some scholars as 'a very incomplete glimpse of the political and economic character of the Galilee and his account is both tendentious and self-serving.'[12] Of particular significance is the comment that 'inequality' was typical of all societies at this time.

The obvious difficulty with the city-state as a community, with its stress on mutual sharing of both burdens and benefits, was the hard fact that its members were unequal. The most troublesome inequality was not between town and country, not between classes, but simply between rich and poor.[13]

---

12 Sakari Häkkinen, 2016, 'Poverty in the first-century Galilee', https://www.researchgate.net/publication/309254500_Poverty_in_the_first-century_Galilee.
13 Douglass E Oakman, 2008, 'Jesus and the Peasants', https://www.academia.edu/3079887/Oakman_D_E_2008_Jesus_and_the_peasants_Cascade_Books_Eugene_Matrix_The_Bible_in_Mediterranean_context_.

Micro Level of First-Century Judaeo-Christian Ecosystem

This state of inequality was endemic across all levels of the ecosystem. In respect of the micro level in relation to village and urban life, the rich were generally elite families known as 'urban elite' composed of the rulers and governing class, including local administration officials. Within the province of Judea, the priestly class—Pharisees and Sadducees—with their families and King Herod and his extended family network would be considered of elite or privileged status. The poor, in the statement above, refers particularly to those identified as having a 'peasant' mentality within the extant peasant society. The definition of a peasant is:

> A peasantry is a rural population, usually including those not directly engaged in tilling the soil, who are compelled to give up their agricultural (or other economic) surplus to a separate group of power holders and who usually have certain cultural characteristics setting them apart from outsiders. Generally speaking, peasants have very little control over their political and economic situation. In Mediterranean antiquity, the overlords of the peasants tended to be city dwellers, and a culture-chasm divided the literate elite from the unlettered villager.[14]

Urban Elites and Peasants

In relation to the urban elite, they perceived and treated the peasants as one mass of the population by creating client-patron relationships that provided the elite with honour and status to exercise political power and wealth.

It has been estimated that only 10%–15% of the provincial population lived in cities that had more than 10,000 inhabitants, with 80%–90% primarily peasants obtaining their living from agriculture. Only a few would be involved in manufacturing activity as we know it today. In such an agrarian society, wealth was based on land ownership like the feudal system of later English practice. The peasants lived mainly in villages that surrounded a city and were exploited by elites extracting agricultural surpluses through taxes and rents. Any so-called benefits provided to the villages were generally supplied as cultic services and administration.[14]

In the New Testament accounts of Jesus' ministry, much emphasis is given to dealings with the poor in response to observed needs. Jesus and his disciples certainly perceived the presence and terrible consequences of poverty and often responded with life-changing outcomes. It is appropriate to further examine who are the poor?

Linguistically, classical Greek (the text of the New Testament (NT)) writings contain two expressions that represent 'poor', πτωχός, representing the destitute beggar/bankrupt, and πένης, the 'working' poor.[14] Nevertheless, scholars have shown that the NT and other later Greek literature tend to use the two terms freely, not restricting them to the classical definitions. Indeed, the vast majority of poor in the NT are πτωχός; the other form, πένης, is rarely found. 'Lazarus the beggar' is an example of the most destitute poor.

In order to understand the attitude of Palestinian-Jewish sources towards poverty, I quote directly:

---

14 M. I. Finley, 1999 'Ancient History – Evidence and Models', https://www.amazon.com/Ancient-History-Evidence-M-Finley/dp/1597400432#reader_1597400432.

It is necessary to be aware of the biblical basis for this attitude, which influenced the sources of the Roman era. The Bible related at length to the poor, for example, in giving them easier conditions to fulfil their obligations toward the Temple. People are warned against taking advantage of the poor or doing them an injustice. In addition, the Bible instructs the people to give special consideration to the poor in monetary assistance, charitable aid, loans, and tithes from the fields. Tithes given to the poor were from agricultural produce: wheat, grapes and olives, which constituted the staple crops in Palestine at the time. The method of allocation to the poor commanded by the Bible was unique. The owner was obligated to leave a corner of his field not harvested.

And there was a certain beggar named Lazarus (Luke 16:20), which was laid at his gate, full of sores, and desiring to be fed with the crumbs which fell from the rich man's table: moreover, the dogs came and licked his sores. This is definitely someone who owned absolutely nothing of his own. On the other hand we read: 'And there came a certain poor widow, and she threw in two mites, which make a farthing.' This woman was 'poor' but had coins to put into the 'treasury' and it is likely that she also had food in her home as well. Here, there are two categories of 'poor': the indigent and the destitute. The destitute are helpless and rely entirely on the generosity of others for their very survival, while the indigent are trying to work and struggle to subsist, but are not able to earn enough to make ends meet. In the NT, Jesus is presented as preaching that one must care for the poor. He instructs his disciples to divide all their belongings amongst the poor. Further, he recommends inviting the poor to communal meals rather than inviting the rich. On the other hand, there is a stark difference between his attitude to illness and handicap, which he promises to cure, and his attitude to the poor, to whom he offers a portion in the 'Kingdom of God.' According to NT sources, in his judgment, money is unimportant; he therefore does not propose a superior social system that would resolve their immediate need for sustenance. He demands total devotion to the poor and sick and transfer of any surplus to them rather than accumulating wealth. In the NT, Jesus is quoted instructing his disciples to give to the poor. However, he does not preach the establishment of a relief organization for helping the poor. ... Jesus's disciples create public relief and care for the poor. Approximately three generations after the beginning of Christianity, that is, at the beginning of the second century CE, there exist nascent public organizations for relief of the poor in Egypt and in Asia Minor. This phenomenon quickly burgeons in the second century and encompasses Christian communities throughout the world.[15]

From another perspective in relation to contemporary Jewish religious practice, rabbinic sources both recognised and distinguished between various poor populations used this differentiation for social organisational purposes.[14] Such social awareness amongst the Jewish leadership in Judea and Palestine at the time of Jesus indicates how traditional Jewish laws and practices would influence His ministry to the poor.

---

15 Ben Z Rosenfeld & Haim Perlmutter, 2020, 'Middle Groups in Jewish Roman Galilee and Jesus and his Disciples' Social Location: New Insights', https://bibleinterp.arizona.edu/articles/middle-groups-jewish-roman-galilee-and-jesus-and-his-disciples-social-location-new.

Rabbinic literature defines five prototypes of 'poor'. Four kinds of poor are defined primarily because of the help to which they are entitled from society. The homeless person receives from the community an allocation of food for basic survival. The destitute person who does not have the bare necessities is entitled to a daily dole from the *tamchui* of the community, as well as the *kupah*—charity collected and distributed by the community. In slightly better condition than the destitute person is the poor man, who is not starving but lacks basic needs. This person is entitled to community support from the *kupah*. One step higher is the man who 'does not have 200 *zuz*,' or 'does not have 50 *zuz* to purchase merchandise,' if he is a merchant. This person has the financial resources not to need help from the community, but he may partake in the tithes allocated to the poor in the field.

Living Traditions and Jewish Culture

In Figure 1.1 (on page 10), at the micro level, the Jewish people of the first century CE practised 'worship-centred living', which, according to Jewish laws, meant taking part in a culturally aware or living tradition. Judaism, as the Jewish religion came to be known in the first century CE, was based on ancient Israelite religion, shorn of many of its Canaanite characteristics but with the addition of important features from Babylonia and Persia. The Jews differed from the Romans and other people in the ancient world because they believed that there was only one God. Like other people, they worshipped their God with animal sacrifices offered at a temple, but, unlike others, they had only one temple, which was in Jerusalem. The Jews also believed that they had been specially chosen by the one God of the universe to serve Him and obey His laws.[16]

In this review of first-century life and practice, variety and commonality are equally important to the understanding of Palestinian Judaism in Jesus' day. Jews agreed on many basic aspects of their religion and way of life, and they agreed that they did not want to surrender their covenant with God to accept the lure of pagan culture, but when it came to details, they could disagree with one another violently. Since God cared about every aspect of life, competing groups and leaders often saw themselves as representing the side of God against his adversaries. Such events can be observed that resulted in violence.

This Jewish religious/cultural identity depends on how one characterises first-century-CE Judaism, which is especially difficult since Judaism in Palestine was highly diverse and included many sects. One may point to certain basic practices that are uniquely Jewish; for example, circumcision, Sabbath observance, avoidance of pork, and the worship of one invisible God.[16] Sanders's description of a 'common Judaism' is highly useful as he focuses on 'a pattern of religion' that includes both practice and basic beliefs, importantly about God's grace and the covenant upon which Torah observance is based. His starting point is to find what 'the priests and the people would agree upon', that is, 'common' Judaism, which was in a sense also normative since it was shared by the majority of the people.[17]

This common Jewish practice was widespread and particularly in villages where Jesus practised His ministry from 29–33 CE. This worship in both temple and synagogue included

---

16 Cecelia Wasson, 2016, 'The Jewishness of Jesus and ritual purity' https://www.researchgate.net/publication/326888106_The_Jewishness_of_Jesus_and_ritual_purity.

17 E. P. Sanders 2016, 'Judaism: Practice and Belief, 63BCE-66 CE' https://www.amazon.com/Judaism-Practice-Belief-63BCE-66-CE/dp/1506406106.

supporting the temple (paying temple tax, making offerings, etc.), keeping the Sabbath, attending synagogue, circumcision, purity observations, and diet.[13] The last five practices, in particular, serve as identity markers of Jews, while 'details of Sabbath and purity practices also identify different groups within Judaism'.[18]

Of particular note is the prominence of the Torah in synagogue services, demonstrating it is founded on a covenantal theology. This practice would, ipso facto, suggest first-century Jews attended such regular services. Indeed, the NT writers comment Jesus taught and 'proclaimed the good news' in synagogues 'throughout all Galilee'.

Indeed, such synagogues have been identified, and in 2019, Mordechai Aviam and R Steven Notley identified the Jewish fishing village of Bethsaida on the banks of Lake Galilee. In addition, early Bronze and middle Bronze Age pieces of pottery were identified showing occupation of the site before the Roman period.[19] Significantly, the archaeologists have confirmed the remains of the legendary Church of the Apostles, and believe it is the one reported in pilgrimage records in the eighth century by pilgrim Willibald, who talks about a church built over the house of Peter and Andrew.[20]

The fact Bethsaida was the hometown of the apostles Peter, Andrew, and Phillip, and is said to be where Jesus planted the seeds of a movement, provides confidence in our understanding of village and urban life between 29–33 CE, and that 'His life

---

18 Douglass E Oakman, 2008, 'Jesus and the Peasants', https://www.academia.edu/3079887/ Oakman_D_E_2008_Jesus_and_the_peasants_Cascade_Books_Eugene_Matrix_The_ Bible_in_Mediterranean_context_.

19 Ariel Sabar, 2016, 'Unearthing the World of Jesus', Smithsonian Magazine, January Washington, DC.

20 Megan Sauter, 2020, 'Excavating El-Araj—a Candidate for Biblical Bethsaida' Biblical Archaeology Society, https://www.baslibrary.org/biblical-archaeology-review/46/2/2.

drew on—or at least repurposed—bedrock Jewish traditions of prophecy, messianism, and social justice critique as old as the Hebrew Bible.'[19] Such discoveries add credence to Jesus spending much time amongst a worshipping-centred people teaching in the synagogues, healing the sick and indigent, and demonstrating miraculous acts in the villages of Capernaum, Chorazin, and Bethsaida.

Some two-hour walk from Bethsaida is the lost village of Magdala, now excavated and revealing not just a synagogue but a flourishing community and the home of Mary of Magdala, a close follower of Jesus.

Images and Conflict

The ruins of Magdala were so well preserved that archaeologist Marcela Zapata-Meza started calling Magdala 'the Israeli Pompeii'. Josephus, the first-century historian, wrote that the people of Magdala eagerly joined the Jewish revolt against Rome in 66 CE. But the Roman legions crushed them, turning the lake 'all bloody, and full of dead bodies.' The city, it seems, was never rebuilt. (Three coins were found at the synagogue from 29, 43, and 63 CE.)

But this is not the only evidence of conflict and violence in the first century CE. There was always tension between the Roman rulers and the Jewish population. 'Pontius Pilate's first serious clash with the Jews took place in his very first year in office when his troops marched into Jerusalem at night with their regimental standards bearing medallions with the emperor's image.' Images and statues were part of the culture of the occupying Roman rulers. But such practices were *verboten* to Jewish sensibilities and worship of the One God. Some took actions into their own hands with deadly results.

In 29–30 CE, Pilate introduced coins engraved with symbols of emperor-worship on one side and Jewish symbols on the other. In 32 CE, he attempted—again—to bring in golden standards honouring Tiberius into Herod's Palace in Jerusalem. In 36 CE, a Samaritan would-be-messiah asked the Samaritan people to go up to Mount Gerizim with him, where he promised to show them sacred vessels hidden by Moses. Pilate blocked their route of ascent with cavalry and heavily armed infantry. In the clash that followed, some were killed, and the rest scattered or taken prisoners. Pilate then executed the ringleaders and those who were most influential.

Meso Level

This meso-level dimension of the ecosystem (Fig. 1.1, page 10) seeks to better understand the role and effect of the exercised authority and power on everyday life in first-century-CE Judea and Palestine. This level is naturally positioned between the understanding of village and urban life and that of the impact of being part of the Roman empire and the expansion of the early Church. Within this meso level of the ecosystem, our understanding is focused on the political, economic, social, and cultural forces at play in terms of power over the urban elite and peasants. Again, this evaluation will facilitate a preparedness to both recognise and discuss opportunities that may have led to innovations as demonstrated by Jesus the entrepreneur.

Besides being an advanced agrarian society, life in the province of Judea was shaped by several dominant forces: the Israelite tradition (linguistic, cultural, and religious heritage), the Roman Empire (political control), and Hellenism (the pervasive cultural influence over the whole Mediterranean and Middle East).[21]

21 K. C. Hanson & Douglas E Oakman, 1998, 'Palestine in the Time of Jesus: Social Structures and Social Conflicts'. Fortress Press, Minneapolis, MN:.

Political forces

Judas Maccabeus was the leader of the Hasmonean clan, and in 167 BCE led the common Jewish people into revolt against their Greek overlords—the Seleucids—and the Hellenised Jewish elite, recaptured Jerusalem, and rededicated the Temple. In 160 BCE, his battlefield death by the Greek Seleucids ushered in an extremely unstable Hasmonean dynasty. This Hasmonean regime in 104 BCE annexed Galilee to Judea and required the local inhabitants to live according to the laws of Judea. Galilee was thus brought together with other Israelite people under the Temple and high priesthood, with the taxation system connected to the temple.[22]

The Roman general Pompeius (Pompey) annexed Syria in 64 BCE. Following continued disputes between the two puppet princes ruling Judea and Galilee, Pompey marched on Jerusalem in 63 BCE and, after much bloodshed, he occupied the temple and brought Roman control to Palestine. Pompey appointed Hyrcanus (one of the princes and of the Hasmonean dynasty) as high priest—basically a political appointment.[23]

At the time of Jesus' birth, 5 BCE, Palestine was under Roman control, but Herod the Great was the loyal and politically crafty client king of the region. He died in 4 BCE. Following the disastrous rule by his son (Herod Archelaus) in the area of Judea, Samaria, and Idumaea, the Roman Emperor Augustus removed him in 6 CE, created the administrative province of Judea and introduced direct Roman rule. This political reality was in place during the whole of Jesus' ministry and death, 29–33 CE. But while it may have made good administrative sense, direct Roman

---

22 Richard, A, Horsley, 2008, 'Jesus in Context: Power, People, and Performance'. Fortress Press, Minneapolis:.

23 https://www.themaparchive.com/pompeys-campaign-against-jerusalem-63-bce.html.

rule was not without its pitfalls. After Archelaus' death, Judea was placed under a Roman governor whose main headquarters were at Caesarea on the coast. The Roman garrison was based there, with forces also stationed in Jerusalem, which would be reinforced at major festivals. The governors were charged with collecting tribute as well as with administering law and order. Initially, they were referred to as prefects, stressing their military role; later, they were called procurators, which strictly refers to their financial responsibilities. They were ultimately subject to the legate in Syria, but this appears only to have taken force in times of crisis. Their power and jurisdiction over all areas of life are well-illustrated by the fact that they could and did appoint and dismiss the high priest at will. They did not, however, always understand the particular sensibilities of the Jews. Pontius Pilate (26–36 CE) offended on a number of occasions, first by introducing standards into Jerusalem bearing embossed images of the emperor (which of course, violated the prohibition against graven images). Further offence was given by his use of Temple funds to construct an aqueduct in Jerusalem. Even after this, he attempted to introduce shields bearing the emperor's name into Jerusalem. In his handling of popular disturbances, he was brutal, and eventually, his harsh treatment of a Samaritan prophet and his followers led to his deposition.[24]

Under the Roman governors, there was plenty of violence in Judea and Galilee. Valerius Gratius (15–26 CE) was the first procurator who arbitrarily appointed and deposed the high priests. Josephus portrayed Gratius as manipulating Jerusalem's temple politics by deposing the incumbent Sadducean high priest Hanan I (6–15 CE), as well as three short-termed successors,

---

24 John Riches, 1990, 'The World of Jesus First-Century Judaism in Crisis' See Chap 1 – 'The Political, Economic, Social, and Cultural Context of First-Century Palestinian Judaism' https://www.cambridge.org/core/books/world-of-jesus/political-economic-social-and-cultural-context-of-firstcentury-palestinian-judaism/78E9FC5FF52226BA04868426D9EDF481.

before finally finding Joseph Kayyafa (Caiaphas), who had a long tenure collaborating with Roman military rule (18–37 CE).[25] He put down two formidable bands of robbers that infested Judea during his government and killed with his own hand the captain of one of them, Simon, formerly a slave of Herod the Great. Gratius assisted the proconsul Quintilius Varus in quelling an insurrection of the Jews.

Economic forces on social life

The economy of first-century Israel was supported by three key segments: agriculture of olives, figs, grains, dates, and vineyards; trade fostered by Israel's key location on the Mediterranean Sea; large government building projects sponsored by King Herod.

Compared to our experience of Western society with a strongly growing economy, recognised class levels and with an established middle class defined by reference to positions within an industrial economy: workers/management; shareholders/wage earners; employed/self-employed/unemployed, it is important to keep in mind such distinctions in first-century Israel, under Roman rule, were of much less significance. Importantly to our understanding of economic life in 1–33 CE, we have noted the strong dependence on an agrarian economy, rich and poor, but also the crucial distinction between slave and free. Jews, because of their own history of liberation 'from the house of slaves', disliked keeping slaves, particularly Jewish slaves, but some still kept them.

Slaves would have been a feature of life in Palestine, though perhaps something that most Jews viewed somewhat from a

---

25 Morten Hørning Jensen, 2012, 'Rural Galilee and Rapid Changes: An Investigation of the Socio-Economic Dynamics and Developments in Roman Galilee, Biblica, Vol. 93, No. 1.

distance. Nevertheless, the threat of being sold into slavery to redeem one's debts must have been a real one for many Jews. Equally, those who engaged in active revolt knew that slavery was one possible outcome. It was the fate of the survivors of the revolt in Sepphoris after Herod's death (Matthew 18:25).

Compared with today's social structure, greater importance was placed on birth order and gender to determine roles and functions within the family and in society at large. Indeed, Palestine, like other surrounding societies, was thoroughly patriarchal. But also, language played a significant role in sharing the wealth of the economy. Greek had been a passport to social status and power. One needed to speak Greek in order to enter the administrative ranks, to trade, to travel, to engage in diplomacy. This aspect was perhaps the most important distinction in Jewish society and where one lived. A great gulf divided town and country. The irony is the fact many of the cities in Palestine identified with Jesus' ministry bore names whose roots were Greek or Latin: Sebaste, Apollonia, Caesarea Panias, Tiberias, Caesarea Philippi, Julias. They were usually controlled by Greek-speaking merchants, officials, and landowners.

It may be surprising to note that the local villages and towns seemed to have been expanding and thriving in the same period that the two urban centres in Jesus' time—namely Sepphoris and Tiberias—were also expanding.

Most of Palestine of course lay outside the cities. Its population was predominantly Jewish and its economy agrarian. Its population lived in towns and villages; the latter being associated with their local town. The land was divided between large estates and small holdings. Agriculture flourished during the time of Jesus and was the basis of a profitable export trade. Crops included wheat, barley, olives, rice, vegetables, flax, balsam, dates, and figs. Reading some contemporary accounts gives the impression of a generally prosperous community. On the other hand, general prosperity depends on the equity of distribution of wealth and goods, more particularly on patterns of land tenure and on the availability of employment. Thus, there are good grounds for supposing that life in rural Palestine was far from easy for peasant farmers and day laborers. Agriculture itself was laborious and the land, possibly the markets, and certainly wages were in the control of a few wealthy landowners. None of this makes for great security or an easy life. Debt, loss of tenancies, and ultimately slavery threatened. At the same time, rural workers would have been aware of the wealth and opportunities offered by the largely Hellenistic cities in their midst, and such prospects no doubt exercised a powerful attraction. Under these circumstances sustaining a traditional Jewish way of life required sustained effort.[26]

Conclusion

In summary, the overall synthesis of this review of political, economic, social, and cultural factors extant in first-century Judea and Palestine appears to point in the direction of a first-century Galilee marked by stability—if not moderate growth—rather than rapid change and/or decline.[26]

Consideration of the performance and impact from actors and relationships contributing to the holistically included stages at the macro and mega levels of this first-century Judaeo-Christian

---

26 John S Kloppenborg, 2000, 'Excavating Q. The history and setting of the sayings gospel,' Fortress Press, Minneapolis, MN.

ecosystem will not be discussed in this volume. Instead, the important and fundamental findings on entrepreneurial behaviour from 5 BCE–33 CE will form a review of the micro and meso levels of the ecosystem. By evaluating the contribution of entrepreneurial behaviour and entrepreneur mindset to Jesus' ministry and community life in general, it is hoped such understanding will provide insight into both the spread and influence of Christian followers on Western civilisation.

Understanding the context for entrepreneurial behaviour in a first-century 'worship-centred living' village and urban environment and the exercise of 'power' and authority over the society will enable an assessment to be made on the influences and opportunities for Jesus to exercise an entrepreneur mindset with his associated social entrepreneurial behaviour between 29–33 CE. These behaviours will be influenced by both external and internal factors such as collegiality, teamwork, and the adoption of a co-creation or innovation collaborative approach that incorporates a 'lived' culture of compassion, care, excellence, and professional practice in the delivery of a new relationship with God—a first-century-CE innovation.

Chapter 2: Jesus the Man

Not only does the Son of God have a fully human body,
but also a fully human mind, heart, and will. [27]

—David Mathis

At the heart of the entrepreneurial process is the entrepreneur[28]: the opportunity seeker, the leader, problem solver, and motivator; the strategist and guardian of the mission, values, and culture of the venture or service. After some forty years of teaching and researching entrepreneurship and mentoring entrepreneurs, it is clear this understanding of the entrepreneur is not simply a function of business processes or management techniques. Rather, and significantly, it is understanding one's inner personal relationship in combining intellectual, emotional, and spiritual intelligence; an entrepreneur's vision; limitless human energy; commitment, drive, and vitality to deliver real benefit to a customer or user. Such behaviour lies in the integration of the intangibles: creativity and ingenuity, intuition, commitment, tenacity and determination, a passion to succeed and excel, leadership and team-building skills, and above all, a human spirit comprising the mental functions of awareness, insight, understanding, judgement, and other reasoning powers. These intangible characteristics are at the very heart of the

---

27 David Mathis, 2016, https://www.desiringgod.org/articles/jesus-is-fully-human.
28 Jeffry Timmons, Murray Gillin, Sam Burshtein and Stephen Spinelli, 2011, 'New Venture Creation: Entrepreneurship for the 21st Century', (Regional Edition) McGraw Hill (Australia).

entrepreneur's humanity that integrates body, soul, and spirit holistically to 'make it happen'.

It is this holistic appreciation of entrepreneurial behaviour that challenges any simplistic argument concerning whether we, as humans, are born with an entrepreneurial gene or develop such behaviours. We are all born with a sense of creativity, and our life experiences will determine how we develop and use this innate quality.

In this book, it will be argued that Jesus exhibited these principles and was indeed a practising entrepreneur delivering a vision of new life behaviours for those followers accepting the message, ethics, and morals for a quality personal and community lifestyle. This was true innovation at its best.

But, before commencing such an analysis, it is necessary to establish the evidence for both the existence and behaviour of Jesus the man. Of course, with a gap of some 2,000 years, there is no definitive physical or archaeological evidence of the existence of Jesus. Both Lawrence Mykytiuk and Bart D Ehrman comment, 'There's nothing conclusive, nor would I expect there to be. Peasants don't normally leave an archaeological trail.'[29] Indeed, 'The lack of evidence does not mean a person at the time didn't exist. It means that she or he, like 99.99% of the rest of the world at the time, made no impact on the archaeological record.'[30] However, the existence of archaeological evidence associated with the community and lifestyle conditions at the time of Jesus are reviewed in Chapter 1 and shows the Jewish people of the first century CE practised a 'worship-centred living' very like that recorded in the Gospels of the Bible.

29 Lawrence Mykytiuk, 2015, 'Did Jesus Exist? Searching for Evidence Beyond the Bible'. Biblical Archaeology Review article, January/February 2015.
30 Bart D Ehrman, 2013, 'Did Jesus Exist?: The Historical Argument for Jesus of Nazareth', Harper Collins USA.

Independent historians from the first century CE have identified the existence of Jesus, called 'the Christ'. Some examples include Tacitus, a Roman historian and politician (56–120 CE), and Josephus, a first-century Romano-Jewish historian who was born in Jerusalem (37–100 CE).

Tacitus presents four pieces of accurate knowledge about Jesus: (1) Christus, used by Tacitus to refer to Jesus, was one distinctive way by which some referred to him, even though Tacitus mistakenly took it for a personal name rather than an epithet or title; (2) this Christus was associated with the beginning of the movement of Christians, whose name originated from his; (3) Christos was executed by the Roman governor of Judea; and (4) the time of his death was during Pontius Pilate's governorship of Judea, during the reign of Tiberius.

Josephus wrote in 62 CE:

> *Being therefore this kind of person [i.e., a heartless Sadducee], Ananus, thinking that he had a favourable opportunity because Festus had died and Albinus was still on his way, called a meeting [literally, 'sanhedrin'] of judges and brought into it the brother of Jesus-who-is-called-Messiah ... James by name, and some others. He made the accusation that they had transgressed the law, and he handed them over to be stoned.*

However, I am fully aware from the biblical references to Jesus that, in addition to the identification of the Christ or Messiah described above, His person embraces a twin nature regarding his humanity and divinity. To assess Jesus the entrepreneur and compare this with accepted entrepreneurs involved in the entrepreneurial process, it will be necessary to establish not only the existence of Jesus but also his humanity—is He of the same body, soul, and spirit of all mankind? To establish this understanding of 'Jesus the man', it will be necessary to first establish the theological understanding of Jesus as being both fully God and fully man. This is not an issue that I am qualified to undertake, and so I am including an extract from an established theologian (with his permission) to clarify the meaning of Jesus' humanity.

The Bible clearly states that Jesus is fully human. Bruce A Ware, an established theologian, (and with permission) explains this dual nature as follows:

> Given that the divine nature in Jesus was eternal and infinite while the human nature in Jesus was created and finite, one of the questions we ponder is just how these two natures could coexist in the one person. Could Jesus as both fully divine and fully human be, for example, simultaneously omnipotent, omniscient, and omnipresent—qualities of his eternal, divine nature—while also possessing a limited and finite human power, a limited yet growing knowledge and wisdom, and a restricted ability to be only in one place at one time—qualities of finite, human nature? It seems clear that some qualities of his eternal, divine nature are simply incompatible with his true and genuine human nature, such that it would be impossible for him truly to live as a human if that so-called human life was also one in which he exhibited fully divine qualities such as omnipotence, omniscience, and omnipresence. In other words, would Jesus be truly and genuinely human if in his human experience he had limitless power, knowledge, wisdom,

and spatial presence? The crux of the answer to these questions comes in how Paul in Philippians 2:5–8 expresses the kenosis, the self-emptying, of the eternal Son as he took on human nature. Here Paul writes: 'Have this mind among yourselves, which is yours in Christ Jesus, who, though he was in the form of God, did not count equality with God a thing to be grasped, but emptied himself, by taking the form of a servant, being born in the likeness of men. And being found in human form, he humbled himself by becoming obedient to the point of death, even death on a cross.' Notice some crucial features of this important passage.

First, Paul makes clear that Christ Jesus, as the eternal Son of the Father, is fully God. He offers two expressions, each of which conveys the full deity of Christ. Paul writes that Christ existed in the 'form of God' (v. 6), using the term morphē, *which refers to the inner nature or substance of something, not its external or outward shape. So, while the English word form can convey merely the outward appearance of something (i.e., the shape or contour or façade of some object), not its inner reality, the Greek word* morphē *conveys just the opposite, as can be seen with Plato's 'forms'—i.e., those substances of ultimate realities such as beauty, truth, justice, goodness, etc., that Plato thought existed eternally and apart from any material representation. The Greek* morphē, *then, is the inner substance or very nature of a thing, not its outer shape or appearance. That Paul intends this understanding can be seen further in his second use of* morphē, *when he says that Jesus took the 'form (*morphēn*) of a servant' (v. 7). Surely it is evident that Paul does not mean that*

Jesus took on merely the outer appearance of a servant, implying perhaps that though he looked like a servant, he was not in his own heart and life a true servant. Just the opposite: Jesus took on the inner substance and very nature, i.e., the form (morphēn), *of what it means to be a servant, and that to its highest expression. As a servant, he served to the utmost, as he was obedient to the point of death, even death on the cross. So again, 'form' (*mor-phē, v. 6, *and* morphēn, v. 7) *must mean the very nature of something, not merely its outer appearance. Therefore, Paul's point in 2:6 is clear: Jesus, being the 'form of God,' exists in very nature as God, with the inner divine substance that is God's alone. He is fully God since he exists 'in the form (*morphē) *of God.'*

*Paul also refers to Christ as possessing 'equality (*isa) *with God' (v. 6), which likewise makes clear his full deity. Nothing is equal to God except God! As God declares of himself, through the prophet Isaiah, 'I am God, and there is no other; I am God, and there is none like me' (Isa. 46:9; cf. Ex. 8:10; 15:11; Deut. 3:24; 2 Sam. 7:22; 1 Kings 8:23; Ps. 71:19; Mic. 7:18). Indeed, there is no god other than the one true and living God—so God is exclusively God—and there is no god who is like the one true and living God—so God is incomparably God. With this background in mind, Paul's declaration that Christ possesses 'equality with God' is stunning. It can mean only one thing: by virtue of the fact that no one can be equal to God but God himself, Christ, who possesses equality with God, must himself be fully God. Of course, as we often find where the deity of Christ is expressed, we see hints or outright declarations that someone other* *than Christ likewise is God. Since he is equal to God, this means that there is another who is God, in relation to whom Christ is his equal. So, as John puts it, the Word is both 'with God' and is 'God' (John 1:1), and Hebrews declares that Christ is the 'exact imprint' of the nature of God (Heb. 1:3). Likewise, here in Philippians 2, Christ is other than the one who is God (understood as the Father, no doubt) while he is also equal to this other one who is God and so is himself fully God.*

Second, when Paul writes that Christ 'did not count equality with God a thing to be grasped' (Phil. 2:6), he cannot mean that Christ gave up equality with God or that he ceased being fully God. Since he is fully God, he cannot cease to be fully God. God is eternal, self-existent, immortal, and immutable, and thus he cannot cease to exist as God, nor can he fail to be fully God. Surely what Paul means is this: Christ being fully God, possessing the very nature of God and being fully equal to God in every respect, did not thereby insist on holding onto all the privileges and benefits of his position of equality with God (the Father) and thereby refuse to accept coming as a man. He did not clutch or grasp his place of equality with the Father and all that this brought to him in such a way that he would refuse the condescension and humiliation of the servant role he was being called to accept. Just how he could accept his calling to become a man while being (and remaining!) fully God, we'll explore next. But here it is crucial to see that Christ's not 'grasping' equality with God cannot rightly be taken to mean that Christ gave up being God or became in any way less than fully God when he took on also a fully human nature. No, rather, he did not grasp or clutch onto the privileged position, rights, and prerogatives that his full equality with God, his Father, afforded him, in order to fulfill his calling to become fully a man who would be, amazingly, servant of all.

Third, as one who is fully God, Christ Jesus 'emptied himself, by taking the form of a servant' (v. 7). The word that here is translated 'emptied himself,' ekenōsen (third aorist indicative of kenoō)*, means literally just this: that Christ 'emptied himself' or 'poured out himself.' Note that Paul is not saying that Christ emptied something from himself or poured something out of himself, as if in so doing he became less fully God than he was before (which, as we have seen, is impossible). Rather, he emptied himself; he poured out himself. That is, all of who Christ is as eternal God, all that he is as the one who is in the form of God and is equal with God, is poured out. Christ, then, as God remains fully God. He loses nothing of his divine nature, and no divine qualities are removed from him as he pours himself out. No, Christ remains in his divine nature fully who and what he is in his existence as the eternal second person of the Trinity. He has eternally been fully God, and now in the incarnation he pours out fully who he is as God, remaining fully God as he does so. The question then becomes just what this means—that Christ, the one who exists in the form of God (*morphē*) and as equal (*isa*) to God, pours himself out (ekenōsen). The answer comes, amazingly, in the three participles (particularly the first one) that follow ekenōsen. Christ poured himself out, taking the form of a servant. Yes, he pours out by taking; he empties by adding. Here, then,* *is a strange sort of math that envisions a subtraction by addition, an emptying by adding. What can this mean?* [31]

Based, then, on the secular historical evidence for the presence of Jesus Christ in the first century CE, the archaeological evidence of a Jewish 'worship-centred community' within Judea and the Galilee, and the clear interpretation from the biblical/theological record that Jesus was 'fully human' and not a 'superman', it is appropriate to examine the actions and practices of Jesus in terms of entrepreneurial behaviours.

In essence, we can then consider Jesus' actions as a model that informs what all people can emulate to varying degrees. These behaviours will be identified from a consideration of His vision, His message, His actions, His passions, and His statements to bring about change that is valued by both the individuals and the community's acceptance of the benefits and life-changes available.

To achieve this examination, it will be necessary to review the life and actions of Jesus from the record of the New Testament and that of the four gospels. It should be possible to show that Jesus identified each specific situation of human and spiritual need as an opportunity and to create an outcome—be it life change or 'miracle'—whereby the recipient valued the benefit. This formulation enables an assessment of how the 'market' (users), as members of the community, understood the spiritual and practical ramifications of Jesus-type behaviour.

The structure of this review will be focused on the understanding of a human being as comprising 'spirit, soul and body' (1 Thessalonians 5:23). See Figure 2.1.

---

31 Bruce A Ware, 2013, The Man Christ Jesus; Theological Reflections on the Humanity of Christ, Crossway.

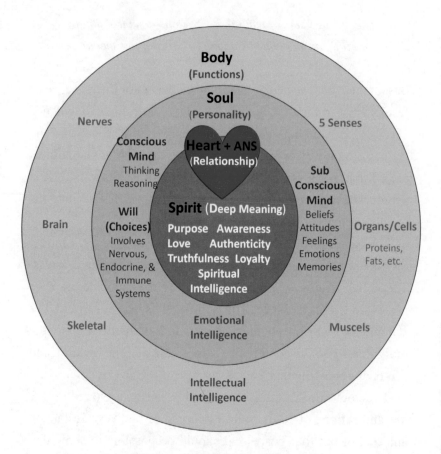

Figure 2.1 'What is Man?' (After Dale Fletcher)[32]

Essentially, humans are made up of physical material, the body (soma), that can be seen and touched as both flesh and bone and expressed in the five senses. The words *soul* and *spirit* are often used interchangeably. I consider they are different expressions of the inner or immaterial aspects of man, which are intangible. We are not simply body and soul, but persons that include the spirit of the creator.

---

32 Dale Fletcher https://www.faithandhealthconnection.org/the_connection/spirit-soul-and–body/.

I define soul and spirit as follows: the soul (psyche)—creativity and ingenuity, intuition, commitment, tenacity and determination, a passion to succeed and excel, emotions, leadership and team-building skills; and spirit (pneuma)—comprising the mental functions of awareness, insight, understanding, judgement, love, authenticity, and other aspects of spiritual intelligence.

Prior to the Enlightenment, philosophers and leaders ascribed the heart, including the autonomic nervous system, as the seat of wisdom and decision-making rather than the brain. In Chapter 3, I will discuss these three elements of the human being in terms of intellectual intelligence (IQ), emotional intelligence (EI), and spiritual intelligence (SI).

Jesus the Man—The Body

The Greek word *soma* in the New Testament refers to the entire material or physical structure of a human being—it is the physical part of a person—and the New Testament is clear that Jesus had a human body. John 1:14—'The Word became flesh.'

We recognise that Jesus, as 'fully' a human being, experienced birth into first-century-CE Judea (Luke 2:7). Importantly, Jesus had a human ancestry (Luke 2:38) and developed like a normal human being (Luke 2:52). Jesus demonstrated the application of His five senses: seeing (eyes), hearing (ears), tasting (tongue), smelling (nose), and feeling (touch) as a baby, boy, carpenter, and itinerant leader of a team. As will be seen in Chapter 4, Jesus exercised all five senses in order to sympathise with humanity. God intended for man to worship Him through those five senses as well as to enjoy life to the fullest. Jesus had the essential elements of a human being—body and spirit (John 19:34, Mark 2:8).

Significantly, Jesus describes Himself as 'Son of Man', the title appearing some eighty-one times in the Greek text of the four canonical gospels. In addition, Jesus delivered his spoken words as a man, teaching and using human terms with human illustrations. Jesus showed all the traits of being human.

Also, Jesus was tempted (Matthew 4:1). It is worth noting only human beings can be tempted. He experienced hunger (Matthew 4:2). Jesus understood what it was like to be thirsty (John 19:28). He knew tiredness (John 4:6), the need for sleep (Matthew 8:24), and knew what it was to experience pain (Luke 24:44) and death (John 19:33).

In summary, the Bible record is clear that Jesus was born with a human body, into a human community, and experienced all the personal realities of living. There was no special treatment given to Jesus while here on earth. He felt the same things every other human being feels. With such a record of human living, we can have confidence in the challenge to assess His compatibility with being a first-century-CE entrepreneur and comparing such behaviour to present-day entrepreneurs.

Jesus the Man–Soul

This is defined by inner self, creativity, intuition, commitment, tenacity, and determination—a passion to succeed and excel, emotions, leadership.

As referred to above, man's physical body functions together with the five senses to enable us to observe the facts and gather the data necessary for living. But there is more—much more—that complements our perception and reality of what it is to be a human being.

Personality

We see such human reality through the observation of our personality—defined as the characteristic sets of behaviours, cognitions, and emotional patterns that evolve from biological and environmental factors. While there is no generally agreed-upon definition of personality, most theories focus on motivation and psychological interactions with one's environment.

Jesus had personality—this can be seen from His outgoing, sociable behaviour and focus on people as described in the Gospels. Such awareness provides an insight into the 'inner' self—thus enabling an examination of Jesus' personality that provides a reasonable assessment of His true or internal mind, soul, or nature as He lived as a man.

Importantly, to know your inner self is to know your purpose, values, vision, goals, motivations, and beliefs. Not what you have been told by others, but what you have discovered for yourself. But personality is not uniquely an aspect of 'man'; it can also be seen and developed in animals, fauna, and flora. So, what was Jesus really like, to those who knew him best and those encountering him for the first time?

Gayle Weinraub (and with permission) comments:

Of course, we can't know for sure since we can't ask him how he was energised (E-extraversion or I-introversion), how he took in information (S-sensing or N-intuition) and used it to make decisions (T-thinking or F-feeling), or how he oriented himself to the outer world (J-judging or P-perceiving). We can get some ideas by reading about him in the Bible, but as with each of us, Jesus himself would have to be the final judge of what his personality type might be.

Using the secular and psychologically based Myers Briggs indicator scale to assess the human behaviour of Jesus as provided in the Gospels, Weinraub has summarised her findings as follows:

Imagine that Jesus had the chance to take a modern personality assessment. What would the results look like? The first letter in his type code—the four letters which denote one's personality type—would have been either E for extroversion or I for introversion. A preference for extroversion means one is energised by the outer world and is active, outgoing, and focused on people and things. People with this preference process outwardly, thinking as they speak, and their motto could be 'Live it, then understand it.'

On the other hand, a preference for introversion means one is energised in his or her inner world and is reflective, focused on thoughts and concepts. These people process inwardly, thinking before they speak, and their motto could be 'Understand it before living it.'

Which of these descriptions sounds most like Jesus? Certainly, he can be seen as outgoing, sociable and focused on people, all characteristics of a preference for extroversion. But what stands out to me like bright stars against a black sky are verses like Mark 1:35, where we are told that '... in the morning, a great while before day, he rose and went out to a lonely place, and there he prayed.' This was after a busy day that had involved teaching and preaching in the synagogues and healing people. And Mark 6:46 says, 'And after he had taken leave of them, he went up on the mountain to pray.'

I believe that Jesus needed this time alone, not only to communicate with God but also to energise himself, either to prepare for what was to come, as in 1:35 or to immediately recharge himself after time with others, as in 6:46. I also believe he understood life before living it and had his thoughts fully formed before he spoke. These are all hallmarks of introversion.

The second letter in Jesus' type code was either S for sensing or N for intuition, two ways of taking in information. Sensing types, who make up as much as 70% of the U.S. population (and I assume of the rest of the world as well), focus on the realities of the present, such as specifics and factual, concrete information. They tend to see the trees rather than the forest. In sharp contrast, intuitive-type people focus on future possibilities, seeing patterns, associations and connections between facts. They tend to see the forest rather than the trees.

I have no trouble seeing Jesus focusing on the importance of each person and taking care of each situation as it arose. He was undeniably great with details. For example, Mark 5:43, which is about raising a girl from the dead, concludes by saying that Jesus '... told them to give her something to eat.'

But what stands out more to me is his interest in the big picture and the future. In Mark 1:17, for instance, we are told that 'Jesus said to them, 'Follow me and I will make you become fishers of men.'' He saw not only who his disciples were, but who they could and would become.

His teaching style also appears to be indicative of intuition. Those with a preference for sensing would probably be more straightforward and easier to understand. They are more down-to-earth and literal in their speech than intuitive folks. Though Jesus spoke about ordinary parts of life for his audiences, I am sure the leap between his earthly examples and their spiritual parallels left most of his followers with rapidly spinning heads. For example, in the Parable of the Sower (Mark 4:3), Jesus taught about farming, which was a regular and prominent aspect of people's lives. But would they naturally make the connection between a farmer sowing seeds and God sowing his word into people's hearts? Mark 4:10 indicates that this parable was not well understood. This fits with the presumption that most of his hearers had a preference for sensing.

Once we take in information, we use it to make decisions. The next letter in Jesus' type code would reflect the way he made decisions: T for thinking or F for feeling. Those with a preference for thinking make decisions on the basis of objective and impersonal criteria. They seek rational order by using logic, and they value justice and fairness. Feeling types, on the other hand, make decisions using subjective criteria as they weigh human values and motives. They value kindness and harmony.

In John 8:3–11, Jesus had an encounter with a woman caught in adultery who, according to the Law of Moses, deserved to be stoned. Several later manuscripts suggest he wrote on the ground a list of all the sins of the scribes and Pharisees who brought the woman to him. Then he said to them, 'Let him who is without sin among you be the first to throw a stone at her (John 8:7).' After the scribes and Pharisees all walked away, he told the woman that he did not condemn her either.

To me, this is a clear indication of a preference for feeling. Justice, valued by thinking types, would have most likely leaned toward her being stoned. Thus John 8:5-6 states that the scribes and Pharisees asked Jesus what he had to say about the woman, who the law commanded should be stoned, 'to test him, that they might have some charge to bring against him.' But kindness, valued by feeling types, liberated her for a fresh start in a life free from the sin that had ensnared her.

On the other hand, though, Jesus often fought against tradition and the status quo, as in Mark 11:15–18 when he overturned the tables of the moneychangers in the temple, and Mark 12:38 when he warned people to beware of the scribes. Perhaps his tendency to turn tradition on its head indicates a preference for thinking rather than feeling. Isabel Myers's brilliant book Gifts Differing, which I highly recommend, says that thinking types 'Contribute to the welfare of society by the intellectual criticism of its habits, customs, and beliefs, by the exposure of wrongs, solution of problems ... ' That does sound a lot like Jesus. Perhaps he was more of a thinker when dealing with the sinfulness of a hard-hearted society and showed his feeling side when dealing with individual sinners who knew they were in need of mercy.

The final letter in Jesus' type code might be the most debatable of all: J for judging or P for perceiving, two ways of orienting oneself toward the outer world. Judging types are interested in controlling their lives, which they like to have settled and planned. They like setting goals, organising, scheduling and deciding. In contrast, flexible and spontaneous perceiving types prefer to let life happen, are undaunted by surprises, and tend to react to life by inquiring about and absorbing it. They prefer adapting to whatever it brings their way and changing as necessary.

Jesus shows the characteristics of a judging type in that he seemed to have a clear plan for his life, to know who he was and what his purpose was, from the beginning of his ministry, if not from the very beginning of his life. Yet, like a perceiving type, he also seemed to be flexible and able to shift gears quickly, not minding terribly when his plans were interrupted. In Mark 6:31, he invited the apostles to join him in escaping to a lonely place for some rest. But a crowd of people met them there and, having compassion on them, Jesus taught them instead of resting.

It might almost be anyone's guess what the fourth letter in Jesus' type code was. Perhaps he did not have a clear preference. But I once read that judgers focus on responsibility while perceivers focus on discovery, two very different life purposes. When looked at this way, I believe his preference, though perhaps only slight or moderate, was most likely for judging.'[33]

Creativity

When human personality is coupled with the identification of opportunities and associated with inner creativity then we find a uniquely human capacity associated with our 'soul' and 'spirit'. Creativity can be defined as a phenomenon whereby something new and somehow valuable is formed. The created item may be intangible (such as an idea, a scientific theory, a musical composition, or a joke) or a physical object (such as an invention, a printed literary work, or a painting).

---

33 Gayle Weinraub, 2016, https://www.truity.com/blog/what-was-jesus%27-personality-type.

In the case of Jesus, His creativity was not only to help His hearers seek salvation but 'to develop the kind of solution-based thinking that would help make the world a better place in which to live.'[34] Jesus saw the opportunities for action in His exposure to the lifestyle and living conditions of the first century CE. Jesus' response to such opportunities conforms with current research understanding of entrepreneurial behaviour: that 'particular people and not others are able to discover and exploit opportunities: the possession of the information necessary to identify an opportunity and the cognitive style necessary to exploit it.'[35]

Jesus's health care ministry, which healed the sick, was not only designed to eradicate debilitating diseases that had both devastated individuals and marginalized them from society, but also designed to creatively and positively change the negative self-concepts these people had acquired as a result of their physical afflictions.[34]

Thus Jesus health care ministry was an exercise in creative problem solving not only medically by healing their afflictions, not only psychologically by transforming their negative self-image into a positive self-image, but also socially by helping those healed persons to become productive citizens in their communities and society.[34]

His creativity is further demonstrated in his human capacity as a teacher.

34 Carlyle Fielding Stewart, III, 2011 'Creative Problem Solving: A Jesus Perspective', A sermon, https://www.carlylestewart.com/creative-solving-problem-a-jesus-perspective/
35 Scott Shane and Sankaran Venkataraman 2000, 'The Promise of Entrepreneurship as a Field of Research,' Academy of Management Review, 25(1): 217–226.

Jesus was an incredibly creative communicator. He used parables when He taught (e.g., Matthew 13:34). He drew in the sand, used a Roman coin, cursed a fig tree, and picked up a piece of bread—in order to explain truth. He divided fish, turned over tables, and put a child on his knee—all to illustrate important lessons. Jesus delivered his life-changing message in dynamic and creative ways. He understood that a point gets to the head while a picture gets to the heart.[36]

Intuition

This creativity and the association with turning opportunities into valued outcomes by those in need is closely coupled with intuition. Intuition is the ability to acquire knowledge, ranging from direct access to unconscious knowledge, unconscious cognition, inner sensing, and inner insight to unconscious pattern recognition and the ability to understand something instinctively without the need for conscious reasoning. Much research has studied this style of decision-making surrounding opportunity recognition, creativity, intuition, and divergent thinking (reasoning) from a cognitive perspective, using both conscious and unconscious processes, including pattern recognition and memory retrieval. However, in considering intuition as a fundamental behaviour of Jesus, I proposed to add to the above understanding by taking an information processing perspective in which intuition is described as a process by which information normally outside the range of cognitive processes is sensed and perceived in the body and mind as certainty of

---

36 Mark Conner, 2016, 'The Theology of Creativity' https://churchleaders.com/children/childrens-ministry-articles/280445-theology-creativity-mark-conner.html.

knowledge or feeling (positive or negative) about the totality of a thing distant or yet to happen.[37]

This aspect of intuition behaviour is called nonlocal intuition and is defined as the body's perception of information about a distant or future event that is not based on reason or memories of prior experience. It will be further discussed under the section on 'Spirit'.

Emotions

Throughout the Gospels, Jesus clearly displays human emotions. Some examples of this human expression are as follows: when Jesus heard the centurion's words of faith, 'he marvelled' (Matthew 8:10). He says in Matthew 26:38 that his 'soul is very sorrowful, even to death'; In John 11:33–35, Jesus is 'deeply moved in his spirit and greatly troubled' and even weeps; John 12:27 records Jesus as saying, 'Now is my soul troubled'; and in John 13:21, he is 'troubled in his spirit'. The author of the letter to the Hebrews writes that 'Jesus offered up prayers and supplications, with loud cries and tears' (Hebrews 5:7).

In summary, we have seen the soul (psyche) of Jesus was that of an ordinary human being, as he had to learn and be instructed in the things of God just like any human being. 'And Jesus increased in wisdom and stature, and in favour with God and man' (Luke 2:52). But without actions, all of the above concepts are just endless layers of abstraction. It will be shown in Chapter 5 that Jesus' actions speak to the community. Indeed, when our actions are a fruit of all of the above, others will receive the fruits of our effort through acts of service.

---

37 Ray Bradley, Murray Gillin, Rollin McCraty and Mike Atkinson, 2011, 'Nonlocal Intuition in Entrepreneurs and Nonentrepreneurs: Results of Two Experiments Using Electrophysiological Measures', International Journal of Entrepreneurship and Small Business. vol 12 (3): 343–372.

Jesus the Man—Spirit

I define spirit as the mental functions of awareness, insight, mindfulness, and conscience. In this section, we will consider that the human spirit is the 'real person', the very core of a person's being, the essential seat of their existence. In some writings, the terms 'soul' and 'spirit' are used interchangeably, but in this discussion of Jesus the man, we will use the concept of the human spirit as having no material body or form but is the spiritual or mental part of being human. As we are considering Jesus the man, the additional conceptualising and understanding of the Holy Spirit as used in the account of Jesus' baptism and that of Pentecost will not be discussed at this time.

Importantly, when non-local intuition and mindfulness—expressed as intention, attention, and attitude—are coupled with spirit, we recognise the reality of our deep inner values that give meaning and purpose to life. In the models of Daniel A Helminiak and Bernard Lonergan, the human spirit is considered to be the mental functions of awareness, insight, understanding, judgement, and other reasoning powers compared to the separate component of psyche, which comprises the entities of emotion, images, memory, and personality.[38]

These deeper values include appreciation and awareness of beauty, wonder, love, creation, and justice. Such inner values and spiritual sensitivities shape our sense of purpose and meaning of life. They include authenticity, truthfulness, joyfulness, curiosity, responsibility, loyalty, and love.[39]

---

38 Daniel A. Helminiak, 2015, Brain, Consciousness, and God: A Lonerganian Integration, State University of New York; Daniel A. Helminiak, 2014, More than awareness: Bernard Lonergan's multi-faceted account of consciousness. Journal of Theoretical and Philosophical Psychology 34(2):116–132.
39 Darius Foroux https://dariusforoux.com/core-values/.

Victor E. Frankl gave an immensely powerful demonstration of how the human spirit can triumph despite the awful conditions of a Nazi concentration camp.

The truth—that love is the ultimate and the highest goal to which man can aspire. Then I grasped the meaning of the greatest secret that human poetry and human thought and belief have to impart: The salvation of man is through love and in love. I understood how a man who has nothing left in this world still may know bliss, be it only for a brief moment, in the contemplation of his beloved.[40]

The Bible says that the human spirit is the very breath of Almighty God and was breathed into man at the beginning of God's Creation: 'Then the LORD God formed a man from the dust of the ground and breathed into his nostrils the breath of life, and the man became a living being' (Genesis 2:7). It is the human spirit that gives us a consciousness of self and other remarkable, though limited, 'God-like' qualities. The human spirit includes our intellect, emotions, fears, passions, and creativity. It is this spirit that provides us with the unique ability to comprehend and understand (Job 32:8, 18).

Having established the principles by which to assess the human spirit of Jesus, it is now appropriate to see such spirituality in action. It is said that actions speak louder than words.

Three examples will be discussed: awareness, authenticity, and love. However, an overarching consideration in reviewing these actions will be the reality of 'relationship' as exercised between giver and receiver in these actions of the human spirit.

---

40 Victor E Frenkel, 1962, Man's Search for Meaning - An Introduction to Logotherapy – From Death Camp to Existentialism. New York: Touchstone Book.

The New Testament states, 'Jesus increased in wisdom and in stature and in favour with God and man' (Luke 2:52). From consideration of the Old Testament view of 'wisdom' and, in particular, that of the Proverbs, and early studies of philosophy, such 'wisdom' is usually referred to as residing in the 'heart' rather than the brain/mind focus of today. But the 'heart' was an expression, not simply as the pump, but as the source of wisdom, love, and spiritual insight.

It was further associated with the connected organs of the body, known today as the autonomic nervous system in which the heart is the central element. Importantly, we now know the heart has intelligence, small compared to the brain, but with an information processing capacity, nevertheless. Such information is transmitted to the brain for the holistic aspects of decision-making.[41]

It is thus essential to consider the role of 'soul' and 'spirit' in human action and the importance of associated relationships between giver and receiver. Such relationships are not simply abstract feelings but the actual exchange of information, sensations, understandings, etc., through our spiritual interconnectivity. This aspect will be discussed further in Chapter 5 along with an understanding of spiritual intelligence and emotional intelligence. Spiritual intelligence is defined as 'the intelligence with which we access our deepest meanings, values, purposes and highest motivation'.[42]

---

41 Rollin McCraty, Mike Atkinson and Ray Bradley, 2004, 'Electrophysiological Evidence of Intuition: Part 1. The Surprising Role of the Heart'. Journal of Alternative and Complementary Medicine, 10(1): 133–143.

42 Danah Zohar and Ian Marshall, 2004, Spiritual Capital, Bloomsbury Publishing, London.

Awareness

Awareness is usually defined as knowledge that something exists or understanding of a situation at the present time based on information or experience perceived in the relationship. Indeed, self-awareness is knowledge and awareness of one's own personality or character.

Many accounts in the Gospels show Jesus as understanding (or being aware) of the people's concerns, even before addressing an individual or community group. In other situations, Jesus was a step ahead of what they were saying, ready to take the conversation to the next level. He had an awareness of people's needs that enabled Him to communicate in ways that truly spoke to the moment. He was aware of their thoughts and what was in their hearts. Consider Luke 5:17–26: 'When Jesus saw their faith, he said, "Friend, your sins are forgiven."' Indeed, the friends of the paralytic man went to great effort to bring this man to Jesus. Jesus did not have to be God to know they had faith. He observed their actions.

At the same time, 'the Pharisees and the teachers of the law began thinking to themselves, "Who is this that speaks blasphemies? Who can forgive sins but God alone?" Jesus knew what they were thinking and asked [...]' (Luke. 5:21–22). Jesus perceived their questions and was clearly aware of their backgrounds. Hence, He redirected the question back onto the Pharisees, knowing His comments would evoke inner realities.

A woman had sneaked up behind Jesus in an anonymous fashion. As his power flowed into her body, Jesus knew something was going on. He stopped in the crowd, having 'realised that power had gone out from him' (Mark 5:30). Jesus turned to his disciples and said, 'Who touched me?' Matthew 9:20–22 explains:

And suddenly, a woman who had flow of blood for twelve years came from behind and touched the hem of His garment. For she said to herself, 'If only I may touch His garment, I shall be made well.' But Jesus turned around, and when He saw her, He said, 'Be of good cheer, daughter; your faith has made you well.'

Indeed, Jesus was very self-aware of His spiritual character. He understood who He was, what His mission was, and how He was going to accomplish the mission (Luke 4:18–19).

Authenticity

Authenticity encompasses the quality and values of being real or true both to yourself and the community and in practising relationships by acting in ways that show your true self and how you feel. In considering this spiritual value as demonstrated by Jesus the man, we can identify two levels at which to judge His authenticity. The first level is His relationship between His inward reality and the second, His actions associated with the outward expression of the inner reality. Authenticity is when these two are in harmony. To succeed in being authentic, you first have to know who your true self actually is.

Regardless, authenticity is a big deal to Jesus. In the twelfth chapter of Luke (12:2–3, *ESV*), He said, 'You can't keep your true self hidden forever; before long you'll be exposed. You can't hide behind a religious mask forever; sooner or later the mask will slip and your true face will be known.' This is contrasted by Jesus saying, 'If I alone bear witness about myself, my testimony is not deemed true' (John 5:31, *ESV*). Looking at His disciples, Jesus said:

Give to everyone who asks you, and if anyone takes what belongs to you, do not demand it back. Do to others as you would have them do to you. 'If you love those who love you, what credit is that to you? Even sinners love those who love them. And if you do good to those who are good to you, what credit is that to you? Even sinners do that. And if you lend to those from whom you expect repayment, what credit is that to you? Even sinners lend to sinners, expecting to be repaid in full. But love your enemies, do good to them, and lend to them without expecting to get anything back. Then your reward will be great, and you will be children of the Most High, because he is kind to the ungrateful and wicked. Be merciful, just as your Father is merciful. 'Do not judge, and you will not be judged. Do not condemn, and you will not be condemned. Forgive, and you will be forgiven. Give, and it will be given to you. A good measure, pressed down, shaken together and running over, will be poured into your lap. For with the measure you use, it will be measured to you.

—Luke 20:30–38, *NIV*

Significantly, when Jesus met the woman at the well in Samaria, she said, 'Sir, I perceive that you are a prophet' (John 4:19).

When Jesus suffered at his concocted trial, Pontius Pilate, the Roman Governor of Judaea, said to Him, 'So you are a king?' Jesus answered, 'You say that I am a king. For this purpose, I was born and for this purpose I have come into the world—to bear witness to the truth. Everyone who is of the truth listens to my voice.' Pilate said to him, 'What is truth?' After he had said this, he went back outside to the Jews and told them, 'I find no guilt in him' (John 18:37–38, *ESV*).

Kullberg writes 'Jesus also lived with authority. He didn't teach chemistry; He turned water into wine. He didn't teach weather patterns; He calmed storms. He didn't teach medicine; He healed hurting people and instructed His followers to heal in His name.' [43]

Love

In defining 'spiritual love' in action, Paul writes in 1 Corinthians 13:4–7:

> *Love is patient and kind; Love is not jealous or boastful; it is not arrogant or rude; Love does not insist on its own way; it is not irritable or resentful; it does not rejoice at wrong, but rejoices in the truth. Love bears all things, believes all things, hopes all things, endures all things.*

Such a statement shows spiritual love rooted in a spiritual connection that helps us find meaning and purpose in our lives. In terms of identifying 'love' as demonstrated by Jesus the man, we can see the close correlation and influence with His relationships between disciples, followers, and the community by engaging in spiritual practices. Such reality demonstrates the interconnectivity between Jesus and His team and followers.

In Matthew 22:37–39 (*ESV*), He said to a lawyer, 'You shall love the Lord your God with all your heart and with all your soul and with all your mind. This is the great and first commandment. And a second is like it: You shall love your neighbour as yourself.'

Jesus also showed us how to love others: 'This is my commandment, that ye love one another, as I have loved you'

43 Kelly Monroe Kullberg, 2009, 'Finding God Beyond Harvard: The Quest for Veritas' Inter Varsity Press, Illinois.

(John 15:12). Love is action. Jesus showed the depths of true love by example: many people had come to hear Jesus teach. They were there a long time and got very hungry. There was only a little bread and fish to feed all of the people. Jesus blessed the food and told His disciples to give it to the people. Everyone had enough to eat, and there was a lot of food leftover. (Matthew 14:13–21); 'I have compassion for these people; they have already been with me three days and have nothing to eat. I do not want to send them away hungry, or they may collapse on the way.' (Matthew 15:32). One day, Jesus saw a man who was blind—he could not see. Jesus blessed the man so he could see (John 9:1–12).

In summary, the extant biographies of Jesus (the books of Matthew, Mark, Luke, and John) show Jesus accepted and loved all people, especially those at the bottom of the social pyramid—poor people, women, outcasts, lepers, children, prostitutes, and tax collectors. But significantly, for our study of Jesus the entrepreneur, He has been shown to be an identified person in history and above all to exhibit the characteristics of a man in terms of body, soul, and spirit.

He didn't teach moral philosophy; He forgave and enabled us to forgive. He didn't teach a course on world hunger; He fed the multitudes and commanded His followers to feed them also.

Chapter 3: Jesus and a Social Entrepreneur Mindset—Are They Compatible?

Entrepreneurial culture and entrepreneur mindset are
inextricably interwoven.

—Dean Shepherd [44]

S ocial entrepreneurship, at its heart, is highly compatible with the values, beliefs, and goals expressed by Jesus in tackling major social issues during His time on earth by teaching us to love and serve one another.[45] Indeed, the application of these principles underpins the commitment to achieve social, economic, and environmental justice for today's citizens.

The focus, in this chapter, is to assess these and other objectives and behaviours, how these may apply to the mission of Jesus, and whether they are compatible with describing a dimension of Jesus the man as a social entrepreneur, and any impact on the community and future human history. By considering an ecosystem concept, it is possible to understand the linkages between entrepreneurial actions, value propositions, and multiple

44 Dean A Shepherd, Holger Patzelt and J. Michael Haynie, 2010. 'Entrepreneurial spirals: deviation-amplifying loops of an entrepreneurial mindset.' Entrepreneurship Theory and Practice, 34(1): 59–82.
45 Susan Calloway Knowles, 2013 https://www.crosswalk.com/family/career/jesus-a-social-entrepreneur.html.

networks or relationships impacting the solution/s to large scale social problems from first-century Judea to today. The method follows the ecosystem process introduced in Chapter 1 and is illustrated in Figure 3.1.

Significantly, this ecosystem model can broaden our appreciation of the contributions from Jesus' birth, formation, and preparation (micro level, Fig. 3.1), and through His period of public ministry (29–33 CE) as expressed in teaching, signs and wonders, relationships, and leadership (meso level, Fig. 3.1), and so form a conceptual base for understanding the holistic expression of Jesus as a social entrepreneur. These concepts will be discussed more fully in Chapters 4 and 5. From our understanding in Chapter 2 of Jesus as 'fully man', we can observe in the ecosystem model (Fig 3.1) the interrelationships between Jesus the person, the influences of the period, and Jesus' social and spiritual impact in the period from the Crucifixion and Resurrection to early Church development and growth.

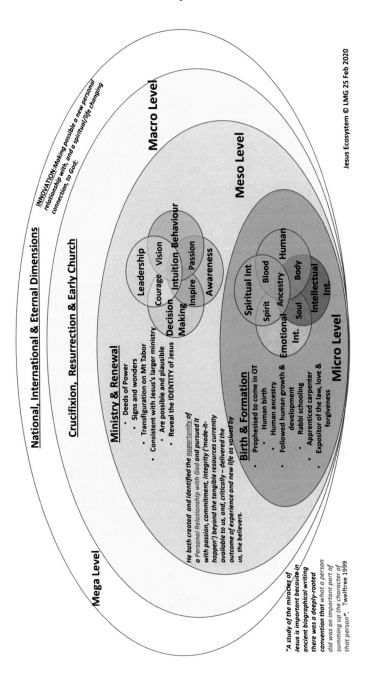

Figure 3.1 Jesus and an entrepreneurial ecosystem of the first century CE

To assess these contributions, it will be necessary to answer the question 'was Jesus really an entrepreneur?' We have established in Chapter 2 that Jesus was 'fully man', but was He a social entrepreneur? Importantly to our study, we know from history and personal experience that the legacy of this first-century-CE ministry and demonstration of faith, love, and serving one another did and continues to impact the development of history, national identity, political ideologies, values and morals, and religious systems. This later period is referred to as the mega level (Fig. 3.1) in this ecosystem. However, in this volume, only the micro and meso levels of the ecosystem will be reviewed in assessing the reality of Jesus the entrepreneur.

To facilitate our assessment of whether Jesus was a social entrepreneur, we need to first understand what it means to be entrepreneurial and then establish what is social entrepreneurship and the way it is practised. Subsequently, we will assess whether Jesus can be considered as having a social entrepreneur mindset. Of course, we will use the experience of recent social entrepreneurs to establish behaviours, beliefs, and practices before comparing them with the biblical examples of Jesus' ministry.

A relevant but controversial aspect of understanding entrepreneurs is whether such individuals are 'born' or 'made'; or are they the outcome of 'nature' or 'nurture'? Entrepreneur researchers, social psychologists, and economic theorists have all speculated whether entrepreneurs are born or made—in other words, whether you're predisposed to become an entrepreneur due to your genetic make-up or whether that disposition comes from your environment, conditioning, or other external influences. Research shows that achieving top performance, whether as an athlete or as an entrepreneur, is more dependent on passion and repeated practice than the inherent 'gift' or skill. 'Passion, an overwhelming drive to reach one's goals, is the single factor that unites all successful people in equal measure.'[46]

In considering Jesus, the Gospel accounts claim Jesus was in the ancestral line of Abraham and King David (Matthew 1:1–17). This claim reinforces the reality that babies derive their exhibited characteristics, features, and genes from their forebears, thus indicating Jesus was born 'fully' man. In addition, His birth fulfilled Old Testament prophecy. Hence, the genetic make-up of Jesus was from King David, who was both an outstanding leader and innovator, with Jesus showing great intellectual talent through His early years. In addition, Jesus received oneness with the Spirit at His baptism. Also, His ministry experience was delivered with love, passion, and commitment in delivering outstanding outcomes. With this background, one could not rule out Jesus as being entrepreneurially oriented.

Another fundamental factor in being entrepreneurially oriented is one's propensity for recognising opportunities: evaluating the potential for a successful application and delivering the opportunity to satisfy a need in the marketplace (business) or amongst users in a communal setting (social). Recognition, evaluation, and action on opportunities are central to the triggering of both entrepreneurial and innovative behaviour, leading to the investment of scarce resources to make the venture happen with the hope of future returns/benefits. At the conceptual level, such opportunity ventures—whether described as commercial or social entrepreneurship—depend on the mission: '[...] in practice, the opportunity dimension of the

46 William Clarke, 2017, https://www.tempstarstaffing.com/2017/05/11/passion-key-success/.

framework is perhaps the most distinct owing to fundamental differences in missions and responses to market failure.'[47]

Commercial entrepreneurship tends to focus on opportunities associated with technological breakthroughs and new needs, whereas social entrepreneurship focuses on serving basic, long-standing needs more effectively, such as aged care, through innovative approaches. For a commercial entrepreneur, an opportunity must have a large or growing total market, create added value, and the industry must be structurally attractive.

For a social entrepreneur, the mission opportunity must be timely, add value, and meet a recognised social need, demand, or service failure and deliver sufficient 'mission market' size and growth to be sustainable amongst the audience or followers. Clearly, the opportunity identified by Jesus ('change societal values and behaviours through a new relationship with God'), the target audience, and the recognised need in the community of the first century CE align with our understanding of social entrepreneurship rather than commercial entrepreneurship. In consideration of the mission concept described in the Gospels and the activities of Jesus in leading the mission, we can conclude that the mission is an example of social entrepreneurship and Jesus is a social entrepreneur. This concept is illustrated in Figure 3.2.

---

47 James Austin, Howard Stevenson and Jane Wei-Skillern, 2006, 'Social and Commercial Entrepreneurship: Same, Different, or Both?' Entrepreneurship Theory and Practice, Vol. 30 issue: 1, page(s): 1–22.

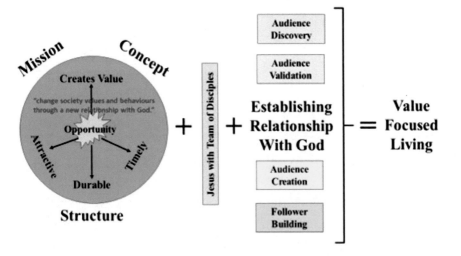

Figure 3.2 Dimensions of Opportunity Recognition in Social Ventures
(Adapted from Gillin & Spring, 2016)[48]

The fact is that Jesus recognised the opportunity to teach the community about a loving Father who created all that exists and who sought a personal relationship between God and man. Such a personal relationship was unheard of prior to Jesus implementing this aspiring undertaking.

A mission of this magnitude required persistence in an unfavourable world that predominantly worshipped idols or false gods. Additionally, Jesus tackled major social issues without seeking the assistance of the ruling government or look to businesses to resolve the problems that He encountered. Jesus took it upon Himself to heal the sick (Matthew 4:23, Mark 7:30, Mark 10:45, Luke 6:6–10, Matthew 15:28–30, Matthew 8:4), to bless (Mark

48 Murray Gillin and Stephen Spring, 2016, ' Entrepreneurship'. In 'Innovation and Entrepreneurship', (eds. D Samson and M Gloet), Oxford Press, Melbourne, pp 215–247.

10:13, Luke 18:15, Matthew 19:13), to wash the feet of his disciples (John 13:1–17), to raise the dead (Mark 5:21–43, John 11:1–45), to feed the masses (Matthew 14:13–21), among other things. It was all in an attempt to bring about a positive change in a sinful world that failed to properly serve its people. [49]

In the broadest sense, social entrepreneurs are innovators who seek new ways of offering solutions to societal challenges. They use entrepreneurial and innovation principles to promote social change. Social entrepreneurs build organisations, create products, and provide services intended to bring positive social change, somewhat irrespective of the bottom line. The goal of the social entrepreneur is to make the world a better place, which may or may not produce a profitable income stream.

In recognition of the impact of the social entrepreneurship initiated by Jesus,

The Roman Emperor Julian, writing in the fourth century, regretted the progress of Christianity because it pulled people away from the Roman gods. He said, 'Atheism [ie. the Christian faith] has been specially advanced through the loving service rendered to strangers, and through their care for the burial of the dead. It is a scandal that there is not a single Jew who is a beggar, and that the godless Galileans care not only for their own poor but for ours as well; while those who belong to us look in vain for the help that we should render them. [50]

49 Bart D Ehrman, 2013, 'Did Jesus Exist?: The Historical Argument for Jesus of Nazareth', Harper Collins USA.

50 John Piper, 2001, Quoting from Roman Emperor Julian in the 4th Century CE, https://www.goodreads.com/quotes/342592-the-roman-emperor-julian-writing-in-the-fourth-century-regretted.

An important corollary to meeting a social need is 'not the existence of the need, but rather whether the necessary resources can be marshalled for the social entrepreneur's innovation to serve that need.' Social entrepreneurship is thus, 'similar to commercial entrepreneurship in that the recognition of opportunities to create or innovate is the initiation point of the entrepreneurial process.'[8] Therefore, while opportunity recognition is central to all processes associated with entrepreneurship, for social entrepreneurship, successful 'exploitation' is dependent on: user discovery, user validation, user creation, and mission building (Figure 3.2).

This concept of social entrepreneurship to solve social problems has existed for ages as a key mechanism to promoting social justice. In New Testament times and the ministry of Jesus, social entrepreneurship (as practised above) was key to the spread of the gospel and social justice in the early church in the Roman Empire. There was no concept of charity to the poor in Roman culture.

However, by caring for those in need who were outside of their own families and communities, Christians acted as evangelists of the new personal relationship with God and as social innovators that through the last 2,000 years have and continue to deliver outpourings of 'love' in practice to the needy and unjustly treated. This aspect is clearly shown in the ecosystem (Fig. 3.1) at the mega Level—'national, international and external dimensions'— where innovation makes possible continuing access to a personal relationship with, and a spiritual/life-changing connection to, God.

In part-answer to the question 'are Jesus and the social entrepreneur mindset compatible,' we can conclude Jesus is very much the social entrepreneur, but taking into account the continuing growth in His followers and the many benefiting from delivered care and love, behaviours, values, and meeting human need in an uncaring society, it is more appropriate to describe

Jesus as the *ultimate social entrepreneur* and perhaps the most successful social entrepreneur of all time.

However, there is a further dimension to our question— that of the social entrepreneur mindset. To explore this aspect further, we will need to examine recent and living examples of outstanding social entrepreneurs to understand the dimensions of any associated mindset, establish extant characteristics, and develop an agreed definition of 'social entrepreneur mindset' to then compare with Jesus the social entrepreneur.

In today's understanding of commerce, international trade, wealth creation, and the ever-increasing dependence on technology-enhanced living, entrepreneurship is usually observed as a major driver of economic growth, job creation, and competitiveness in local and global markets. Such a concept involves reallocating resources to a new use that produces a preferred outcome in line with market and user needs/demands. Thus, entrepreneurship is a planned behaviour. It is not the product of unconscious and unintended antecedents, but rather is a 'conscious and intended act' that is 'aimed either at creating a new venture or creating new values in existing ventures.'[51] This act is the response to an entrepreneur mindset.

By way of illustration, the distinctive behaviours that we associate with entrepreneurs such as Bill Gates, Rupert Murdoch, Richard Pratt, Richard Branson, Thomas Edison, or Steve Jobs are not their wealth, but rather their vision of a better tomorrow and their achievements in building viable enterprises that turn those visions into reality, at a profit.

Many successful entrepreneurs are found outside traditional business enterprises, launching ventures that bridge the gap

---

51 Donald Kuratko and David Audretsch 2009, 'Strategic Entrepreneurship: Exploring Different Perspectives of an Emerging Concept', Entrepreneurship Theory and Practice, Vol 33, Issue 1.

between the commercial sector and the social one. For example, Dr Fred Hollows established a not-for-profit program based in Australia to treat cataract sufferers in the developing world at no cost to those patients and established factories in Eritrea and Nepal to manufacture intraocular lenses for transplant. It is estimated that over one million people can see today because of initiatives instigated by Hollows.[52]

Significantly, entrepreneurs who create or recognise opportunities and then seize and shape them into high-potential ventures/services think and do things differently from conventional business managers. They operate in an entrepreneurial domain, a place governed by creative modes of action and dominated by passionately focused driving forces. Consider, for example, the Brotherhood of St Laurence® (BSL). This social enterprise was established during the Great Depression as the vision and creation of Fr Gerard Tucker, a man who combined his Christian faith with a fierce determination to end social injustice.

The Brotherhood has developed into an independent organisation with strong Anglican and community links. Their vision is 'an Australia free of poverty'. The Brotherhood delivers programs and services to support disadvantaged people of all ages to build better lives for themselves. BSL aims to develop innovative services that support social change and help achieve its vision by:

- empowering themselves and the people they work for
- developing and building community capacity, as part of the community

52 Fred Hollows quoted in Gillin And Spring (2016) - (http://www.hollows.org.au/Fred-Hollows).

- creating and developing enterprise projects and ventures as catalysts for individual and community transformation.

Such a social enterprise is a business. But the BSL is a business with a difference. All profits made by the social enterprise are reinvested back into the community to develop much-needed services and resources. Each social enterprise is run in a socially responsible and entrepreneurial manner, and the business itself often provides an unmet service to the community: e.g., In 2000, BSL acquired Modstyle—an importer and wholesaler of optical frames to meet their social market; BSL community stores, selling recycled clothing and homewares; Hunter Gatherer® stores, selling hand-picked retro clothing; a No Sweat Shop® accredited fashion label; and accessories and homewares sourced from young independent designers.[53]

Social Entrepreneurship:

> *Social entrepreneurs are not content*
> *just to give a fish or teach how to fish.*
> *They will not rest until they have*
> *revolutionized the fishing industry.*
> —Bill Drayton, CEO and founder of Ashoka

Importantly, and from the example of Fr Tucker above, it is clear that the application of entrepreneurship concepts and behaviours can be, and are, exhibited in many socially directed and delivered ventures/enterprises that seek to turn recognised opportunities into an outcome that meets personal/community need.

---

53 Brotherhood of St Laurence https://www.bsl.org.au/about/our-history/.

Such social entrepreneurship has become a global movement—a movement with a goal to effect positive social change. But are all social services entrepreneurial and innovative? Opportunities in social sectors, including environmental, poverty, aging, and human rights issues, etc., are driven by large, complex problems. Perhaps we can be so bold as to call such social problems 'wicked problems.'[54] In the early 1970s, wicked problems were contrasted with tame problems. In other words, the linear and traditional approaches to solving tame problems were being used on social issues with little success. Further observation indicated that these problems were ill-defined, so the perception of the actual problem was the symptom of another problem. As such, 'wicked problems became characterised as malign, vicious, tricky, and aggressive.'[54]

As with any emerging area of intellectual and practical significance, it is important to have a guiding definition for the purpose of shared understanding and discussion. Two definitions of social entrepreneurship are noted:

Social entrepreneurs play the role of change agents in the social sector by (1) adopting a mission to create and sustain social value (not just private value); (2) recognising and relentlessly pursuing new opportunities to serve that mission; (3) engaging in a process of continuous innovation, adaptation, and learning; (4) acting boldly without being limited by resources currently in hand; and (5) exhibiting heightened accountability to the constituencies served and for the outcomes created.[55]

---

54 Jeffrey Timmons, Murray Gillin , Sam Burshtein and Stephen Spinelli.. 2011 'New Venture Creation – Entrepreneurship for the 21st Century, McGraw-Hill, Australia (Pacific Edition) PP 240.

55 Gregory Dees, 1998, 'The Meaning of Social Entrepreneurship', Kauffman Foundation and Stanford University, Kansas City and Pao Alto.

Social entrepreneurship arises from an unconscious spirit of generosity within various people who produce a facility to envision, resource, and enable effective actions that otherwise exist as an unmet need. Need is lessened by a social entrepreneur who possesses unique qualities to match the need. [56]

These definitions share a common theme: their method and execution are entrepreneurial in thinking and action, while their mission and purpose are driven by social need and benefit. Four examples follow to illustrate the central position of meeting social need and delivering a benefit to the user:

The Prince's Trust

Entrepreneurship is a way of thinking, reasoning and acting that is opportunity obsessed, holistic in approach, and leadership balanced. [57]

—Jeffry Timmons (1998)

This is a charity in the United Kingdom founded in 1976 by HRH Charles, Prince of Wales, to help vulnerable young people get their lives on track. It supports eleven- to thirty-year-olds who are unemployed and those struggling at school and at risk of exclusion. Many of the young people helped by the Trust are in or leaving care, facing issues such as homelessness or mental health problems, or have been in trouble with the law—indeed a 'wicked' problem.

---

56 Loris Gillin, 'Social Value Creation: Core Determinant from the Impact of Social Entrepreneurship', PhD Thesis, Swinburne University of Technology, 2005.

57 Jeffry Timmons 1998, 'America's entrepreneurial revolution', Franklin Olin Graduate School of Busines, Babson College MA.

The Trust runs a range of training programmes providing practical and financial support to build young people's confidence and motivation—over 950,000 young people have been helped to turn their lives around; it has created 125,000 entrepreneurs and given business support to 395,000 people in the UK. From 2006 to 2016, its work for the youth has been worth an estimated £1.4 billion.

Significantly, during the COVID-19 pandemic, HRH the Prince of Wales says young people in the UK need help 'more than ever' as he acknowledges the impact of the pandemic.[58]

In 2015, the Prince's Trust International was launched at the Commonwealth Heads of Government Meeting in Malta. It is an independent charity, with HRH the Prince of Wales as its founder and president. As in the UK, PTI supports young people in Australia, Canada, the Caribbean, Greece, India, Jordan, Malta, New Zealand, and Pakistan. Over 10,000 young people across the world have experienced the support of the Trust, with 66% successfully entering work, education, or training. This is an exciting time for Prince's Trust International as they implement a new five-year strategy designed to help 100,000 young people over the next five years and raise £50 million in order to transform their lives.[59]

In 2015, *The Telegraph* reported, 'Evergreen Prince has changed the world':

> *In 1969 Prince Charles lobbied the Prime Minister, Harold Wilson concerning the fate of Atlantic Salmon. That intervention preceded the foundation of either Friends of the Earth or Greenpeace, and the Prince—who turns 65*

---

58 Princes Trust, https://www.princes-trust.org.uk/about-the-trust/news-views, June 2020.

59 HRH Prince Charles, June 2020, https://princestrustinternational.org/about-us/.

on Thursday (14, Nov. 2015)—has continued to be ahead of his time, with a remarkable eye for issues that will later become widely adopted. In 1970, he advocated new regulatory standards for pollution, and he was pressing for action on global warming in the late Eighties.

Sir Richard Branson, in referring to the work of the Prince's Trust, says 'that the sooner young people start learning about entrepreneurship, the better, as the skills that can be gained are manifold.'[60] Penny Junor, in her book, says:

[Prince Charles] has helped where no bank manager would have considered their application—even if they had known how to apply for a loan. Prince Charles believed in their potential and has put time, thought, effort and money into helping through the Prince's Trust and its various offshoots.[61]

Muhammad Yunus

Born 28 June 1940, Yunus is a Bangladeshi social entrepreneur, banker, economist, and civil society leader who founded the Grameen Bank and pioneered the loan concepts of microcredit and microfinance.[62] From the 1970s, using this concept, these loans were given to entrepreneurs too poor to qualify for traditional bank loans. In 2006, Yunus and the Grameen Bank were jointly awarded the Nobel Peace Prize 'for their efforts through microcredit to create economic and social development from below'. The Norwegian Nobel Committee

60 The Telegraph- September 15, 2014.
61 Penny Junor, 1998, 'Charles Victim or Villain', (pp.54).
62 http://www.muhammadyunus.org.

said that 'lasting peace cannot be achieved unless large population groups find ways in which to break out of poverty' and that 'across cultures and civilisations, Yunus and Grameen Bank have shown that even the poorest of the poor can work to bring about their own development'.

Yunus co-founded Yunus Social Business (YSB) as a global initiative. YSB creates and empowers social businesses to address and solve social problems around the world. As the international implementation arm for Yunus' vision of new, humane capitalism, YSB manages incubator funds for social businesses in developing countries and provides advisory services to companies, governments, foundations, and NGOs.

The belief that money and wealth are the ultimate good has, Yunus thinks, given rise to a 'wicked problem' comprising three great societal ills: unemployment, as competition increases for a set number of jobs; environmental destruction, which is accepted as a side-effect of economic growth; and poverty, an inevitable consequence of wealth concentration.

In his latest book, *A World of Three Zeros,*[63] Yunus discusses a new concept of business: the 'social business', which has the objective of addressing a social problem rather than accumulating wealth. Sitting in between for-profit and non-profit enterprises, the social business satisfies the selfless component of human instinct, so far ignored by an economic theory (and system) driven by selfishness. Humans, Yunus says, 'are both selfish *and* selfless,' and they should be allowed (and educated) to measure business success not just in terms of monetary gain but also in the ability to improve society.

Yunus, who has seen social businesses flourish thanks to microfinance loans, rests his vision of a new system on two core

63 Muhammad Yunis, 2017, 'A World of Three Zeroes - The New Economics of Zero Poverty, Zero Unemployment, and Zero Carbon Emissions.' Hachette Books NY.

principles. The first is that people are born to be entrepreneurs, but this nature gets constrained in a system that teaches them to be merely job seekers, limiting job creation to a privileged few. The second is that some people would fulfil that natural inclination by starting businesses that do not have wealth accumulation as their only goal if only they thought doing so were an acceptable measure of success.

And if wealth were not the only yardstick, Yunus says, new objectives and goals would open up in front of our eyes. People would solve unemployment by becoming, in larger numbers, job creators rather than job seekers. As a result, they would stay out of poverty, having access to capital as long as they can create a sustainable business, even if it doesn't produce enormous wealth. And they would protect the environment by considering it a resource, not merely fuel to more wealth creation.

Florence Nightingale

Florence has many titles to her name. She has been known as the Lady of the Lamp and the Mother of Modern Nursing.[64] The Crimean War (October 1853) was a brutal battle fought between an alliance of Britain, France, Turkey, and Sardinia against the Russian Empire. A tragic outcome for Britain was that thousands of its young men were sent to the front to give their all, but many young men wound up wounded and sick at the British hospital in Constantinople. It is worth noting that the majority of deaths were not a result of combat but rather disease. For example, 2,755 of the British Empire's force were killed in action compared with the 17,580 who died of disease. Even when brought to the hospital in Scutari, the patients were 'swarming with vermin, huge lice crawling all about their persons and clothes. Many

64 Barbara C. Phillips, www.NPBusiness.ORG/florence/.

were grimed with mud, dirt, blood and gunpowder stains. Several were completely prostrated by fever and dysentery.' Nightingale comments that 'the sight was a pitiable one and such as I never before witnessed ...' This was the situation when Nightingale, and her nurses, arrived at Scutari, near Constantinople, on 3 November 1854, and recognised the conditions were dire—indeed a 'wicked' problem. The dirty and vermin-ridden hospital lacked even basic equipment and provisions. The medical staff were swamped by the large number of soldiers being shipped across the Black Sea from the war in the Crimea with the majority of casualties suffering from disease rather than from battle wounds.

But it did not deter Florence Nightingale and her group of thirty-four nurses. They accepted the challenge and worked tirelessly improving the medical and sanitary arrangements at Scutari by setting up food kitchens, treating the wounded, cleaning the soldiers, and washing their linen and clothes. Their work in Crimea set the standards for modern professional nursing. Importantly, Florence Nightingale drew upon her entrepreneurial talents of organising, structuring, persuading, and creating. She helped her patients, or 'customers', and provided overwhelming value to them. This was innovation in action. The team created something different, something new out of the individual parts and delivered a service valued by all in the hospital. This response to a dire need amongst these military casualties was not an end in itself. On return to England, Nightingale committed her total energy, and indeed her life, to applying these experiences to improving the provision of health care to the community at large using her entrepreneurial behaviour to deliver universal access to 'patient-centred' care. This legacy is indicated by abstracts taken from her obituary.

The obituary for Florence Nightingale appeared in *The Times* on 15 August 1910.[65] Amongst many references to the outstanding contributions to nursing care in her life, it is noted that:

> *a fund for a national commemoration of her services had been started, the income from the proceeds, £45,400, being eventually devoted partly to the setting up at St. Thomas's Hospital of a training school for hospital and infirmary nurses and partly to the maintenance and instruction at King's College Hospital of midwifery nurses. For herself she would have neither public testimonial nor public welcome.*
>
> *[...]*
>
> *The demand for district nurses soon became so great that more were clearly necessary, and Miss Nightingale was consulted as to what should be done. She replied that all the nurses then in training at St. Thomas's were wanted for hospital work, and she recommended that a training school for nurses should be started in Liverpool.*
>
> *[...]*
>
> *Great and most beneficent changes, again, have followed the substitution in workhouse infirmaries of trained nurses for the pauper women to whose tender mercies the care of the sick in those institutions was formerly left. It was a 'Nightingale probationer,' the late Agnes Jones, and twelve of her fellow-nurses from the Nightingale School at St. Thomas's who were the pioneers of this reform at the Brownlow-hill Infirmary, Liverpool; and it was undoubtedly the spirit and the teaching of Florence Nightingale that inspired them*

---

65 https://vauxhallhistory.org/florence-nightingale-times-obituary/.

in a task which, difficult enough under the conditions then existing, was to create a precedent for Poor Law authorities all the land over.

[...]

Midwifery was another branch of the nursing art which Florence Nightingale sought to reform.

The Times concludes with a statement that surely underlines the personal values to support patient-centred care:

At her own request the money which would have been spent on a gold casket was devoted to charity, the sum of 100 guineas being given instead to the Hospital for Invalid Gentlewomen; and the casket presented to Miss Nightingale was of oak.

Rosie Batty AO

Born in 1962, Batty is an English-born Australian domestic violence campaigner and 2015 Australian of the Year. Domestic violence is a worldwide 'wicked' problem with no—as yet—legislated or community solution. Her entrepreneurial behaviour in articulating a nationwide campaign for action began in 2014 after her eleven-year-old son Luke Batty was murdered by his father, Greg Anderson.

In April 2013, Anderson wielded a knife at Luke when they were alone inside his car, reportedly telling him that 'it could all end with this'. Batty decided that she could no longer support Anderson in having contact with Luke. After she reported the incident to police, the court ordered that Anderson could have no further contact with his son, and an intervention order naming both Batty and Luke as protected persons was granted. In July 2013, Anderson challenged the decision in a court hearing and was granted access to Luke in public when he was playing sport.[66]

Rosie Batty knows pain no woman should have to suffer. Her son was killed by his father in a violent incident in February 2014, a horrendous event that shocked not only the nation but the world. Greg Anderson murdered his eleven-year-old son Luke and was then shot by police at the Tyabb cricket oval. Rosie had suffered years of family violence and had had intervention and custody orders in place in an effort to protect herself and her son. She believes the killing was Greg's final act of control over her.

Since those events of 2014, Rosie has become an outspoken crusader and entrepreneur against domestic violence, winning hearts and minds all over Australia with her compassion, courage, grace, and forgiveness. In the wake of the tragedy, Rosie's advocacy work has forced an unprecedented national focus on family violence, with the Victorian Labor government establishing Australia's first royal commission into family violence and committing a further $30 million over four years to protect women and children at high risk of family violence. The then-Victorian Police Commissioner Ken Lay called it 'the Rosie Batty factor'. In January 2015, Rosie was named Australian of the Year for 2015.

In 2016, then-Prime Minister Malcolm Turnbull said of domestic violence in Australia that 'cultural change requires a great advocate and Rosie has been able to do that in a way that I think nobody has done before'.

On 10 June 2019, Batty was appointed an Officer of the Order of Australia in recognition of her 'distinguished service to the

---

66 Rosie Batty with Bryce Corbett , A Mother's Story, 2015 Harper Collins.

community as a campaigner and advocate for the prevention of family violence'.

Batty is considered to have had a significant influence on national public attitudes, philanthropy, government initiatives and funding, support services and police and legal procedures related to domestic violence in Australia and established the Luke Batty Foundation to give voice to women and children affected by the trauma of domestic and family violence.

Jesus' Vision and Mission

In seeking to review the vision and mission of Jesus from the perspective of social entrepreneurship, and in particular His entrepreneurial behaviour, it is helpful to use the adapted Timmons Model[54] (Figure 3.3) to evaluate the different elements contributing to value-focused-living through a personal relationship with God (Fig. 3.1). In this adapted model (Fig. 3.3), Jesus, as a social entrepreneur, is shown as the founder and the fulcrum for balancing primary components; namely, a people-centred opportunity; resources—comprising human, financial, and spiritual; and a team of disciples to deliver the ministry of a new relationship. Of course, the mission is subject to the external factors of exogenous forces, ambiguity, uncertainty, and the spiritual context for the message, much of which was discussed in Chapter 1, 'Introduction to the First Century CE'.

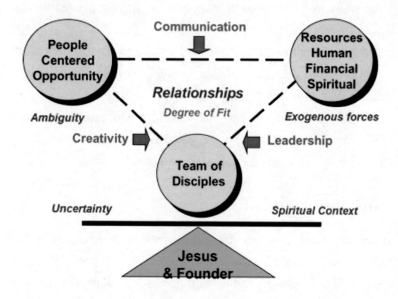

Figure 3. 3 Social Opportunity Process Model (Adapted from Timmons)

The components in the process model certainly apply to social entrepreneurship, but the model requires a few contextual changes. Social opportunities, for example, are driven not only by markets but also by mission and social needs. The managing team—and the external stakeholders—are especially important here because collaboration across boundaries is paramount in social entrepreneurship. Similar to traditional start-ups, the art of bootstrapping is a necessary method of resource acquisition in the early stage of not-for-profit and social-focused ventures. Importantly, capital markets, sponsorship, donations, and philanthropy exist to resource social entrepreneurs in their mission/not-for-profit sectors.

Social entrepreneurship seeks to solve wicked problems, and such problems cannot be solved alone or even with a small start-up team. The environment to solve social problems requires a spirit of collaboration, and therefore, in the social entrepreneurship context, the management team—with its external stakeholders—is particularly important. The four case examples above illustrate the importance to the social entrepreneur of recognising the 'wicked' problem. However, in meeting the community's needs, the examples fully demonstrate the personal characteristics required to make it happen and, even more significantly, the mind and spirit of a true entrepreneur.

Starting a social venture from an entrepreneurial vision is exciting and demanding, but the means to enable sustainability and long-term service/delivery of the vision in meeting users' needs requires a multi-skilled team and access to ongoing resources. Recent research shows a propensity to run out of resources has bedevilled the not-for-profit/social entrepreneurship organisation for generations, therefore, the highest priority of any not-for-profit venture is to 'manage the risk' associated with achieving the social value identified for 'meeting a need'.

For the case of Jesus in first-century-CE Judea and Galilee, sustaining His ministry to the community as a not-for-profit activity, He used the principles of simplicity, team input, donations, and loyal followers. Jesus was able to meet the needs of His hearers. This aspect will be more fully discussed in Chapter 6.

Sustaining the social venture requires collaborative and interactive association/alliance in an enablement way with others outside the organisation. The Enablement Effectiveness Model, Figure 3.4, provides a representation of the integration of motivated visionaries and necessary resources to achieve sustainable value creation for the stakeholders/users. Both social entrepreneurs and support teams are integral to the success of the social venture in fulfilling an identified need and fulfilling collaborative enablement. Being opportunity/mission conscious, a social entrepreneur inspires, and the team gives support. A contagion passes between them.

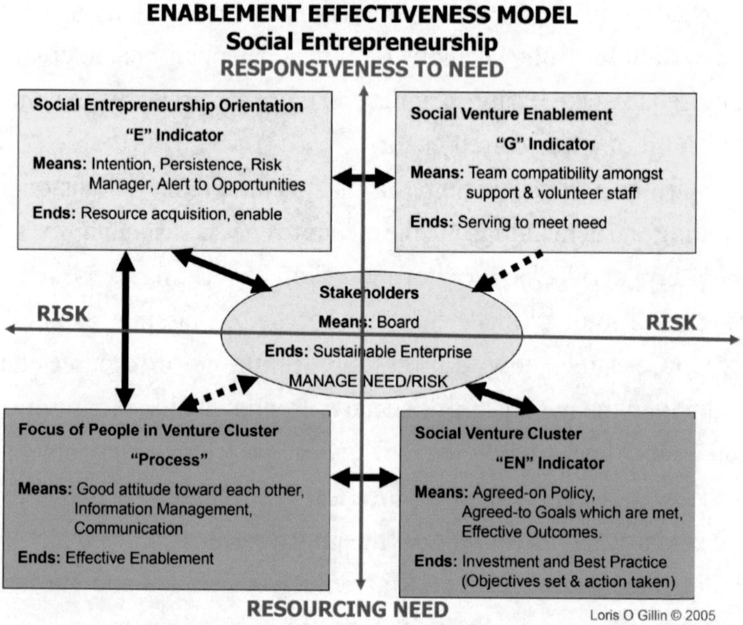

Figure 3.4 Enablement Effectiveness Model for Social Entrepreneurs (Loris O Gillin, 2006)[67]

Using this model, we can show Jesus the entrepreneur ('E' Indicator, Fig. 3.4) as driving the ministry from within with vision, passion, and enthusiasm; those who support (ministry enablers) are drawn to the project from outside with a commitment to the cause (or inspired following). Together, these factors catalyse the energy to provide the holistic resources to meet the mission's

67 Loris Gillin, 2006, 'A Model for Social Value Creation Within Social Entrepreneurship Ventures: Governance and Stakeholder Factors', AGSE Entrepreneurship Research Exchange, Auckland. NZ.l.

needs. Importantly, Jesus as the social entrepreneur combines: leadership; spiritual energy; intentional action, perseverance, responsiveness to risk, and alertness to opportunity in driving the ministry forward.

So this sustainable ministry can be represented on two axes, with the vertical axis showing the upper half based on 'responsiveness to need' and the lower half based on 'resourcing need' (Fig. 3.4). The other parameter—risk—can be managed by considering not only the value added but also the value lost to various related groups with assessed consequences. Being opportunity mission-conscious to the 'need', the model indicates Jesus, the social entrepreneur, as responding to the need through inspirational/spiritual leadership, and the team giving passionate and committed support. In respect of resourcing the need, the opportunity is enabled through association with clusters of empowering organisations and/or actors acting with strategic intent and due process throughout the community resource chain. These organisations/actors invest not only with capital but with skills, specialisations, and services to address best practices. In today's world, a further factor for the enterprise success requires a purpose-driven board that leads to professional-style governance that can work cooperatively and yet be a sounding board to the social entrepreneur.

In 2013, the International Council for Small Business (ICSB) met to explore the potential disconnect between the twentieth-century entrepreneurial point of view in business and the evolving twenty-first-century focus on achieving sustainable needs. The main question posed by ICSB was, 'How should entrepreneurship be defined in a changing world?' This was to be a search for a new definition of entrepreneurship, with a particular emphasis on how entrepreneurial behaviour relates to social issues in today's world.[68]

By 2016, a new working term evolved to describe a new model of entrepreneurship: 'humane entrepreneurship', based on the idea that entrepreneurs should extend their priorities beyond their profit margin toward their employees, people, environment, and society, where entrepreneurship is considered as a strategic posture. This concept can be expressed as:

> *A behavioral model of entrepreneurship is suggested because behaviours rather than attributes are what give meaning to the entrepreneurial process. An individual's psychological profile does not make a person an entrepreneur. Rather, we know entrepreneurs through their actions. In short, behavior is the central and essential element in the entrepreneurial process.*[69]

The proposed 'humane entrepreneurship' model was based on entrepreneur orientation (EO) theory, corporate social responsibility (CSR) theory, and servant leadership theory (SLT),[70] which is capable of better facing the pressures and expectations of sustainability that have been growing in organisational environments. This model is better suited to taking on the challenges of the twenty-first century by identifying and exploiting entrepreneurial opportunities

68 Roberto Parente, Ayman El Tarabishy, Massimiliano Vesci, Antonio Botti, 2018, 'The Epistemology of Humane Entrepreneurship: Theory and Proposal for Future Research Agenda', Journal of Small Business Management, Vol. 56.
69 Covin, J. G., and D. P. Slevin (1991). 'A Conceptual Model of Entrepreneurship as Firm Behavior,' Entrepreneurship Theory and Practice 16(1), 7–25.
70 White book (2016). Humane Entrepreneurship. Available https://docs.wixstatic. com/ugd/ cc1725_c642180108094a59b1c53bb81a8b6d2b.pdf.

through the active involvement of people inside and outside organisational boundaries.[71]

Indeed, these three principles of EO, CSR, and SLT are readily identifiable as elements contributing to the ministry of Jesus and the team in first-century-CE Judea and Galilee. Maybe the Jesus-led mission was the first example of this humane entrepreneurship model.

Applying the framework[72] for analysing the role of entrepreneurial orientation (EO) in social contexts, a pioneering study of Australian aged care facilities[73] identified that, in addition to the dimensions of EO—innovativeness, proactiveness, risk-taking, autonomy and competitive aggressiveness—the additional dimensions of 'governance' and 'trust' were essential elements for facility, board, and staff delivery of valued services to residents in these high performing aging facilities. Importantly, this study concluded that such facilities, operating as social entrepreneurial ventures, were characterised by both the senior operational leadership and board members exercising an entrepreneur mindset (see next section) in delivering service delivery to residents in need.

Earlier research on the strategic intent of entrepreneurs within entrepreneurially led companies noted the preconditions for their success or failure fits well with the concept of humane entrepreneurship with its focus on entrepreneur strategic posture

71 Roberto Parente, Ayman El Tarabishy, Antonio Botti, Massimiliano Vesci & Rosangela Feola (2020): https://doi.org/10.1080/00472778.2020.1717292.

72 Tom Lumpkin, Todd Moss, David Gras, Shoko Kato, and Alejandro Amezcua, (2013), 'Entrepreneurial processes in social contexts: how are they different, if at all?', Small Business Economics 40(3):1–23.

73 Lois Hazelton, 2012, 'Governance and Stewardship in the Aged Care Industry: Evaluating a model for Corporate Social Entrepreneurship - The relationship of Board culture To entrepreneurial behaviour' Thesis, University of Adelaide.

and how entrepreneurial behaviour relates to social issues in today's world.[74] The core sample of entrepreneurs interviewed all showed, to varying degrees, both moral and professional commitment to their chosen entrepreneurial goals, team, and venture. Individual entrepreneurs in the study were mapped by reviewing their education, character propensity, and prior career experiences, but significantly, a common thread became evident with every interviewee. That thread is best coined as the 'spiritual' driver—and relates to the holistic reality of the entrepreneur as both body and spirit.

This intensely human dimension of 'spirit' motivates the entrepreneur to drive him or herself beyond the accepted normal standards of business activity and focus to achieve the sought-after level of success that transcends the merely financial or material. This is the success that also seeks the genuine recognition of one's peers, family, and staff, and, perhaps more importantly, one's inner self. A phrase recorded by one interviewee epitomises the reality of 'spirit' existence:

> *I do not really care that I may be forgoing large salary opportunities and large-company benefits by working in my own small entrepreneurial company; what I'm doing is what I choose to do because I want to and because it gives me great satisfaction to build something worthwhile and to do it with a group of people that I am proud to work with.*

Figure 3.5 shows how this 'human spirit' dimension encapsulates the entrepreneurial values of the entrepreneurs interviewed.

---

74 Robert Ipasso, 2002, The strategic intent of entrepreneurs within entrepreneurially led companies and the preconditions for their success or failure, Thesis, Swinburne University of Technology, Australia.

Figure 3.5 Visual Interpretation of Entrepreneurial Values (Ipasso, 2002)

Entrepreneur Mindset

The concept of an 'entrepreneur mindset' seeks to encapsulate the importance of the 'whole' being to the expressed behaviour of the entrepreneur committed to making it happen. Such a concept integrates the realities of intellectual intelligence, emotional intelligence, and spiritual intelligence in delivering entrepreneurial outcomes leading to user-valued innovations.

Entrepreneur mindset is a way of thinking about opportunities that surface in the firm's external and internal environment and the commitments, decisions, and actions necessary to pursue them, especially under conditions of uncertainty that commonly accompany rapid and significant environmental changes.[75] Entrepreneurs are, by definition, ordinary people

---

75 Duane Ireland, Michael Hitt and David Sirmon, 2003, 'A Model of Strategic Entrepreneurship: The Construct and Its Dimensions', Journal of Management 29(6).

who do extraordinary things. For fifty years, researchers have sought unique explanations for why entrepreneurs do what they do. In the past twenty years, the focus has been on the entrepreneurial mindset, or, as in this book, seeking to understand the entrepreneur mindset of Jesus as an outstanding example of social entrepreneurship. Recent research by Pidduck, Clark, and Lumpkin have shown that entrepreneurial mindset is:

> *a goal orientation formed through dispositional beliefs (a belief that is not currently being considered by the mind) about entrepreneurship and opportunity beliefs (feasibility and market fit of a venture idea), which results in entrepreneurial behaviours.*[76]

The focus for discussion in this section is informed by research conducted in a financial services firm[77] and with nurses who become practitioners, not just of their profession but of entrepreneurial behaviour,[78] and from my understandings of Jesus and His leadership of the mission team of disciples. Such behaviour is often equated with the cultivation of innovation culture as the organisation's most precious asset and a strong indicator of a healthy and successful organisation/mission. The question is, 'What gives rise to achieving such a culture?'

---

76 Pidduck Robert, Clark Daniel and Lumpkin Tom, 2021 Entrepreneurial mindset: Dispositional beliefs, opportunity beliefs, and entrepreneurial behavior, Journal of Small Business Management, DOI: 10.1080/00472778.2021.1907582.

77 Murray Gillin, 2020, 'Facilitating intuitive decision-making and an entrepreneurial mindset in corporate culture – a case study' - (Chapter 17) 3rd Handbook of Intuition Research Ed. Marta Sinclair, Handbook of Intuition as Practice, Edward Elgar Publishing, Cheltenham.

78 Murray Gillin and Lois Hazelton, 2020, 'Bringing an entrepreneurial mindset to health care: a new tool for better outcomes,' Journal of Business Strategy, https://doi.org/10.1108/JBS-03-2020-0049.

Significantly, consideration is given to the umbilical link between thoughts, beliefs, and actions leading to practice amongst the team of an entrepreneurial culture. Indeed, your mindset in such a culture is your individual collection of thoughts and beliefs that shape your thought habits and ongoing actions. Your thought habits affect how you think, what you feel, and what you do. Your mindset impacts how you make sense of the world and how you make sense of yourself. Such mindsets are linked inextricably to behaviours that lead to developing recognised opportunities into growth-oriented innovations that meet user needs.

An important aspect in developing an entrepreneurial mindset is associated with understanding how your attitudes develop a settled way of thinking or feeling toward team members or about the service/product, and typically reflected in the entrepreneur's behaviour. Jesus reflected an amazing synergy between articulated attitudes and personalised behaviours in setting the cultural ambience for the mission. The resulting entrepreneur mindset is a growth-oriented perspective through which individuals promote flexibility, creativity, continuous innovation, and spiritual renewal. In other words, even under the cloak of uncertainty, the entrepreneurially minded can identify and exploit new opportunities because they have cognitive abilities that allow them to impart meaning to ambiguous and fragmented situations.

But an organisation/mission, of itself, is not entrepreneurially minded—the behaviour that may be present within the organisation/mission is driven by the human propensity to be entrepreneurial as expressed by leaders and staff identifying opportunities with application to the marketplace. Such innovation does not happen by accident or from outside consultants. Rather, the best innovation comes from within, from people across all levels of the organisation/mission and social ecosystem.

Entrepreneurship and innovation are inherently human behaviours and generated most effectively when staff/team work together. But how does one engage strategically to empower, educate, support, and create the cultural shift that facilitates innovation? Indeed, healthcare professionals or the disciples of Jesus may not think of themselves as 'entrepreneurial', so how can the individual's and team's mindset be changed to be both entrepreneurial and innovative? How does an organisation/mission then value and act on the contribution from practitioners/disciples to ensure the authenticity of the exercise? The developed and validated entrepreneur mindset audit tool (see Chapter 5) can individually assess the management/staff/team behaviour and use that data/knowledge so the operational team can learn about and facilitate entrepreneurial behaviour and effective collaboration.

When adopting an entrepreneur mindset approach to mission practice, the disciples/actors increase their ability to sense opportunities and mobilise the resources and knowledge required to exploit them by the creation of 'value' through effective innovation. Indeed, no matter how entrepreneurial either an individual's mindset or an organisation's culture is, interdependencies exist between the manager's mindset and the disciples/organisation culture such that 'entrepreneurial culture and entrepreneur mindset are inextricably interwoven.'[79] In practice, the concept of cognition and decision-making, emotions/gut-feel/intuition, and reasoning form a continuum of information processing, so 'contrasting emotion with cognition is therefore pointless'.[80]

79 Dean Shepherd, H Patzelt, & J.M. Haynie, 2010. 'Entrepreneurial spirals: Deviation-amplifying loops of an entrepreneurial mindset.' Entrepreneurship Theory and Practice, 34(1): 59–82.

80 Jonathon Haidt, 2013. 'The righteous mind.' New York: Vintage Books.

Being entrepreneurial is essentially about thinking and doing something that is new or new to the mission with the determination to bring any benefit to account and achieve a desirable goal or outcome. It is about assessing a situation, designing alternatives, and choosing a new way—or perhaps a combination of ways—that may lead to something better. In professional healthcare practice, this results from applying nursing care, care procedures, technology, image processing, pharmacology, data acquisition, and analysis (as examples) by exploiting opportunities that solve problems and deliver solutions. Indeed, this same approach is used in Chapter 5 to assess the social entrepreneur mindset of Jesus.

An entrepreneurial mindset is not achieved by writing business plans. Such a mindset is achieved and exercised by developing the personal attributes and behaviours associated with recognising opportunities and pursuing them with passion and commitment, seeking necessary physical, human, and financial resources to make it happen.

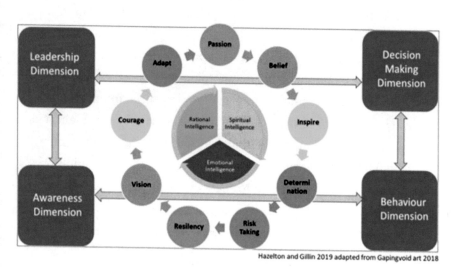

Hazelton and Gillin 2019 adapted from Gapingvoid art 2018

Figure 3.6 Entrepreneur Mindset model—personal insight
(Gillin & Hazelton 2020)

Figure 3.6 illustrates the multi-layer nature of personal attributes and performance contributing to exercising an entrepreneur mindset.[81] Significantly, Jesus, like us, was born with body, soul, and spirit and demonstrated the capability for the integration of rational, emotional, and spiritual intelligence to evaluate recognised and potential opportunities. This reality has been referred to as the outworking of a 'righteous mind'.[82]

Firstly, rational intelligence, which includes calculating or logical thinking, is basic to all our cognitive behaviours, but it is not the whole story in identifying how we think and act. Secondly, emotional intelligence, defined as instinct, intuition, and the 'heart', contributes to our perceptions of opportunities, reality, and decision-making within our respective ecosystem and identifies with one's ability to understand and feel for other people and members of the team. It is about relationships and a capacity to read the social and practice situation environment one is in. Thirdly, spiritual intelligence refers to our capacity to access our deepest meanings, values, purposes, and motivations.[83]

Non-local intuition is strongly associated with spiritual intelligence by accessing the richness of imagination, insight, deep values, and meaning. These three concepts form the basic building blocks to establishing an entrepreneurial mindset.

The middle ring (Fig. 3.6) represents a synthesis of the traits associated with entrepreneurial characteristics and behaviours, including the attributes of passion, belief, inspiration, determination, risk-taking, resilience, vision, courage, instinct, and adaptation to produce an action-centred entrepreneur

81 Laurence Gillin & Lois Hazelton, 2020, "Bringing an entrepreneurial mindset to health-care: a new tool for better outcomes", Journal of Business Strategy, Vol. ahead-of-print No. ahead-of-print. https://doi.org/10.1108/JBS-03-2020-0049.

82 Haidt, J. 2013. The righteous mind. New York: Vintage Books.

83 Dana Zohar and Ian Marshall, 2004, 'Spiritual Capital - Wealth We Can Live By.' Bloomsbury Publishing, UK.

mindset. This holistic insight integrates what were traditionally considered narrow personality traits, personality dispositions, and cognitive processes with the spiritual aspects of human cognition, decision-making, and proactive behaviours within the organisation/mission. The Gospels provide a rich source to identify such personality traits in Jesus.[84]

The four mindset dimensions (outer four points Fig. 3.6) comprise the concepts of: leadership, decision-making, behaviour, and awareness, all derived from the integration of the identified intelligence states and the ring of attributes associated with the entrepreneur's holistic involvement in a culture of entrepreneurial thinking, practice, and behaviour.

Here, I will summarise the four dimensions associated with a make-it-happen entrepreneur mindset. A fuller discussion of these dimensions will be explored in Chapter 5 using the findings based on a study of nursing entrepreneurs and the Gospel record of Jesus and His mission.

Leadership

The leadership style of entrepreneurially behaving leaders is strongly characterised by a 'collaboration' value-based approach to leadership in group work and organisation management. Such leadership is determined in terms of one's propensity to act collaboratively and/or be directive. From both the nursing study and Gospel accounts of Jesus reviewed in Chapter 6, collaboration plays a strong role in future strategic thinking, particularly in identifying possible collaboration arrangements which may benefit the achievement of goals or strengthen the impact one is

---

84 Kelly Shaver Jan Wegelin and Immanuel Commarmond, 2019, 'Assessing Entrepreneurial Mindset: Results for a New Measure,' Discourse and Communication for Sustainable Education 10(2):13–21.

trying to make. It is top-of-mind and not all are operationalised, as only those with a good chance of adding value are pursued. The directive characteristic is not top-of-mind and comes into play when required to execute necessary action to achieve goals and it is necessary to manage the business. Examples of these measurements will be discussed in Chapters 5 and 6 in regard to the social entrepreneur mindset of Jesus.

Decision-making

Decision-making is a critical aspect of entrepreneurial behaviour. Indeed, the literature shows the interplay between rational and intuitive decision-making is not well understood. Both of these characteristics contribute to effective patient-centred decision-making in nursing and person-focused decision-making by Jesus and discipleship team-leading delivered love and care in the mission. However, healthcare decision-making is often 'rule driven' rather than 'data driven'.[85] Many organisations are moving towards becoming more data-driven, yet it is a slow process hindered by the lack of investment in systems. A fatal flaw here is when management thinking is focused on policies and practices associated with financial solutions alone.

Behaviour

It is clearly established in the literature that entrepreneurial corporations are characterised by a proactive component of entrepreneurial orientation (EO), serving to prepare for, intervene in, or control an expected occurrence or situation, and are proactive in causing change and not simply reacting to change

85 Hazelton Lois, 2012, Thesis – 'Governance and Stewardship in the Aged Care Industry: Evaluating a model for Corporate Social Entrepreneurship – The relationship of Board culture to entrepreneurial behaviour', University of Adelaide.

when it happens. Similarly, *proactive* has the same meaning when applied to the entrepreneur mindset and is a well-established characteristic of an entrepreneur and has been identified as a major characteristic in the ministry of Jesus. This is the opposite of a reactive behaviour where the individual or organisation reacts to events or situations rather than acting first to change or prevent something.

> *When operating with proactive behaviours and within an organisation where the board and executive team have an agreed plan it is possible to grow an organisation and develop innovative services and programs which add value. However, where this has not been the case, I have found the need to find an exit pathway as reactive pathways involve you in continually 'putting out fires' and are exhausting and unsustainable.*[78]

Awareness

Awareness is usually defined as: the knowledge that something exists; understanding of a situation at the present time based on information or experience. Indeed, self-awareness is knowledge and awareness of one's own personality or character. Together, cognition and spirituality form the natural characteristics for an aware person. Cognition is the mental process involved in knowing, learning, and understanding things. Spirituality is the quality of being concerned with human spirit or soul as opposed to physical or material things. Jesus fully reflects this spiritual characteristic throughout His recorded ministry. This reflection is fully incorporated in the model of entrepreneur mindset (Fig. 3.6), where the rational, emotional, and spiritual intelligence are at the core of the holistically focused entrepreneur. Of course, such characteristics are not absolutes or mutually exclusive, but in the entrepreneur mindset, the spirituality characteristic is very much associated with entrepreneurial activity and behaviour.

These mindset behaviours are present at all levels of entrepreneurial action and are characteristics that play a strong role when patient-centred care is important, for example, when care is being delivered and/or in system changes to create more value for patients. This same principle applies in other person-centred missions providing beneficial values to the user.

Conclusion

The above discussion demonstrates the close correlation between opportunity-focused entrepreneurs with a holistic application of their entrepreneur mindset and outcomes that benefit the community in which the entrepreneur is involved.

In addition, successful social entrepreneurs build a mission/organisation, establish high personal values, make significant and passionate contributions to the mission and community outreach, and deliver a real and perceived value by users that results in the user exchanging 'wealth' to gain access to the benefit. Such a result describes effective innovation. Also, social entrepreneurs build organisations where economic value and societal contribution are two sides of the same coin. They identify opportunities to solve problems related to spiritual wellbeing, relationship values, education, health care, poverty, and the environment—to name a few. They are 'cause-fighters' and 'change-agents' using the fundamental principles of entrepreneurship to promote positive change and permanent impact.

In answer to our full question concerning compatibility between Jesus and a social entrepreneur mindset, it is confirmed from this overview of Jesus' personal behaviours and mission practices, He exhibited a well-rounded social entrepreneur mindset. Further research on this aspect of Jesus will be presented in Chapters 5 and 6.

Chapter 4: Entrepreneurial Formation of Jesus

There is one thing more powerful than all the armies in the world, and that is an idea whose time has come.[86]

—Victor Hugo

The argument as to whether entrepreneurs are born or made— the result of nature or nurture—has raged for many years. There is no universal answer, and science has not identified an 'entrepreneur gene'. As with all human beings, entrepreneurs come into this world with a body, soul, and spirit and access to their endowed levels of intellectual intelligence (IQ), emotional intelligence (EI), and spiritual intelligence (SI). In Chapter 2, we showed that Jesus was born as 'fully man' and lived his life as a Jewish son with a family and experienced education and synagogue learning, was apprenticed to a trade, and was familiar with the community and Roman governance until age thirty and prior to His baptism and ministry.

Indeed, Jesus would exhibit certain traits that would characterise His behaviours. However, no-one is born with all the traits necessary to be one hundred percent successful on their own. Using the endowed intelligence associated with IQ, EI, and SI, every successful entrepreneur learns new traits

86 Victor Hugo, 1964, The Future of Man. From the series Great Ideas of Western Man.

and seeks mentorship and effective living relationships as an absolute must.

This whole-of-life perspective acknowledges that entrepreneurs are developed over time, gaining experience and learning to make it happen. The environment that a person lives in and the experiences faced forms the entrepreneur. This approach to assessing the 'formation' years of Jesus recognises that entrepreneurship behaviour is not an 'either/or' understanding of born-or-made/nature-or-nurture concepts, but rather a balance of these concepts with skills learned beyond these black or white perspectives.

As mentioned in Chapter 3, entrepreneurs are defined as being opportunity-focused, passionately committed to delivering change that both solves an identified problem and meets the needs of the user of the product or service.

Indeed, such entrepreneurs 'are aggressive catalysts for change within the marketplace. They challenge the unknown and continuously create breakthroughs for the future.'[87]

In Chapter 3, we concluded that Jesus, during His ministry from 29–33 CE, behaved as a social and skilful entrepreneur by shaping and creating the opportunity ('change society values and behaviours through a new relationship with God') to meet the needs of His followers and hearers. This modern title of social entrepreneur, first coined by William (Bill) Drayton, founder of Ashoka, and pioneer in the field of social entrepreneurship since 1980, sought new ways to solve social problems and promote social justice. This concept of social justice is therefore, as old as Jesus in the first century CE.

Drayton viewed the primary objective of social entrepreneurship as systemic change.

---

[87] Donald F. Kuratko and Richard M. Hodgetts, 2003 'Entrepreneurship: Theory, Process, Practice.' South-Western College Pub, USA.

The job of the social entrepreneur is to recognise when a part of society is not working and to solve the problem by changing the system, spreading solutions, and persuading entire societies to take new leaps. Social entrepreneurs are not content just to give a fish or to teach how to fish. They will not rest until they have revolutionised the fishing industry. Identifying and solving large-scale social problems requires social entrepreneurs because only entrepreneurs have the committed vision and inexhaustible determination to persist until they have transformed an entire system.[88]

Importantly, such entrepreneurship is fundamentally a human activity and builds on the whole-of-life-experiences and formation that are associated with establishing the person's values, morals, integrity, and focused energy to deliver outcomes that are valued and sought by community users.

Having established that Jesus existed in the first century CE and confirmed that Jesus was 'fully' man, it is time to assess how the early life and formation of Jesus impacted His social entrepreneurial behaviour during His period of ministry.

By considering the ecosystem concept (Figure 3.1), the linkages between entrepreneurial actions, value propositions, and multiple networks or relationships impacting the solution/s to the large-scale social problems from first-century Judea to today can be observed. The method follows the process used in Chapter 1 (Fig. 1.1). Significantly, this ecosystem model can establish our appreciation of the contributions from Jesus' birth, formation, and preparation (micro level, Fig. 4.1), and through His period of public ministry (29–33 CE) as expressed in teaching, signs and wonders, relationships and leadership (meso level, Fig.

---

88 William Drayton, 2002, 'The Citizen Sector: Becoming as Entrepreneurial and Competitive as Business,'California Management Review. 44:120–133.

3.1), and so form an understanding of the holistic expression of Jesus as a social entrepreneur. At the macro level, (Fig. 3.1) the model accommodates understanding of Jesus' social and spiritual impact in the period from the Crucifixion and Resurrection to early Church development and growth.

From history and personal experience, it is evident the legacy of this first-century-CE demonstration of social entrepreneurship and leadership did and continues to impact the development of history, national identity, political ideologies, values and morals, and religious systems. This period is referred to as the mega level (Fig. 3.1) in this ecosystem. However, in this volume, only the micro and meso levels of the ecosystem will be reviewed in assessing the reality of Jesus the entrepreneur.

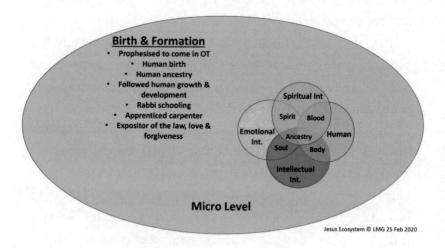

Jesus Ecosystem © LMG 25 Feb 2020

Micro level: 5 BC–29 CE

The micro level of Fig. 4.1 is predominantly concerned with identifying the influence of Jesus' birth and formative early years, before 28 CE, and to assess how such upbringing may have impacted His behaviours, personality, and spiritual awareness on the development of an entrepreneurial mindset, to be assessed within the meso level of Fig.3.1, 'Ministry & Renewal', in Chapter 5.

In Chapter 1, we demonstrated that first-century Judea and Galilee was characterised by an endemic level of inequality, Jews living under Roman Empire rule, and experienced continual political unrest. It was in such an environment that Jesus was born in 5 BCE. Significantly, the Gospel accounts claim Jesus was in the ancestral line of Abraham and King David (Matthew 1:1–17). This claim reinforces the reality that babies derive their exhibited characteristics, features, and genes from their forebears, thus indicating Jesus was born 'fully' man. In addition, His birth fulfilled Old Testament prophecy.

Recent archaeological evidence suggests that first-century Nazareth was a community with a population of around 1,000. Although under Roman control, the community strongly rejected Roman objects, values, and practices. Such Roman culture was regarded as impure and not part of the true Jewish way of worship, living, and community responsibility.[89] As seen in Chapter 1, Nazareth was a classic example of 'worship-centred living'. This was fundamentally at odds with the more liberal interpretation of Jewish life when mixed with Roman values and practices, as was the case in the nearby city of Sepphoris, 6.5 kilometres northwest of Nazareth and capital of Galilee during the time of Jesus.

It's known that the people of Sepphoris, including much of its substantial Jewish population, led lives that were highly influenced by Greek and Roman culture. By contrast, the new evidence suggests very clearly that the people of Nazareth lived purely Jewish lives—and kept to all the major ritual law.

---

89 Ken Dark, 2020, https://www.livescience.com/jesus-home-nazareth-discoveries.html.

These findings confirm that the community of Nazareth can be described as a town in which Jewish worship, rituals, education, and lifestyle was in accord with Jewish teachings and culture. Jesus' early life was formed in this very principled culture. In Chapter 3, it was established that at the core of the entrepreneur is the integration of intellectual intelligence, emotional intelligence, and spiritual intelligence of the human being. The following exploration will seek to establish that Jesus' formation in early life developed these three functional levels of intelligence.

Some Christian authors have described Jesus as an entrepreneur but limited their assessment to His time as a craftsman and head of a family business in Nazareth. Significantly, Laurie Beth Jones coined the term 'spiritreneur' to describe those who fully integrate their soul in a workplace enterprise. By answering yes to either of two questions—'would I be doing this work even if I weren't getting paid?' and 'am I doing this work as unto the Lord?'—one can be considered as on their way to 'spiritreneurship.'[90] Although such a Christian emphasis on practising enterprise leaders may provide valuable insight into value-driven entrepreneurship, it is not the focus of this chapter.

Rather, we are now in a position to assess Jesus the man as both entrepreneur and leader of an entrepreneurial endeavour that delivered effective and valued outcomes, physical and spiritual, to citizens and community. Significantly, this endeavour was not limited to the few years of His earthly life but was taken up by a committed team of disciples, followers, and evangelists to deliver an ongoing impact to person centred values and community values of compassion, equality, justice and freedom which was seen in Chapter 1 as 'worship-centred living'.

---

90 Laurie Beth Jones, 2002, Jesus Entrepreneur, Using Ancient Wisdom to Launch and Live Your Dreams, Crown ce.

Intellectual Intelligence

Although we have minimal written evidence describing the education of Jesus per se, we do have the archaeological evidence that positions first-century-CE Nazareth as committed to Jewish culture. It is, therefore, reasonable to consider that this lifestyle included traditional education and schooling practices. Such communities placed a high value on education and commitment to a formative experience that enabled the young to fully appreciate and honour the Jewish cultural heritage. That being said, the town rabbi and synagogue would be pivotal in the education and formation of Jesus. Josephus wrote:

> [...] *above all we pride ourselves on the education of our children, and regard as the most essential task in life the observance of our laws and of the pious practices based thereupon, which we have inherited.*[91]

With such a cultural background, it is reasonable to suggest the education of Jesus would include a focus on developing and increasing intellectual intelligence (IQ), comprising both the intellect—referred to as the mental *capacity* for material reality—and the mental *ability* to compute the components of material reality. Human intelligence defines the intellectual power of humans, which is marked by complex cognitive feats and high levels of motivation and self-awareness.[92] Intelligence is:

> *a very general mental capability that, among other things, involves the ability to reason, plan, solve problems,*

---

91 Flavius Josepheus, Early 2nd Century, The Life. Against Apion (Book 1:60), Harvard University Press, 1926.
92 Tirri, Nokelainen (2011). Measuring Multiple Intelligences and Moral Sensitivities in Education. Moral Development and Citizenship Education. Springer.

think abstractly, comprehend complex ideas, learn quickly and learn from experience. It is not merely book learning, a narrow academic skill, or test-taking smarts. Rather, it reflects a broader and deeper capability for comprehending our surroundings-'catching on,' ' making sense' of things, or 'figuring out' what to do.

This deep focus on IQ is a primary building block in Jesus' formation and provides for the development of creative insights into opportunity recognition and evaluation, and essential decision-making elements characteristic of the entrepreneur.[93]

In the first century CE, responsibility for the first level of formal education belonged to the father. As soon as the child was able to speak, he was to be taught some Bible verses. The learning of the Hebrew 'alef-bet' began at about age three. The focus at the start was to train the memory, and the letters were learned both forwards and backwards. Since written documents were rare and accessible to only a few, memory was in many ways more important than the ability to read.

At five years of age, one is ready for the study of the Written Torah, at ten years of age for the study of the Oral Torah, at thirteen for bar mitzvah [the religious coming-of-age ceremony], *at fifteen for the study of halachot* [rabbinic legal decisions], *at eighteen for marriage, at twenty for pursuing a vocation, at thirty for entering one's full vigour...*[94]

---

93 Linda S. Gottfredson, 1994, The Wall Street Journal copyright, Dow Jones & Company, Inc.

94 Laan, Ray Vander, 2006. In the Dust of the Rabbi Discovery Guide (That the World May Know) (pp. 25–26). Zondervan. Quoting Rabbi Judah ben Tema in (Ethics of the Fathers 5:21).

Given the high probability that Jesus experienced this approach to his education and formation, it is appropriate to compare the experiences of Jesus recorded in the Gospels:

1. Jesus 'grew in wisdom' as a boy (Luke 2:52),
2. Jesus reached the 'fulfilling of the commandments' indicated by his first Passover at age twelve (Luke 2:41—47) where 'they found him in the temple, sitting in the midst of the teachers, both hearing them, and asking them questions',
3. Jesus learned a trade with his father (Matthew 13:55),
4. Jesus spent time with John the Baptist, a rabbi (John 3:22—26; 4:1—3),
5. Significantly, 'Jesus himself, when he began to teach, was about thirty years of age', (Luke 3:23), providing strong evidence He was considered a rabbi as 'He entered into the full vigour of His ministry.' Another confirming evidence of both His teaching and leadership occurs where 'the people who heard Jesus teach recognised that he taught with authority' (See Matthew 7:28—29; 21:23—27; Mark 1:27—28). Such recognition can add further understanding:

In fact, Jesus best fits the type of rabbi believed to have Semikhah, the authority to make new interpretations of the Torah. Most teachers of the law could only teach accepted interpretations. Teachers with authority, however, could make new interpretations and pass legal judgments.[94]

Another confirmation of Jesus' recognised intelligence and leadership amongst the disciples and followers was their trust in Jesus the rabbi. As rabbi, Jesus was the driving motivation of each disciple's life! For years, each disciple wanted to hear everything the rabbi said, know everything the rabbi knew, and do everything the rabbi did. Today, we can see a similar loyalty, respect, and commitment amongst an entrepreneurial team and the entrepreneur leader.

Emotional Intelligence

Clearly, intellectual intelligence is basic to all human cognitive behaviours, but it is not the whole story in identifying the contributions to the development and formation of Jesus in the period before His ministry from 29–33 CE. Importantly, emotion, instinct, intuition, and the 'heart' contribute to human perceptions of opportunities, reality, and decision-making within daily life. Of course, such emotions and behaviours occur simply because we are human, just as Jesus was human.

Little evidence is available to inform our understanding of EI in Jesus during the early school years, family life, and formation to age thirty. However, and as reviewed more fully in the next level of the ecosystem (meso), it will be shown that Jesus demonstrated a strong propensity for EI behaviour in His dealings with individuals, community, and in the leadership of the disciples and close followers and is linked to the assessment of Jesus the entrepreneur. Recent research demonstrates a link between academic learning performance and EI. 'It is not enough to be smart and hardworking—to have the added edge for success, students must also be able to understand and manage emotions to succeed at school.'[95] Such a finding supports the concept that Jesus was both an excellent student and developed effective EI. Studies have shown that people with high

95 Carolyn McCann, et al 2020, Emotional Intelligence Predicts Academic Performance: A Meta-Analysis,Psychological Bulletin, 2020, Vol. 146, No. 2, 150–186.

EI have greater mental health, job performance, and leadership skills. Because of the brain's plasticity, it is possible to change behaviours and attitudes, enhance positive emotions and diminish negative emotions, and thus to actually change the brain itself.

Indeed, such behaviour could not have been an instantaneous expression from 29 CE but would be evident through Jesus' early life and formation. The following comments will provide an understanding of this human behaviour using some examples from His time of ministry and leadership. EI identifies with our ability to understand and feel for other people and staff; it is about relationships and the capacity to read the social situation we are in.

Emotional intelligence has been defined, by Peter Salovey and John Mayer, as 'the ability to monitor one's own and other people's emotions, to discriminate between different emotions and label them appropriately, and to use emotional information to guide thinking and behaviour.' This definition was later broken down and refined into four proposed abilities: to

- perceive emotions accurately,
- use emotions to facilitate decision-making,
- understand emotions, and
- manage emotions to up-regulate positive emotions and down-regulate negative emotions.[96]

In a recent book entitled *The Emotional Intelligence of Jesus*,[97] the authors ask: 'Are we justified in claiming to know anything about Jesus' emotional intelligence?'

96 Peter Salovey, Lohn Mayer, and David Caruso, (2004), "Emotional Intelligence: Theory, Findings, and Implications", Psychological Inquiry, pp. 197–215.

97 Roy, M. Oswald and Arland Jacobson. 2015. The Emotional Intelligence of Jesus. Rowman & Littlefield Publishers.

Though we are aware that we cannot peer into the mind and soul of Jesus, the Gospels can inform us about Jesus' emotional intelligence. There are several ways we can legitimately assess the emotional intelligence of Jesus. First, we can examine a few explicit statements in the Gospels about Jesus' emotional states (e.g., that he had compassion). Second, we can make inferences from the sayings of Jesus about assumptions or views he held. For example, Jesus' saying about taking the log out of your own eye before you try to take the speck out of your neighbour's eye (Matthew 7:3–5) clearly indicates that Jesus understood the need for self-awareness. Third, we can make claims about Jesus as he is portrayed in Gospel accounts. In this case, we are doing the same thing that Shakespeare scholars might do with a character such as Hamlet. Whether these portraits of Jesus in the Gospels are historically accurate is not our concern because we are making claims only about Jesus as a literary character in the Gospels. Fourth, and in some ways the most interesting, we can explore the emotional intelligence implicit in Jesus' admonitions. For example, what kind of emotional intelligence would be required to love one's enemies or to forgive without limit? In fact, we believe that careful attention to Jesus' sayings about forgiveness and love of enemies is of special importance. These reflect a profound understanding of human nature that can be articulated in terms of emotional intelligence.

Such EI reflects human abilities to join intelligence, empathy, and emotions to enhance thought and understanding of interpersonal dynamics. Empathy is typically associated with EI, because it relates to an individual connecting their personal experiences with those of others. Such awareness adds to effective decision-making. Goleman defines EI as the effective awareness and control of one's own emotions and those of other people.[98] In a large research study of senior executives across the USA, Goleman observed that EI accounted for 67% of the abilities deemed necessary for superior performance in leaders and mattered twice as much as technical expertise or IQ.[99]

The four emotional competencies identified by Goleman are:

1 Self-awareness (emotional self-awareness),
2 Self-management (achievement orientation, adaptability, emotional self-control, positive outlook),
3 Social awareness (empathy, organisational awareness),
4 Relationship management (conflict management, coach and mentor, influence, inspirational leadership, teamwork).

Figure 4.2 shows the relationship between competencies and will be discussed by way of application to Jesus and entrepreneurship in the meso level.

98 Goleman, D. (1995). Emotional intelligence: Why it can matter more than IQ. London, UK: Bloomsbury.
99 Daniel Goleman, 2005, Emotional Intelligence: Why It Can Matter More Than IQ, Bloomsbury, London.

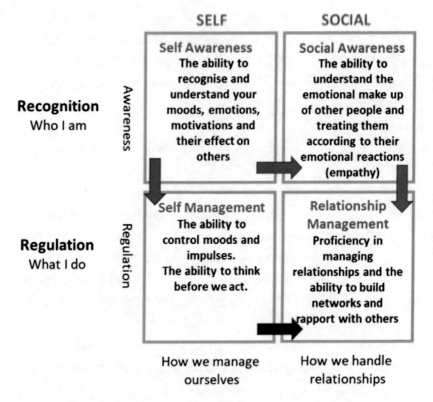

Figure 4.2 EI Competencies After Daniel Goleman 2005

Oswald and Jacobson recount an excellent example of high emotional intelligence as demonstrated by Jesus:

Early in the morning he [Jesus] came again to the temple. All the people came to him and he sat down and began to teach them. The scribes and Pharisees brought a woman who had been caught in adultery; and making her stand before all of them, they said to him, 'Teacher, this woman was caught in the very act of committing adultery. Now in the law Moses commanded us to stone such women. Now what do you say?' They said this to test him, so that they might have some charge to bring against him. Jesus bent down and wrote with his finger on the ground. When they kept on questioning him, he straightened up and said to them, 'Let anyone among you who is without sin be the first to throw a stone at her.' And once again he bent down and wrote on the ground. When they heard it, they went away, one by one, beginning with the elders; and Jesus was left alone with the woman standing before him. Jesus straightened up and said to her, 'Woman, where are they? Has no-one condemned you?' She said 'No-one, sir.' And Jesus said, 'Neither do I condemn you. Go your way, and from now on do not sin again.' (John 8:2–11)2 These are similar, yet unique, situations involving a hostile crowd. It is our suggestion that when asked what should be done with this woman, Jesus stooped to write with his finger on the ground to give him time to figure out how to manage this emotionally charged situation. He does not want to be accused of ignoring the law of Moses. The scribes and Pharisees assume that he is not fully Torah observant and therefore set a trap for him. Jesus expresses no disagreement with the Torah: she should be executed. But he insists that whoever is without sin should follow the Torah and cast the first stone. At this, his opponents melt away, leaving no-one to condemn the woman. Jesus, not having been a witness to the adultery, does not condemn her, either. The story portrays Jesus as a very quick thinker, someone able to defuse a situation of potential danger both to the woman and to him. At the same time, Jesus is portrayed as remarkably sympathetic to a marginalised woman. Throughout his ministry, Jesus was empathic to the plight of women.[97]

Spiritual Intelligence

Spiritual intelligence (SI) is a higher dimension of intelligence (IQ and EI) that activates the qualities and capabilities of the authentic self (or the soul) in the form of wisdom, compassion, integrity, joy, love, creativity, and peace. Spiritual intelligence results in a sense of deeper meaning and purpose and fulfills the 'innate human need to connect with something larger than ourselves.'[100] Indeed, it will be shown Jesus displayed deep spiritual intelligence in His 'ability to behave with wisdom and compassion while maintaining inner and outer peace (equanimity) regardless of the situation.'

In considering the development and formation of Jesus in the period to age thirty years, we note there is minimal direct evidence as to His SI but, given the strong exposure to Jewish culture in Nazareth, commitment to religious-based education, and His later learning at the feet of Rabbis it is reasonable to posit that Jesus would have been schooled in and became aware of the spiritual reality of being a Jew and the associated life values. Indeed, the Torah makes clear 'So God created man in his own image' (Genesis 1:27, *RSV*). Such an image can be interpreted to include the power to think, to have emotions, and to experience real energy interconnectivity resulting from the inbuilt structure and energy circuits within our being. Developing awareness, connecting to, and using responsibly is the hallmark of SI and such expression of this power within can be developed and experienced. 'He has made everything beautiful in its time; also, He has put eternity into man's mind.' (Ecclesiastes 3: 11, *RSV*)

In addition, SI is associated with creativity that is both innate and learned. As we have seen, Jesus achieved a high level of understanding during His formative years with the ability to

---

100 Cindy Wigglesworth, 2012 'SI21: The Twenty-One Skills of Spiritual intelligence.' New York: Select Books.

synthesise and reformulate spiritual truths as a twelve-year-old in the temple, where everyone 'was amazed at his understanding and his answers' (Luke 2:46–47) or to paraphrase at His spiritual intelligence astounded those who listened to Him.

With such an understanding, it is clear 'man' has the capacity and inner being to connect his spirit holistically with both body and soul or, as in the terms developed above, with the body's functional reality and emotional awareness. Importantly, all of Creation is basically a function of energy and interconnectivity which provides the framework for our higher levels seeking to understand human meaning, performance, and satisfaction (see Chapter 5). Abraham Maslow first enunciated the concept of a 'hierarchy of needs' that described an organised scale of our motivations from what he called 'deficiency needs'—such as survival and security and to belong or be loved—to our 'higher needs', such as self-esteem, self-actualisation, and peak experience.

This insight morphed into the realisation of the essential role 'motivations' play in driving our behaviour and also our thinking. In considering the business mindset, Danah Zohar and Ian Marshall explored the means for moving from a short-term gain and material-focused business culture to a culture driven by fundamental values and a deep sense of meaning in achieving a common goal that can be both profitable and responsible. Zohar and Marshall identified such a transition involves the need to make a choice, to exercise freedom, and to act with responsibility. They named this 'inner voice' Spiritual Intelligence (SI).

Spiritual Intelligence is defined as:

> *[...] the intelligence with which we address and solve problems of meaning and value, the intelligence with which we can place our actions and our lives in a wider,*

richer, meaning-giving context, the intelligence with which we can assess that one course of action or one life-path is more meaningful than another.[101]

Using this definition, Zohar and Marshall extended Maslow's original six motivations to sixteen: eight positive ones and eight negatives. These are arranged in a hierarchy from -8 to +8 and have the unique property that the positive and negative legs of the scale mirror one another (See Figure 4.3). Thus +3, *power within*, mirrors and is paired with -3, *craving*; +1, *exploration*, mirrors and is paired with -1, *self-assertion*, and so on. As implied by the numbering, it is better to have a motive of +3 than one of +1, but it is also better to be at a -1 than at a -4. Our personal effectiveness increases and our behaviour improves or has a more positive outcome as we progress upwards along the scale. A leader driven by *fear* (-4) will adopt far more reactive and defensive strategies than a counterpart who is driven by *self-assertion* (-1). *Fear* leads to behaviour that is risk-averse, or perhaps desperate; *self-assertion* may lead to overconfidence or carelessness.[97]

101 Danah Zohar and Ian Marshall (2004), Spiritual Capital – Wealth We Can Live By. Bloomsbury Publishing, London.

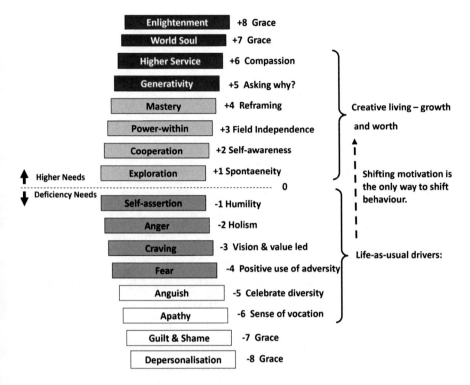

Figure 4.3 How SI Processes act on Motivations (Zohar & Marshall, 2004)[97]

Danah Zohar has described her early life as stuck in the lower motivation levels of (-4, *fear* and -6, *apathy*) and then undergoing a sudden shift to higher motivations (+4, *mastery,* and +6, *higher service*). Zohar says:

> *This sudden shift was brought about through two of the transformative principles of SI coming to bear on her life and original motives. It was like being shot full of new energy. These were the principles of positive use of adversity (see Fig 4.3) (turning my patriotic fear into a*

mastery of physics), and sense of vocation (turning my apathy into a heartfelt wish to serve my country).

Significantly, I found a similar explosive release of energy when experiencing a transformative change from the motivation level of +1, *exploration,* and +2, *cooperation,* behaviours. I had become complacent within my career. The transformative change came as my 'eureka' moment and involved embracing the liberating motivations (+4, *mastery,* and +6, *higher service*).

Using the SI principles of spontaneity (turning my sense of exploration into a mastery of entrepreneurship) and self-awareness (turning my gregariousness and cooperation into a committed mission to grow entrepreneurs throughout society), this was essentially a spiritual experience.

These two examples provide an insight into the application of SI principles when bringing change within a human being able to deliver valued outcomes. Figure 4.3 correlates twelve of the sixteen motives that drive behaviour with the twelve processes of change (principles) that give SI its active and transformative power to effect change in personal and cultural opportunities.

This insight correlates with understanding how Jesus' formative years prepared Him to fulfil His mission in altering human behaviour and values. It is reasonable to posit that Jesus fully understood the motivation to 'be about His Father's business' (Luke 2:49) by exercising intelligent choice and emotional freedom to act with responsibility in the coming mission of the ministry. This response to what we called an 'inner voice' is fully consistent with Jesus expressing spiritual intelligence (SI). It is reasonable to suggest, from consideration of the motivations described in Fig. 4.3, His shift to the highest motivations (+6 *higher service*; +7 *world soul*; +8 *enlightenment*) are associated with the principles of *compassion* and *grace*.

Zohar also observes that:

> ... *motives are attractors in the shared field of consciousness theory. They are just energy states, not consciously chosen. Energy is distributed among them- reaching equilibrium scattered among these states. By contrast, SI qualities require acts of consciousness and will. They can be freely chosen. They have the force to pump energy into the motivational states and to redistribute human energies into higher-energy motivational was His states (into new attractors).*

Creativity is desirable but costly. It is calculated that as much personal energy, per unit of time, is expended on a 'creative thought' as it does to play a game of football. An SI transformative process to shift motives requires one to pump energy into the system. This energy has to come from somewhere. We will return to this concept in Chapter 7.

Decision-making style

Our consideration of Jesus from birth and the formative years to age thirty has identified inner forces at work. It is clear, even at age twelve, that He understood the impact of these forces on the forthcoming mission—'I must be about My Father's business'—a mission that was associated with changing behaviours and understanding the holistic concept of intelligence and a values-driven focus for human beings. It is worth noting most scholars agree that what differentiates entrepreneurs from other actors in society is their behaviour.[102] Importantly, entrepreneurial behaviour is shown to be the interplay between rational and intuitive decision-making and expressed as an individual's 'cognitive style index' (CSI).[103] Likewise, in terms of the cognitive basis of making moral judgments and decisions, social psychologist Haidt identifies the crucial components as 'intuition and reasoning.'[104] Within this context, Kreuger emphasises the significance of entrepreneurial intentions, entrepreneurial attitudes, deep cognitive structures, and deep beliefs. [105] All these findings demonstrate the importance of a holistic view of entrepreneurial behaviour, opportunity focus, decision-making and the spiritual/moral understandings that drive the successful entrepreneur's mindset.

In concluding this chapter on assessing the development and formation of Jesus for His public mission, it is appropriate to evaluate, as far as is possible, His decision-making style in the strategic decisions and actions necessary to bring effective change from His message and power. It is acknowledged Jesus had a relationship with a higher power (God), but we will continue to evaluate the human dimensions of His life and practices. From the literature, it is established that entrepreneurs are strongly associated with a propensity for intuitive-style decision-making rather than a propensity for analytical decision-making when prosecuting entrepreneurial opportunities.

102 Ray Bradley, Murray Gillin, Rolin McCraty, and Mike Atkinson, 2011, 'Nonlocal Intuition in Entrepreneurs and Nonentrepreneurs: Results of Two Experiments Using Electrophysiological Measures,' International Journal of Entrepreneurship and Small Business. vol 12 (3): 343–372et al., 2011).

103 Allinson, W.C., & J. Hayes.1996. The Cognitive Style Index: A measure of intuition-analysis for organizational research. Journal of Management Studies, 1: 119–135.

104 Haidt, J. 2013. The righteous mind. New York: Vintage Books.

105 Kreuger, N.F. Jr. 2007. What lies beneath? The experiential essence of entrepreneurial thinking. Entrepreneurship Theory and Practice, 31(1): 123–138.

To help in the assessment of Jesus' decision-making style, I intend to apply the instrument developed by Alison and Hayes. Of course, it is not possible to request Jesus to fill out the CSI index (see Appendix 4.1) or to be in any way definitive about Jesus' decision-making style. However, given the apparent entrepreneurial behaviour of Jesus, it is reasonable to assume his decision-making style would be similar to current entrepreneurs. In order to test this proposition, I requested a number of entrepreneurs familiar with the development of this book and, importantly, familiar with the mission and history of Jesus to answer the questions (Appendix 4.1) as they perceived Jesus might have responded to such questions. Using this 'purposefully selected panel', no single-bias will prevail. It should be noted from Figure 4.4 that successful entrepreneurs are skewed towards the intuitive decision-making end of the continuum.

Over many years, the author has used the CSI measure to initially screen and identify serial entrepreneurs participating in a study of 'heart rate variability', intuition, opportunity decision-making, and entrepreneurial behaviour.[106] From 2004 to 2020, some 400 serial entrepreneurs, postgraduate students studying for a Master of Entrepreneurship, and financial services managers seeking to improve their entrepreneurial behaviour/culture inside the organisation have completed a CSI measure. Analysis and interpretation of these results found the CSI score to be a robust and reliable indicator of entrepreneurial intent. Given this finding, and the need to maintain consistency with these previous studies,

---

106 Frank LaPira and Murray Gillin, 2006, 'Non-local Intuition and the Performance of Serial Entrepreneurs,' , Journal of International Entrepreneurship and Small Business, Vol 3 #1, pp 17–35.

all measures of decision-making style in this study are based on the standard CSI measure.[107]

Figure 4. 4 shows an assessment of the CSI index score for Jesus as 19 (on a continuum scale of 0–76). The average score of 19 was derived from ten participants with a score spread of 9 to 28. Against the average findings from other groupings as identified above, it is clear that the selected panel considers Jesus had a very high propensity for intuitive decision-making, even stronger than that assessed from testing serial entrepreneurs. This finding in no way implies Jesus did not apply analytical skills to strategies and decision-making during His life. The finding is Jesus exhibited a higher propensity for intuitive decision-making compared to His analytical decision-making actions.

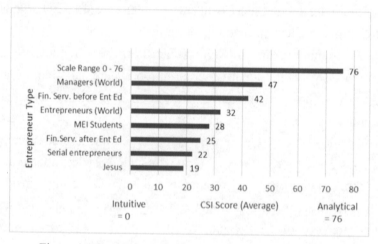

Figure 4.4 Cognitive Style Index scores (Average of Type)

107 L Murray Gillin, 2020, 'Facilitating Intuitive Decision-making and an Entrepreneurial Mindset in Corporate Culture – A Case Study.' (Chapter 17) 3rd Handbook of Intuition Research Ed. Marta Sinclair, Handbook of Intuition as Practice, Edward Elgar Publishing, Cheltenham, UK/Northampton, MA, USA.

Conclusion

Our exploration of the birth and formation of Jesus to age thirty years, and before commencing His public ministry, has concluded He was at a high level of intellectual intelligence (IQ), leading to a deeply human understanding of knowledge (religious and secular), the politics of the day, the associated economics, and the stresses of community life. His emotional intelligence (EI) was well-honed through the development of strong family relationships, experience in the family business, and involvement with community pressures on living and health through difficult times under Roman control.

This strong demonstration of personal self-awareness, self-management, and relationship management enabled Jesus to exercise a social awareness in His ability to understand the emotional make-up of friends and community in ways that met their emotional needs and reactions. Importantly, we conclude that Jesus both understood and embraced the whole concept of spiritual intelligence (SI).

His quest for understanding and recognising the true inner self and His response to the inner call provided the crucial component of inner peace and confidence. Such inner peace and calling cannot be undervalued as it forms the foundation of Jesus' authentic behaviour and is not corrupted by compliance with fears, doubts, and the corrupted opinion of others. As will be discussed in later chapters, insights will be provided into the relationship with inner peace and SI observed in the period of public ministry.

In summary, Figure 4.5 illustrates the reality of IQ, EI, and SI in preparing Jesus for His public ministry. Chapter 5 will identify how Jesus both recognised opportunities for change, used dynamic entrepreneurial processes that delivered true innovations that were valued, and met the needs of individuals and the community. Such an entrepreneurial mindset delivers world-changing entrepreneurial performance.

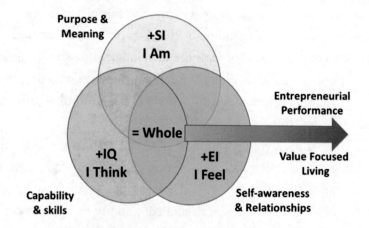

Figure 4.5 Holistic Relationship of IQ, EI, and SI to Entrepreneurial Performance: IQ + EI + SI = Value-Focused Living.

Appendix 4.1

COGNITIVE STYLE INDEX

NAME...

AGE ....

OCCUPATION...

SEX ....

People differ in the way they think about problems. Below are 38 statements designed to identify your own approach. If you believe that a statement is *true* about you, answer T. If you believe that it is *false* about you, answer F. If you are *uncertain* whether it is true or false, answer? This is not a test of your ability, and there are no right or wrong answers. Simply choose the one response which comes closest to your own opinion. Work quickly, giving your first reaction in each case, and make sure that you respond to every statement.

Indicate your answer by completely filling in the appropriate oval opposite the statement:

T True   ? Uncertain   F False

T ? F

1. In my experience, rational thought is the only realistic basis for making decisions.

☐ ☐ ☐

2. To solve a problem, I have to study each part of it in detail.

☐ ☐ ☐

3. I am most effective when my work involves a clear sequence of tasks to be performed.

☐ ☐ ☐

4. I have difficulty working with people who 'dive in at the deep end' without considering the finer aspects of the problem.

☐ ☐ ☐

5. I am careful to follow rules and regulations at work.

☐ ☐ ☐

6. I avoid taking a course of action if the odds are against its success.

☐ ☐ ☐

7. I am inclined to scan through reports rather than read them in detail.

☐ ☐ ☐

8. My understanding of a problem tends to come more from thorough analysis than flashes of insight.

☐ ☐ ☐

9. I try to keep to a regular routine in my work.

☐ ☐ ☐

10. The kind of work I like best is that which requires a logical, step-by-step approach.

☐ ☐ ☐

11. I rarely make 'off the top of the head' decisions.

☐ ☐ ☐

12. I prefer chaotic action to orderly inaction.

☐ ☐ ☐

13. Given enough time, I would consider every situation from all angles.

☐ ☐ ☐

14. To be successful in my work, I find that it is important to avoid hurting other people's feelings.

☐ ☐ ☐

15. The best way for me to understand a problem is to break it down into its constituent parts.

☐ ☐ ☐

16. I find that to adopt a careful, analytical approach to making decisions takes too long.

☐ ☐ ☐

17. I make the most progress when I take calculated risks.

☐ ☐ ☐

18. I find that it is possible to be too organised when performing certain kinds of task.

☐ ☐ ☐

19. I always pay attention to detail before I reach a conclusion.

☐ ☐ ☐

20. I make many of my decisions on the basis of intuition.

☐ ☐ ☐

21. My philosophy is that it is better to be safe than risk being sorry.

☐ ☐ ☐

22. When making a decision, I take my time and thoroughly consider all relevant factors.

☐ ☐ ☐

23. I get on best with quiet, thoughtful people.

☐ ☐ ☐

24. I would rather that my life was unpredictable than that it followed a regular pattern.

☐ ☐ ☐

25. Most people regard me as a logical thinker.

☐ ☐ ☐

26. To fully understand the facts, I need a good theory.

☐ ☐ ☐

27. I work best with people who are spontaneous.

☐ ☐ ☐

28. I find detailed, methodical work satisfying.

☐ ☐ ☐

29. My approach to solving a problem is to focus on one part at a time

☐ ☐ ☐

30. I am constantly on the lookout for new experiences.

☐ ☐ ☐

31. In meetings, I have more to say than most.

☐ ☐ ☐

32. My 'gut feeling' is just as good a basis for decision-making as careful analysis.

☐ ☐ ☐

33. I am the kind of person who casts caution to the wind.

☐ ☐ ☐

34. I make decisions and get on with things rather than analyse every last detail.

☐ ☐ ☐

35. I am always prepared to take a gamble.

☐ ☐ ☐

36. Formal plans are more of a hindrance than a help in my work.

☐ ☐ ☐

37. I am more at home with ideas rather than facts and figures.

☐ ☐ ☐

38. I find that 'too much analysis results in paralysis'.

☐ ☐ ☐

Chapter 5: Entrepreneur Mindset of Jesus

*We think sometimes that poverty is only being
hungry, naked and homeless. The poverty of being
unwanted, unloved and uncared for is the greatest
poverty. We must start in our own homes to remedy
this kind of poverty.*

—Saint Mother Teresa

Following our consideration and discussion of the birth and formation of the soon-to-be Jesus the social entrepreneur (Chapter 4) at the micro level of the ecosystem, this chapter evaluates the entrepreneurial mindset of Jesus during His ministry and commitment to effect 'change to societal values and behaviours through a new relationship with God.'

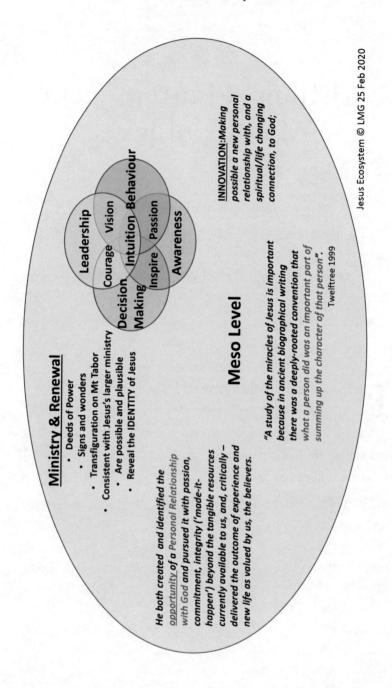

Figure 5.1 Meso Level of Ecosystem and Jesus the Social Entrepreneur

This meso-level dimension of the ecosystem (Fig. 5.1) (29–33 CE) seeks to understand the ministry of Jesus. This awareness will facilitate both our recognition and evaluation of the opportunity Jesus followed during this period of ministry, commencing at His baptism in 29 CE.

Based on this understanding of the mission and the entrepreneurial behaviour exercised by Jesus and His leadership of the team of disciples, we will seek to identify Jesus' entrepreneur mindset, His source of energy and power, and the added value to followers accepting the life change.

Besides being an advanced agrarian society, life in the province of Judea was shaped by several dominant forces: the Israelite tradition (linguistic, cultural, and religious heritage), the Roman Empire (political control), and Hellenism (the pervasive cultural influence over the whole Mediterranean and Middle East).

Contrary to the beliefs of many people in the first century CE, and particularly in our current era, the primary purpose of Jesus was not to heal the sick or perform other signs and wonders— although these were important—but to 'change societal values and behaviours through a new relationship with God.' This was the true vision driving Jesus during His time on earth. Indeed, we showed in the preceding chapter that Jesus recognised His mission 'to be about My Father's business' when aged twelve. Now at age thirty, He is ready to commit all to the mission and make the vision a reality. This passionate, courageous, and committed approach to delivering such a change in personal behaviour and societal values is characteristic of a social entrepreneur, and first defined by Drayton as:

The job of the social entrepreneur is to recognize when a part of society is not working and to solve the problem by changing the system, spreading solutions, and persuading entire societies to take new leaps. Social entrepreneurs are not content just to give a fish or to teach how to fish. They will not rest until they have revolutionized the fishing industry. Identifying and solving large-scale social problems requires social entrepreneurs because only entrepreneurs have the committed vision and inexhaustible determination to persist until they have transformed an entire system.[108]

As established in Chapter 3, being socially entrepreneurial is essentially about thinking and doing something that is new, or new to the organisation/society, with the determination to bring the benefit into use and achieve a desirable goal or outcome for the user. As noted in Chapter 3, the entrepreneur mindset is not achieved by writing business plans and studying economics. Such a mindset is achieved and exercised by developing the personal attributes and behaviours associated with recognising opportunities and pursuing them with passion and commitment and seeking necessary physical, human, and financial resources to make it happen. Jesus was shown to be a classic example of a social entrepreneur (Chapter 3) and have a mindset in harmony with the integration of IQ, EI, SI, and 'His Father's business' that delivers a relationship for value-focused living.

It is worth noting that successful social entrepreneurs are highly valued, committed, and passionate in delivering valued service, and are recognised for their contribution to society. Significantly, the Nobel Peace Prize has been awarded to social entrepreneurs addressing 'wicked problems' in the community:

---

108 William Drayton, 2002, California Management Review. 44:120–133.

Muhammad Yunus (2006) is a Bangladeshi social entrepreneur, banker, economist, and civil society leader who founded the Grameen Bank and pioneered the loan concepts of microcredit and microfinance. He received the Nobel Peace Prize ' for their efforts to create economic and social development from below. Lasting peace cannot be achieved unless large population groups find ways in which to break out of poverty. Micro-credit is one such means. Development from below also serves to advance democracy and human rights.' Yunus and Grameen Bank have shown that even the poorest of the poor can work to bring about their own development and achieve the highest levels of repayment of loans in the world.

Saint Mother Teresa (1979) was awarded the Nobel Peace Prize for her work in bringing help to suffering humanity. 'She placed special emphasis on the spirit that has inspired her activities, and which is the tangible expression of her personal attitude and human qualities. A feature of her work has been respect for the individual human being, for his or her dignity and innate value. The loneliest, the most wretched and the dying have, at her hands, received compassion without condescension, based on reverence for man.'

Malala Yousafzai (2014) received her joint Nobel Peace Prize 'for their struggle against the suppression of children and young people and for the right of all children to education. Children must go to school and not be financially exploited. It is a prerequisite for peaceful global development that the rights of children and young people be respected. In conflict-ridden areas in particular, the violation of children leads to the continuation of violence from generation to generation'.

In addition, both Gandhi and Wilberforce are classic examples of highly motivated and spiritually aware social entrepreneurs:

Mohandas Gandhi (1869–1948) was nominated five times for Nobel Peace Prize but without success. However, he became the strongest symbol of non-violence, the 'symbol of peace', and the 'unelected spokesman of non-violence' of the twentieth century. In recognising the needs of humanity, he especially devoted himself to the service of the poor, the distressed, and the oppressed millions everywhere.

William Wilberforce (1759–1833) Wilberforce underwent a spiritual rebirth that changed his life and led him to become an evangelical Christian. This spiritual conversion led him to change his lifestyle and began his lifelong concern for reform, particularly his desire to see the end of the slave trade and of slavery.

Social entrepreneurship is a way of thinking, reasoning, and acting that is opportunity-obsessed, holistic in approach, and leadership balanced for the purpose of value creation and capture.[109] Such entrepreneurship results in the creation, enhancement, realisation, and renewal of value, not just for the entrepreneur but for all participants and stakeholders. At the heart of delivering on the vision of Jesus is the creation and/or recognition of the opportunity, followed by the will, energy, and initiative to seize this opportunity. It requires a willingness to take risks—both personal and societal—but in a way that balances the personal risk to the entrepreneur with the benefits to meet the needs of potential users of the services offered.

109 Jeffrey Timmons, Murray Gillin, Sam Burshtein and Stephen Spinelli. 2011 'New Venture Creation – Entrepreneurship for the 21st Century, McGraw-Hill, Australia (Pacific Edition).

Typically, social entrepreneurs devise ingenious strategies to marshal their limited resources.

In attempting this review and assessment of Jesus as an entrepreneur, it is to be clearly understood that I seek to increase our wonder and faith in the mission and sacrifice Jesus made in bringing a new relationship with God, which is freely available to all who choose this life change. Indeed Jesus used such a concept when He said (Matthew 5: 17), 'Think not that I am come to destroy the law, or the prophets: I am not come to destroy, but to fulfil.' These words would seem to point chiefly to Jesus' mission and work as a teacher. He came to fill up what was lacking, to develop hints and germs of truth, to turn rules into principles. So too, this review attempts to add to our understanding of Jesus the man but recognising the amazing synergy between Jesus being fully man and fully God (see comments by Bruce Ware in Chapter 2). Just as the mathematical and analytical contributions by Albert Einstein and Stephen Hawking have opened a way to understanding the physics of energy and matter surrounding the origins of the universe, they have not decreased our wonder of the universe but significantly enhanced our capacity to express wonder at Creation and thereby God.

There is general agreement that the period of ministry for Jesus commenced immediately after His baptism in the Jordan River by John the Baptist and the descending of the Spirit of God like a dove and alighting on Him. Matthew 3: 17 records, 'And a voice from heaven said, "This is my Son, whom I love; with him I am well pleased."' This is significant as it represents the first public demonstration in which Jesus is called the beloved Son of God. This can be interpreted that, to this time, no-one other than His mother Mary was aware of another dimension to Jesus the man living in Nazareth and discussed fully in Chapter 2. The text in Matthew would suggest that, when Jesus came up out of the water, the Spirit began to officially work in Him, which signified that God's incarnate flesh had begun to fulfil His ministry and had begun the work to deliver the potential for real change in the personal lives of followers and thereby establish a new relationship with God.

By considering the birth and formation of Jesus in Chapter 4, we established Jesus both lived in and was educated in the traditional Jewish culture, was relaxed and confident discussing interpretations of the Torah with teachers in the temple at Jerusalem, and learnt first-hand leadership of family life and business together with understanding the significance of family and community relationships. We concluded that Jesus exercised high levels of intellectual intelligence (IQ), emotional intelligence (EI), and significantly to this experience of baptism, was high in spiritual intelligence (SI).

Also discussed in Chapter 4 was an assessment of Jesus' propensity for intuitive decision-making. From the assessment of experienced contributors to entrepreneurial activity, it was indicated that Jesus would have exhibited strong intuitive behaviour and at a similar level as serial entrepreneurs. Such intuitive propensity is associated with what is defined as non-local intuition:

A process by which information normally outside the range of cognitive processes is sensed and perceived in the body and mind as certainty of knowledge or feeling (positive or negative) about the totality of a thing distant or yet to happen. [110]

---

110 Rollin McCraty, Mike Atkinson and Raymond Trevor Bradley, 2004, 'Electrophysiological Evidence of Intuition: Part 1. The Surprising Role of the Heart,' Journal of Alternative and Complementary Medicine 2004; 10(1): 133–143.

It suggested that our human capacity to receive and process information about non-local events appears to be a property of all physical and biological organisation and is likely due to the inherent interconnectedness of everything in the universe. During His early years, Jesus would have been aware of this human and spiritual capability to process such information from without himself. It is emphasised such information processing is not a 'magical'-type event. We, as humans, are constructed totally of energy and matter and all communication and power transfer is by energy wave transmission, whether locally or even from within the universe. With a physics understanding of the created universe, it can be suggested that the same physics principles apply to the communication between God and Jesus as for the 'voice' of the Spirit of God at Jesus' baptism. A fuller explanation of this spiritual communication and power transfer will be provided in Chapter 7. Following the baptism, it is recorded in Matthew 4:1–11 that 'at that time Jesus was led by the Spirit into the desert to be tempted by the devil. He fasted for forty days and forty nights and afterwards was hungry.'

Here, we have communication with a dark force and the 'Spirit' response from Jesus, an interplay of power that is a precursor to the fulfilment of Jesus' mission and end of life events (crucifixion and resurrection). It is worth noting that recent research on intuition suggests that it is possible to access intuitive intelligence more frequently by quieting mental chatter and emotional unrest and by paying attention to one's intuitive guidance.[111] This observation is consistent with Jesus' increasing spiritual awareness whilst meditating, praying, and communing with God during the desert retreat.

---

111 Petitmengin-Peugeot C. 1999 The intuitive experience. In: The view from within. First-person approaches to the study of consciousness. Varela FJ, Shear J, editors. Imprint Academic: London; 43–77.

Significantly, when Jesus returned (from the wilderness) in the power of the Spirit and entered into Galilee, He returned to the synagogue in Nazareth where He stood and chose to read a scroll of the prophet Isaiah:

> *And he came to Nazareth, where he had been brought up; and he went to the synagogue, as his custom was, on the sabbath day. And he stood up to read; and there was given to him the book of the prophet Isaiah. He opened the book and found the place where it was written, 'The Spirit of the Lord is upon me, because he has anointed me to preach good news to the poor. He has sent me to proclaim release to the captives and recovering of sight to the blind, to set at liberty those who are oppressed, to proclaim the acceptable year of the Lord.' And he cl osed the book, and gave it back to the attendant, and sat down; and the eyes of all in the synagogue were fixed on him. And he began to say to them, 'Today this scripture has been fulfilled in your hearing.*
>
> —Luke 4:16–21, *RSV*

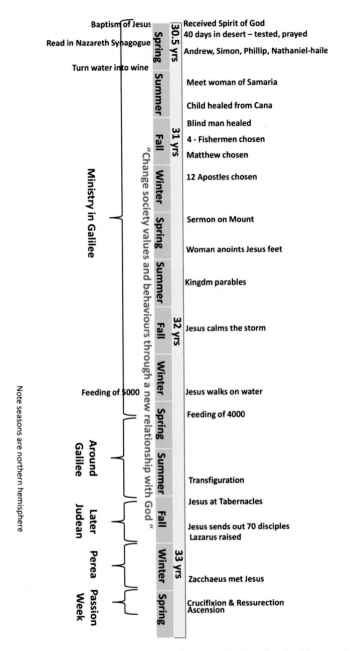

Figure 5.2 Timeline for Jesus and Events Referred to in Chapter 5

With this emphatic statement of who Jesus is and the purpose of His upcoming ministry to all those who will listen, it is timely to discuss Jesus' mission in terms of concepts used to assess the entrepreneurial nature of the process. Figure 5.2 places the 'opportunity' firmly at the centre of the mission concept as 'change societal values and behaviours through a new relationship with God.' To be effectively received, the opportunity must be timely, durable, valued, and attractive (see Fig. 3.1). However, the model (Fig. 3.1) links the establishment of a personal relationship with God as requiring the development of an audience/hearers who will be responsive. A fundamental contribution to the overall process is the leadership of Jesus and His team of disciples. Taken together, true value-focused living is the outcome.

Of particular note to the success of this model is the reference to leadership and the selected team of disciples. McKinsey & Co practice the policy 'if you can attract enough good people to your cause, you can climb any mountain, win any battle, kill any dragon, do whatever you want. In other words, with talent, anything is possible'—such practice is not a set of superior Human Resources processes but a mindset that emphasises the importance of talent to the success of the organisation.[112]

The premise of our consideration of Jesus as an outstanding example of a social entrepreneur is grounded in the definition: 'Entrepreneurship is a way of thinking, reasoning, and acting that is opportunity-obsessed, holistic in approach, and leadership balanced for the purpose of value creation and capture.'[113]

Such social entrepreneurship results in the creation, enhancement, realisation, and renewal of value, not just for the team delivering the value, but for all the users of the service, and

112 Ed Michaels, Helen Handfield-Jones, and Beth Axelrod, 2001, Harvard Business Press, ISBN 978-1-57851-459-5.

113 Jeffrey Timmons, 2011, New Venture Creation.

stakeholders. At the heart of the social entrepreneurship, process is the creation and/or recognition that the opportunity for change exists, followed by the will, energy, and initiative to make the opportunity a reality. It requires a willingness to take risks—personal, social, and economic—but in a very calculated fashion in order to constantly shift the odds of success, balancing the personal risk with the potential added value for users of the new relationship. We will see how Jesus devises difficult to understand strategies and practices to deliver true relationship change reality.

True entrepreneurial leaders inject imagination, motivation, commitment, spirituality, passion, tenacity, integrity, teamwork, and vision into their enterprise. Even so, entrepreneurs, as did Jesus, face daunting dilemmas and hence must make decisions despite ambiguity and contradictions—an environment typical of 'wicked' problems in social and community change. The social entrepreneur demonstrates a behaviour of continuous renewal because the entrepreneur is never satisfied with the status quo of the opportunity. The result of this value creation process is that the total culture grows in purpose and society benefits.

Purpose/Mission

As discussed in Chapter 4, Jesus, at age twelve, expressed understanding for His true purpose, which was to do 'my Father's business' (Luke 2: 49). It is likely Jesus did not fully appreciate the full extent of the 'Father's business' until His baptism at age thirty and the forty days spent in the desert fasting and praying with God. The disciple John records (John 1:14): 'The Word became flesh and made his dwelling among us. We have seen his glory, the glory of the one and only Son, who came from the Father, full of grace and truth.'

However, on entering into His full-time ministry, following the desert experience, Jesus made very clear the mission He was committed to over the next three years was 'preaching the truth'. Mark 1:35–39). In Luke 19:10, Jesus confirmed His fundamental mission on earth was to fulfil God's plan 'to seek and to save the lost'. Jesus knew that God's plan for Him was to die on the cross as atonement for the sin of those who put their faith in Him, i.e., through establishing a new relationship with God. Jesus did not passively wait for the lost to come to Him, but He went after them. He explained His active mission in a parable found in Luke 15:1–7. In this parable, Jesus weaves a story about a man who loses his sheep and leaves the rest of his herd to find the one lost sheep. Jesus concludes this parable by saying, 'There will be more joy in heaven over one sinner who repents than over ninety-nine righteous persons who need no repentance.'

In seeking to review the vision and mission from the perspective of Jesus' entrepreneurial behaviour, it is helpful to use the adapted Timmons Model (Figure 3.2) to evaluate the different elements contributing to the person-centred value-focused living and a relationship with God. In the adapted model, Jesus is shown as the founder and the fulcrum for balancing primary components: namely, a people-centred opportunity; resources, comprising human, financial, spiritual; and a team of disciples to deliver the ministry of new relationships. Of course, the mission is subject to the external factors of exogenous forces, ambiguity, uncertainty, and the spiritual context for the message, much of which was discussed in Chapter 1—'Introduction to the First Century CE'.

Opportunity

As first presented (Fig. 3.1), the opportunity and challenge for Jesus to make it happen can be summarised as changing societal values and living through a new relationship with God. Using an adapted opportunity screening guide (Appendix 5.1), we seek to identify indicators of the challenge which complement the passion and commitment of Jesus and His team of disciples to deliver change and new life to the people-followers during this three-year period.

This assessment is important to establishing the entrepreneurial mindset of Jesus. To make the assessment more manageable, the screen is divided into sections, addressing:

1. Public following;
2. Competitive advantages;
3. Value creation and costs;
4. Strategic differentiation;
5. Personal criteria;
6. Leadership and management team; and
7. Harvest issues.

The results are summarised and discussed in terms of the characteristics exhibited by Jesus the entrepreneur in fulfilling His mission. These specific entrepreneurial characteristics were identified in Fig. 3.5 (Chap. 3) and represent a synthesis of the traits associated with entrepreneurial characteristics and behaviours, including the attributes of passion, belief, inspiration, determination, risk-taking, resilience, vision, courage, instinct, and adaptation to produce an action-centred entrepreneurial mindset. This holistic insight integrates what were traditionally considered narrow personality traits, personality dispositions, and cognitive processes with the spiritual aspects of human cognition, decision-making, and proactive behaviours within the ministry.

Public following

As discussed in Chapter 1, 'Introduction to the First Century CE', the social compact was strained to crisis point and characterised by exploitation, violence, poverty, and spiritual segregation. Indeed, during Jesus' formation and preparation for ministry, He was fully aware of this crisis in human and spiritual values, so it is very appropriate to recognise the need (Fig. 5.3) for a relationship-changing experience amongst the community as of very high potential. In seeking to attract committed followers in Galilee, Jesus' 'vision and mission' recognised the downside of the crisis in the human condition and so preached a new way to follow God in worshipful living—one not based on the past, religion, wealth, or political status, but on personal need and expressed as:

> *The Spirit of the Lord is upon me, because he has anointed me to preach good news to the poor. He has sent me to proclaim release to the captives and recovering of sight to the blind, to set at liberty those who are oppressed, to proclaim the acceptable year of the Lord.*
>
> —Luke 4:18–19, *RSV*

In Matthew 4: 23–25, we read:

> *And he went about all Galilee, teaching in their synagogues and preaching the gospel of the kingdom and healing every disease and every infirmity among the people. So his fame spread throughout all Syria, and they brought him all the sick, those afflicted with various diseases and pains, demoniacs, epileptics, and paralytics,*

and he healed them. And great crowds followed him from
Galilee and the Decapolis and Jerusalem and Judea and
from beyond the Jordan.

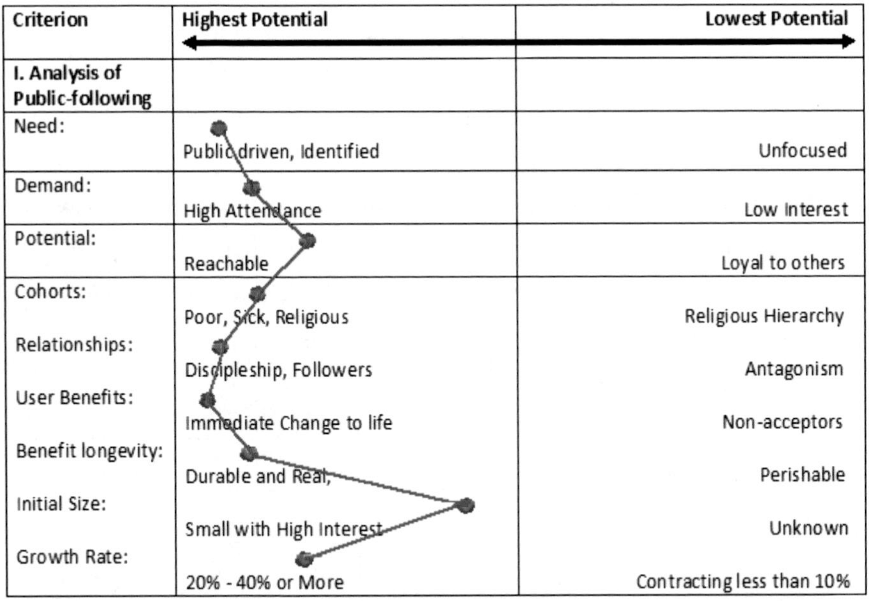

Criterion	Highest Potential	Lowest Potential
I. Analysis of Public-following		
Need:	Public driven, Identified	Unfocused
Demand:	High Attendance	Low Interest
Potential:	Reachable	Loyal to others
Cohorts:	Poor, Sick, Religious	Religious Hierarchy
Relationships:	Discipleship, Followers	Antagonism
User Benefits:	Immediate Change to life	Non-acceptors
Benefit longevity:	Durable and Real,	Perishable
Initial Size:	Small with High Interest	Unknown
Growth Rate:	20% - 40% or More	Contracting less than 10%

Figure 5.3 Opportunity Screening Profile Public-Following

This passage is important both thematically and structurally
in Matthew's Gospel as it highlights the beginning of Jesus'
public ministry in Galilee. This example confirms the validity
of showing a high potential rating for demand, potential and
the cohorts of poor, sick, and religious. Even at this early stage,
growth rate was significant as Jesus' fame spread throughout
all of Syria. Indeed, this first screen profile (Fig. 5.3) shows
Jesus leading and meeting the high potential measures for a
very timely and effective ministry by meeting the need for and
growing cohorts of disciples and new relationship followers
expressing real user benefits.

Competitive Advantages

When describing Jesus' behaviour in teaching a new relationship with God for His followers, it is appropriate to consider any perceived competitive advantages that Jesus may have over the traditional teachings of the Pharisees, Sadducees, and Scribes in Judea and Galilee. Competitive advantage (Fig. 5.4) is generally considered as the delivery of a superior outcome to that provided by the established organisation groups. Importantly, Jesus was providing much greater personal value through differentiating the message from the traditional options available to the community. Competitive advantage results from Jesus matching His core competencies to the opportunity.

Criterion	Highest Potential	Lowest Potential
2. Competitive Advantages		
Know Active Opponents:	Identified and Confronted	Unknown
Identified Expertise:	Multi-skilled from Various careers	All from Same Industry
Contacts and Networks	Community, Religious, Political	Individualistic
Point of Difference:	Clear and Demonstrable	None
Response/ Lead Time	Immediate	Indeterminate
Scalable:	Operational Plan in Place	No capacity or Plan

Figure 5.4 Opportunity Screening Profile for Competitive Advantages

During the formation and development of Jesus to 'be about His Father's business' (Luke 2: 49) and the commencement of the full ministry in Judea and Galilee, one thing is certain: He knew all about the active competitors to the message and hence could both identify their purpose and confront the falsehood. Two examples will suffice. After Jesus had fed the 4,000:

And the Pharisees and Sadducees came, and to test him they asked him to show them a sign from heaven. He answered them, 'When it is evening, you say, "It will be fair weather; for the sky is red." And in the morning, "It will be stormy today, for the sky is red and threatening." You know how to interpret the appearance of the sky, but you cannot interpret the signs of the times. An evil and adulterous generation seeks for a sign, but no sign shall be given to it except the sign of Jonah.' So, he left them and departed.

—Matthew 1:1–4, *RSV*

In the interchange with the woman caught in adultery, John 8:2–11 (*RSV*) provides an excellent account of Jesus knowing His opponents (Scribes and Pharisees):

Early in the morning he came again to the temple; all the people came to him, and he sat down and taught them. The scribes and the Pharisees brought a woman who had been caught in adultery, and placing her in the midst, they said to him, 'Teacher, this woman has been caught in the act of adultery. Now in the law Moses commanded us to stone such. What do you say about her?' This they said to test him, that they might have some charge to bring against him. Jesus bent down and wrote with his finger on the ground. And as they continued to ask him, he stood up and said to them, 'Let him who is without sin among you be the first to throw a stone at her.' And once more he bent down and wrote with his finger on the ground. But when they heard it, they went away, one by one, beginning with the eldest, and Jesus was left alone with the woman

standing before him. Jesus looked up and said to her,
'Woman, where are they? Has no-one condemned you?'
She said, 'No-one, Lord.' And Jesus said, 'Neither do I
condemn you; go, and do not sin again.'

Such a 'point of difference' was immediately clear and demonstrable to all who listened to Jesus. The response was immediate and effective. Jesus' entrepreneurial characteristics in meeting the challenge were inspirational, learned, and compassionate.

Value Creation/Costs

In the ministry of Jesus and the disciples, value-creation was never attributed to a focus on profit from sales, etc., but to the changed lives of His followers, their growth in numbers and a significant community impact within Judea and Galilee. Jesus, as founder and entrepreneur, was responsible for the organisation of the human, financial, and spiritual resources to keep the ministry functioning.

In terms of financial costs and living expenses, it is clear they were resourced from self-funding team members, supporters and/ or sponsors. In the Sermon on the Mount, Jesus made clear:

> *Therefore, I tell you, do not be anxious about your life,*
> *what you shall eat or what you shall drink, nor about your*
> *body, what you shall put on. Is not life more than food,*
> *and the body more than clothing?*
>
> —Matthew 6:25, *RSV*

Interestingly, Joanna (Luke 8: 3), the wife of Chuza, Herod's steward, was an upper-class woman married to a man who was intelligent and capable enough to manage the complicated household of Herod Antipas, the son of Herod the Great, the violent and ambitious head of Judea. Clearly, Joanna would be uniquely positioned to help Jesus with her resources, being both wealthy and having palace connections. She attends to him during his life, and, the Gospels tell us, after his death, as one of the trio of women who go to his tomb and find it empty. Other wealthy and influential sponsors included Nicodemus and Joseph of Arimathea.

Criterion	Highest Potential	Lowest Potential
3. Value Creation/Costs		
Investment/ Development Costs:	Resourced from Team Members	Need Venture Capital
Fixed Costs:	Low. Incremental Requirements	High Requirements
Variable Costs:	Low. Incremental Requirements	High Requirements
Time to Pay Own Way:	Less than a Year	Greater than Four Years
Time to Breakeven	Less than a Year	Greater than Four Years
Return on Invested Energy:	40% or More New Followers	Less than 5% New Followers

Figure 5.5 Opportunity Screening Profile for Value Creation/Costs

With this background, it is clear that fixed and variable costs were low and met as demand requires, so it is appropriate to use this 'resource management' approach as a contributor to a successful mission. It is salutary to remind ourselves of the enormous costs and resources to mount a similar evangelical mission in today's circumstances.

In assessing 'return on invested energy' in lieu of the normal ROI as of high potential, it is to reflect the benefits resulting from the team's characteristics of 'determination', 'commitment', and 'personal energy' expended by the team to achieve success.

Strategic Differentiation

In considering the potential for strategic differentiation in Jesus' ministry, it is necessary to consider the 'degree of fit' between the opportunity, resources, and the team. From an entrepreneurial perspective, the primary entrepreneurial focus of Jesus' ministry was on teaching to bring change to the hearers and their experience in a new relationship with God. We can ask was His teaching fit for purpose? Such a term is defined as 'something that is fit for purpose is good enough to do the job it was designed to do.' The teaching was clearly designed for the job and meets the further aspect of the definition where 'quality is inextricably linked with being fit for purpose.'

Importantly, Jesus exercised passion, courage, learning, and risk-taking as He sought to teach the Gospel of God. In addition, the signs and wonders Jesus performed testified to the truth of His message, but they were not ends in themselves. Preaching the truth about the kingdom of God and how one may receive it by trusting only in Christ formed the bulk of His message, and this message of faith and repentance surpassed all of Jesus' miracles in terms of importance. People travelled far and wide just to hear him. The lessons He taught spread like fire and literally changed the world. Indeed, this summary is consistent with the assessment in Figure 5.6 of 'degree of fit for purpose' as having a very high potential for the success of the ministry.

Criterion	Highest Potential ←	Lowest Potential
4. Strategic Differentiation		
Degree of Fit for Purpose:	High	Low
Team:	Best in Class; Excellent Collaborators	B Team; Minimum Collaboration
Ministry Management::	Superior Service Performance	Perceived as Unimportant
Timing:	'Rowing With the Tide'	'Rowing Against the Tide'
Flexibility:	Able to Adapt. Commit/decommit quickly	Slow; Stubborn
Application Orientation:	Always Searching for Applications	Operating in a Vacuum
Freedom of Choice:	No Compulsion on Followers	Absolute Control
Delivery Channels:	Acceptable; Networks in Place	Unknown; Inaccessible
Room for Error:	Forgiveness	Unforgiving; Rigid Strategy

Figure 5.6 Opportunity Screening Profile for Strategic Differentiation

It is not surprising that examination of the principles and techniques used by Jesus the master teacher are freely available in the literature to guide 'teachers' in delivering learning outcomes that are effective and valued by their students. It is observed He taught with authority (Mark 1:22), told countless stories and parables (Luke 18:1), used poetic form (Luke 6:37–38), using object lessons (John 13:3–17), and teachable moments (Matthew 22: 37–39).

As founder, Jesus took full responsibility to recruit a team to balance His opportunity and available resources. When Jesus called the first four disciples, who were fishermen, to follow him, he said, 'Come, follow me, and I will send you out to fish for people.' (Mark 1:17). When Jesus began the process of calling his disciples to follow him, he started with men who had something in common. The act of Christ in recruiting the first disciples is a lesson in how important it is for any leader to begin with people who share common traits and values. These four men did not have to explain themselves to one another; neither did they have to learn each other's backgrounds. The final team could be considered 'best in class'. This action enables the establishment of stability before diversity and conflict come along.

Of course, errors can be made, as is evident from the accounts of the disciples' actions, but Jesus was the ultimate entrepreneurial leader and knew the importance of showing forgiveness when the action or ignorance was acknowledged.

Peter, the disciple, would never forget that terrible moment following his denial and when the eyes of he and Jesus met. Luke records the incident and says, 'the Lord turned and looked upon Peter' (Luke 22:61). In that one glance, Peter saw the depth of his own failure. He realised that he had just done the very thing that Jesus had foretold, the one thing that Peter had insisted he would never do—he had disowned his beloved Master. It was a low point for Peter, perhaps the worst moment of the worst day of his life. Yet he was forgiven and continued as a man of great faith, he still had an opportunity to recover from his mistakes and to learn one of Jesus' greatest lessons. Such a mindset demonstrated by Jesus is the hallmark of an 'entrepreneurial mindset'.

Personal Criteria

Great leaders, and particularly those providing entrepreneurial leadership, led by example and from the inside out of their mission/ organisation. Such leadership and personal determination to make it happen is directly correlated with the leader's commitment to the enterprise goals, the wellbeing of staff, and meeting the needs of users. This first-century-CE mission/ministry, led by Jesus, is clearly of high potential (Fig. 5.8). Entrepreneurship theory identifies the importance of personal criteria and inner qualities to achieving enterprise success. Such consideration is not focused on the material elements of the opportunity but on the 'qualities, goals and fit' of the entrepreneur's personal criteria to deliver high potential outcomes (Fig. 5.7).

Criterion	Highest Potential	Lowest Potential
5 Personal Criteria		
Qualities, Goals and Fit: Enablement	Getting what You Want; but Wanting what You Get	Surprises
Committed to Mission:	Focused	Un-focused
Connected to Creative Source:	High Levels of Communication	Free-wheeling
Holistic Approach: Stress Tolerance	Fully Integrated with Mission	Self-centred
	Thrives Under Pressure	Cracks Under Pressure

Figure 5.7 Opportunity Screening Profile for Personal Criteria

It is the personal character of the entrepreneur that will ensure the delivery of value-based outcomes to meet the needs of users. At the core of this expressed character is integrity, and without integrity, no-one would follow Jesus, and if no-one is following Jesus, there is no new relationship with God.

When considering one's personal integrity, it is helpful to use a 'spiritual' understanding of inner self—and considered in more detail in Chapters 6 and 7. From this perspective, the spiritual values of integrity, honesty, goodness, compassion, graciousness, humility, cooperation, intuition, trustworthiness, respect, justice, self-control, and service contribute to a holistic understanding of the entrepreneur.

Importantly, Jesus did not say, 'Look at me as the leader,' but actively empowered others. A perfect example of this was in his healing of a man with leprosy:

> And a leper came to Jesus, beseeching Him and falling on his knees before Him, and saying, 'If You are willing, You can make me clean.' Moved with compassion, Jesus stretched out His hand and touched him, and said to him, 'I am willing; be cleansed.' Immediately the leprosy left him, and he was cleansed.'
>
> —Mark 1:40–45

Jesus practised daily 'connecting to creative source' through prayer: 'After he had dismissed them, he went up on a mountainside by himself to pray' (Matthew 14:23); 'Very early in the morning, while it was still dark, Jesus got up, left the house and went off to a solitary place, where he prayed' (Mark 1:35).

Leadership and Management Team

Jesus' leadership style is diametrically opposed to that of the business world. He declared that in the Kingdom, greatness belongs to the servant, and that distinction grows from child-like humility (Matthew 18:4). Jesus taught that leaders were to serve others, not to be served by them. Such a 'servant'-style commitment provides the basis for the highest potential outcome in the provision of a targeted social entrepreneurial and value-driven mission.

With this mindset, Jesus proceeded to recruit an 'entrepreneurial team' (called disciples) to collaborate in delivering the mission to the peoples of Judea and Galilee. Initially, Jesus began with a core group—Peter, Andrew, James, and John—that had something in common: they were fishermen.

This stage was followed by selecting disciples that would add to the skill set by introducing new thoughts, ideas, and vision, and provide diversity to the group (Matthew—tax collector). Such a team, committed and trained by Jesus, were able to both spread the message enthusiastically and be robust enough to cope with fear, tension, and conflict. To reinforce the commitment to servanthood behaviour, Jesus called the disciples to himself and said: 'You know that the rulers of the Gentiles lord it over them, and those who are great exercise authority over them. Yet it shall not be so among you; but whoever desires to become great among you, let him be your servant' (Matthew 12:25–26).

Using this instruction, Jesus emphatically declared that in the Kingdom, greatness belongs to the servant and that distinction grows from child-like humility (Matthew 18:4). The disciples were to serve others, not to be served by them. In this way, the team developed high potential in delivering the message of the Kingdom.

Criterion	Highest Potential	Lowest Potential
6 Leadership / Management Team		
Entrepreneurial Team	All-star Combination; Servanthood	Weak or Solo Entrepreneurs
Life and Spiritual Expertise:	Top of the Field; Super Record	Underdeveloped
Integrity:	Highest Standard	Questionable
Intellectual Honesty:	Know What They Do Not Know	Not Interested in Lack of Knowledge

Figure 5.8 Opportunity Screening Profile for Leadership/ Management Team

Harvest Issues

It is clear that Jesus was fully supportive of a growth strategy for this opportunity and presented the mission as a challenge to both the disciples and the followers to take specific action while on this earth.

Criterion	Highest Potential	Lowest Potential
7 Harvest Issues		
Growth Potential:	A World Following	Local Only Strategy
Growth Strategy:	To Judea and Beyond	Local Only
Role of Holy Spirit:	Personal Communion, & Actions	Not Considered
On-going Mission Leadership	Spirit-led and Empowered	Self-centred
Persecution:	Turn the Other Cheek	Give-in

Figure 5.9 Opportunity Screening Profile for Harvest Issues

Then Jesus came to them and said,

> *All authority in heaven and on earth has been given to me.*
> *Therefore, go and make disciples of all nations, baptising*
> *them in the name of the Father and of the Son and of the*
> *Holy Spirit, and teaching them to obey everything I have*
> *commanded you. And surely I am with you always, to the*
> *very end of the age.*
>
> —Matthew 28:18–20

In issuing this challenge, Jesus invokes the 'name of the Father and of the Son and of the Holy Spirit'—the Spirit being significant in the growth of the Church over the next 2,000 years. Consideration of these developments is part of the 'macro' and 'mega' dimensions of the eco-system (Figure 3.1).

Jesus—Social Entrepreneur

From recent research, Loris Gillin[114] validated a social entrepreneur indicator based on faith-based CEOs' responses to the key dimension of entrepreneurial motivation and expressed as *intentional action, persistence, risk, network orientation,* and *alertness to opportunities.* Measures of these dimensions were evaluated against the entrepreneur's responses to a series of assertions (see Appendix 5.2). Specifically, the concept of motivation incorporated responses based on *a conviction of the heart, a vision, a compulsion to respond,* and *an intuitive response.* This approach is shown to correlate strongly with the commitment of social entrepreneurs to identify a need and satisfy that need amongst users.

---

114 Loris Gillin, 2006, Social Value Creation – as a Core Determinant from the Impact of Social Entrepreneurship, Thesis, Swinburne University of Technology.

Having screened the opportunity profile associated with Jesus' mission (above) as of high potential and identified multiple characteristics exhibited by Jesus in leading the mission and ministry, it is appropriate to apply, as far as is possible, the entrepreneurial indicator to Jesus' teaching, healings, and spiritual actions and behaviours. Figure 5.10 compares the results from the research samples of Australian and USA social entrepreneur CEOs with an estimated response from Jesus, as the founder of Jesus' mission. Clearly, it is not possible to obtain a personal response from Jesus but, given the extensive accounts of Jesus' ministry in the Gospels and the detailed screening of the opportunity, a considered assessment of the questions and index scoring in Appendix 5.2 is included in Figure 5.10.

Item.	Key Dimensions	High Indicator Response Levels - Australian/USA, CEOs' as Social Entrepreneurs	Assessed Response of Jesus as a Social Entrepreneur
	Intentional Action		
2		I draw on latent ability to perform…	✔
3		If task too difficult, I know so.	✔
4		Do not give up on task though difficult.	✔
13		I respond to cause with intent & action	✔
6		I persevere because I like to break thru.	✔
	Persistent/ Obsessive/ Depressed		
11		I can persist…..for years.	✔
12		I practice 'follow-through' above 86%.	✔
14		I feel personally responsible to make things better.	✔
17		I express my spirituality	✔
	Depression Profile		✔
		I get depressed and work harder.	✔
		I get depressed and bounce back.	✔
		Never get depressed.	✔
	Risk		✔
15		The means for me to live are not assured, even 'though I contribute to others with time and expertise.	✔
27		I have given a lot of thought to risk management.	✔
30		I was prepared to roll up my sleeves and get my hands dirty.	✔
	Alertness to Opportunities		✔
34		I continue to be alert to opportunities which emerge.	✔
35		I have my own way of mobilizing resources when necessary to exploit an opportunity– Human, Physical, Capital.	✔

Figure 5.10 Results & Analysis of Indicators for Social Entrepreneurial Behaviour

It is presumed Jesus would exhibit a strong congruence with the other respondent's response levels to intentional action, persistence, risk, and alertness to opportunities, and to such a degree that one could observe Jesus behaved as an entrepreneur during His period of ministry, 29–33 CE.

Interesting, both the Australian and USA entrepreneurs and Jesus acknowledge their spirituality (Q 17) in responding to cause (Q 13), to make things better (Q 14), see it as their duty (Q 15), and contribute time and expertise (Q 16).

This recognition of Jesus as a social entrepreneur is further enhanced when comparing indicator index results with the Australian and USA average social entrepreneur index. The index is a continuum from a score of 0 (entrepreneurial) to a score of 56 (non-creative). Figure 5.11 shows Jesus with an excellent assessed score of 6 with the USA group at twelve and the Australian group at 10.

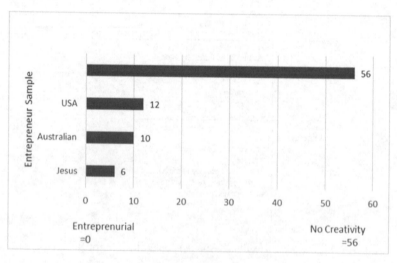

Figure 5.11 Social Entrepreneur Index Score

Jesus—Entrepreneur mindset

Having assessed Jesus as a dynamic and spiritually aware social entrepreneur, acting with passion, commitment, and strong leadership, it is not surprising that the resultant ministry He founded grew strongly, built, as it was, on the added value followers received and experienced in their personal lives. From screening both the potential and delivery of the mission opportunity, it is clear that by being entrepreneurial in such a new ministry, Jesus brought essentially a revolutionary approach to meeting the needs of the community, based on experiencing a new relationship with God through personal acceptance of the preached message.

Indeed, this impact and success, at the cost of the founder's life, was not achieved by writing business plans or the manipulation of high-tech marketing social platforms. Indeed, Jesus demonstrated the personal attributes and behaviours associated with recognising the mission opportunity and pursuing it with vision, courage, inspiration, intuition, and passion as identified in Figure 5.1, and by bringing the necessary physical, human, and financial resources together to make it happen. In Chapter 3, we discussed the multi-layer nature of personal attributes and performance contributing to exercising an entrepreneurial mindset (Fig. 3.6). At the formative and developing stage in Jesus' life (see Chapter 4), we established the reality of Jesus' holistic integration of intellectual intelligence (IQ), emotional intelligence (EI), and spiritual intelligence (SI) into the man that emerged to found the new mission.

Importantly, and identified in the screening of the opportunity above, the entrepreneurial characteristics and behaviours (first reviewed in Chapter 3 and included in the model at Fig. 3.6) of Jesus include those high-performance social entrepreneurship attributes of passion, belief, inspiration, determination, risk-taking, resilience, vision, courage, instinct, and adaptation so necessary to delivering action-centred and value-centred outcomes.

As defined in Chapter 3:

> *Entrepreneur mindset is a way of thinking about opportunities that surface in the firm's external and internal environment and the commitments, decisions, and actions necessary to pursue them, especially under conditions of uncertainty that commonly accompany rapid and significant environmental changes.*[115]

Significantly, there is an umbilical link between our thoughts, beliefs, and actions leading to our expressed behaviour. The functional mindset thus impacts how you make sense of the world and how you make sense of yourself. Such mindsets are linked inextricably to behaviours that lead to developing recognised opportunities into growth-oriented and value-adding innovations that meet user needs. But a mission organisation, of itself, is not entrepreneurially minded—the behaviour that may be present within the mission organisation is driven by the human propensity, spirit, and energy to be entrepreneurial as expressed by leaders and staff identifying the opportunities with application to user needs and perceived value. Importantly, no matter how entrepreneurial either an individual's mindset or an organisation's culture is, interdependencies exist between the founder's mindset and the staff/mission culture such that

---

115 Duane Ireland, Michael Hitt and David Sirmon, 2003, 'A Model of Strategic Entrepreneurship: The Construct and Its Dimensions,' Journal of Management 29(6).

'entrepreneurial culture and entrepreneurial mindset are inextricably interwoven.'[116]

The four mindset dimensions (outer four points Fig. 3.6 and comprising the basis for the entrepreneurial audit (Appendix 5.3)) are *leadership, decision-making, behaviour, and awareness* (see Chapter 3), and are derived from the integration of the identified intelligence states with the attributes identified above to produce an action-centred entrepreneurial mindset. This holistic insight integrates what were traditionally considered narrow personality traits, personality dispositions, and cognitive processes with the spiritual aspects of human cognition, decision-making, and proactive behaviours within the mission enterprise. These four dimensions (Fig. 5.12) form the axes of the entrepreneurial mindset chart. Each dimension is scaled in terms of two alternative characteristics (in bold black type) and measured on a five-point scale (see audit Appendix 5.3).

As derived in Chapter 3, each of the four mindset dimensions is rated in terms of one's propensity to act in two contrasting characteristic styles. Completion of the audit provides a measure for each of the eight characteristics—two for each mindset dimension—giving a pictorial expression of entrepreneurial mindset when plotted on the 'radar' chart.

---

116 Dean Shepherd, H Patzelt, & J.M. Haynie, 2010. 'Entrepreneurial spirals: Deviation-amplifying loops of an entrepreneurial mindset.' Entrepreneurship Theory and Practice, 34(1): 59–82.

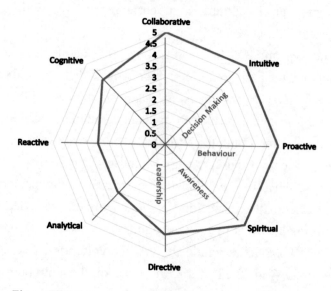

Figure 5.12 Entrepreneurial Mindset for Jesus Entrepreneur
(After Gillin & Hazelton 2019)

The leadership dimension is thus a balance between acting collaboratively and acting in a directive style. In seeking to assess Jesus' leadership of the mission and informed from the gospel record, it is concluded He exhibited a strong collaborative style of leadership but was directive when necessary.

Decision-making is a critical aspect of entrepreneurial behaviour. As shown in Fig. 4.4 (Chapter 4), Jesus exhibited a very strong intuitive decision-making index score: 19. This propensity is reflected in the high intuitive characteristics associated with His recorded examples of decision-making (Fig. 5.12). However, it is noted Jesus also exhibited analytical characteristics during His ministry. Both of these characteristics contribute to effective person-centred decisions.

In all organisations or missions, there is a behavioural need to intervene in, or control an expected occurrence or situation, by being proactive in causing the change and not simply reacting to change when it happens. The Gospels describe the many times Jesus acted proactively to support change in religion, justice, healing, and secular authority. Of course, Jesus did include in His ministry parables that were a reaction to the status quo. These two characteristic levels are included in Figure 5.12.

Awareness is usually defined as knowledge that something exists or as the understanding of a situation or a subject at the present time, based on information or experience. Indeed, self-awareness is knowledge and awareness of one's own personality or character. Together, cognition and spirituality form the natural characteristics of an aware person. Cognition is the mental process involved in knowing, learning, and understanding things. Spirituality is the quality of being concerned with the human spirit or soul as opposed to physical or material things. Figure 5.12 shows Jesus exhibiting a strong spirituality characteristic with a balance on cognition.

In summary, this assessment of the entrepreneurial mindset of Jesus, and charted in Fig. 5.12 shows a complete skewing of Jesus' mindset towards leading in a collaborative style, strong intuitive decision-making, behaving proactively, and a highly developed spiritual awareness as compared with the cognitive, directive, reactive, and analytical characteristics of linear thinking and leadership.

Appendix 5.1

Jesus Ministry—Opportunity Screening Profile

Criterion	Highest Potential ◄——————►	Lowest Potential
I. Analysis of Public following		
Need:	Public driven, Identified	Unfocused
Demand:	High Attendance	Low Interest
Potential:	Reachable	Loyal to others
Cohorts:	Poor, Sick, Religious	Religious Hierarchy
Relationships:	Discipleship, Followers	Antagonism
User Benefits:	Immediate Change to life	Non-acceptors
Benefit longevity:	Durable and Real,	Perishable
Initial Size:	Small with High Interest	Unknown
Growth Rate:	20%—40% or More	Contracting less than 10%
Criterion	Highest Potential ◄——————►	Lowest Potential
2. Competitive Advantages		
Know Active Opponents:	Identified and Confronted	Unknown
Identified Expertise:	Multi-skilled from Various careers	All from Same Industry

Contacts and Networks	Community, Religious, Political	Individualistic
Point of Difference:	Clear and Demonstrable	None
Response/ Lead Time	Immediate	Indeterminate
Scalable:	Operational Plan in Place	No capacity or Plan

Jesus Ministry—Opportunity Screening Profile

Criterion	Highest Potential ←	→ Lowest Potential
3. Value Creation/ Costs		
Investment/ Development Costs:	Resourced from Team Members	Need Venture Capital
Fixed Costs:	Low. Incidental Requirements	High Requirements
Variable Costs:	Low. Incremental Requirements	High Requirements
Time to Pay Own Way:	Less than a Year	Greater than Four Years
Time to Breakeven	Less than a Year	Greater than Four Years
Return on Invested Energy:	40% or More New Followers	Less than 5% New Followers
Criterion	Highest Potential ←	→ Lowest Potential
4. Strategic Differentiation		

Degree of Fit for Purpose:	High	Low
Team:	Best in Class; Excellent Collaborators	B Team; Minimum Collaboration
Ministry Management::	Superior Service Performance	Perceived as Unimportant
Timing:	'Rowing With the Tide'	'Rowing Against the Tide'
Flexibility:	Able to Adapt. Commit/decommit quickly	Slow; Stubborn
Application Orientation:	Always Searching for Applications	Operating in a Vacuum
Freedom of Choice:	No Compulsion on Followers	Absolute Control
Delivery Channels:	Acceptable; Networks in Place	Unknow n; Inaccessible
Room for Error:	Forgiveness	Unforgiving; Rigid Strategy

Jesus Ministry—Opportunity Screening Profile

Criterion	Highest Potential	Lowest Potential
	←	→
5 Personal Criteria		
Goals and Fit:	Getting what You Want; but Wanting what You Get	Surprises
Committed to Mission:	Focused	Un-focused
Connected to Creative Source:	High Levels of Communication	Free-wheeling
Holistic Approach:	Fully Integrated with Mission	Self-centred

Jesus the Social Entrepreneur

Stress Tolerance	Thrives Under Pressure	Cracks Under Pressure
Criterion	Highest Potential ⟵	Lowest Potential ⟶
6 Leadership / Management Team		
Entrepreneurial Team	All-star Combination; Free Agents.	Weak or Solo Entrepreneurs
Life and Spiritual Expertise:	Top of the Field; Super Record	Underdeveloped
Integrity:	Highest Standard	Questionable
Intellectual Honesty:	Know What They Do Not Know	Not Interested in Lack of Knowledge
Criterion	Highest Potential ⟵	Lowest Potential ⟶
7 Harvest Issues		
Growth Potential:	A World Following	Local Only Strategy
Growth Strategy:	To Judea and Beyond	Local Only
Role of Holy Spirit:	Personal Communion, & Actions	Not Considered
On-going Mission Leadership	Spirit-led and Empowered	Self-centred
Persecution:	Turn the Other Cheek	Give-in

Appendix 5.2

SOCIAL ENTREPRENEURSHIP INDICATOR

Was there at any point before start-up ... Please circle

A conviction of heart?

A vision?

A compulsion to respond?

An intuitive response?

Circle options where appropriate or given, please circle 'true' or 'false' to the following:

T True   ? Uncertain   F False

                                                    T ? F

1. I draw on/do not draw on latent ability to perform a task.

                                                    ☐ ☐ ☐

2. I merely rely on good luck to perform well.

                                                    ☐ ☐ ☐

3. If the task is too difficult, I know so.

☐ ☐ ☐

4. If the task is too difficult I 'give it away'.

☐ ☐ ☐

5. Even if a task is not too difficult, if it requires a lot of effort I 'give it away'.

☐ ☐ ☐

6. I persevere because I like to 'break through'.

☐ ☐ ☐

7. 'Why work hard if people-relating things come more easily!'

☐ ☐ ☐

8. Everything I do needs to have a supply of good luck.

☐ ☐ ☐

9. Across life, I have showed persistence when ....
....

10. In this non-profit venture (NPV) I am *persistent obsessive*. In what way? ....
....

11. I can persist for: days / weeks / months / years.

12. I practice 'follow-through' at a rate of 10% 20% 30% 40% 50% 60% 70% 80% 90% 100%

13. I, personally, respond to a cause ... by feeling driven/ compelled feeling inspired with intent and action.

☐ ☐ ☐

14. In the social field, I feel personally responsible to make things better.

☐ ☐ ☐

15. The 'means' for me to live are assured, so I want to contribute to others with my time and expertise.

☐ ☐ ☐

16. I feel it a duty to respond in this way.

☐ ☐ ☐

17. I express my spirituality in this way.

☐ ☐ ☐

18. I am charged with acting entrepreneurially towards those in need.

☐ ☐ ☐

19. I have followed a vision and it has failed, but that does not mean I am a failure.

☐ ☐ ☐

20. I get depressed for ... a day ... a few days a couple of weeks ... longer.

☐ ☐ ☐

21. I get depressed and withdraw.

☐ ☐ ☐

22. I get depressed and work harder.

☐ ☐ ☐

23. I get depressed and bounce back.

☐ ☐ ☐

24. I obsess over wishing I could do even better.

☐ ☐ ☐

25. Before becoming a social entrepreneur I decided against doing something else which was...
....
....

26. Having said that, I chose the 'subjective return' to becoming an entrepreneur, and decided against the 'subjective expected return' to doing something else. What I now have is the 'subjective relative return' to social entrepreneurship made up of:

1. Personal characteristics: Please circle family background, personal history and educational achievements:
Parents/Married/Separated/Mother living/Father living/
Siblings/Sisters/Brothers.
My birth order Oldest /2nd/born 3rd/born 4th/born 5th born/Youngest.

2. In 2020 the institutional and economic variables I operate in are ....
....

27. I have given a lot of thought to risk management.

☐ ☐ ☐

28. The costs of setting up the venture I work in were covered before commencement.

☐ ☐ ☐

29. A breakdown of those costs is as follows: ....
....

30. I was prepared to roll up my sleeves and get my hands dirty.

☐ ☐ ☐

31. I was prepared to roll up my sleeves and get my hands dirty even if nobody else joined in support.

☐ ☐ ☐

32. I believe the venture I work in has broken down resistance to change amongst others.

☐ ☐ ☐

33. The community of which we are a part has moved from Little entrepreneurship/Medium entrepreneurship/High entrepreneurship.

34. I continue to be alert to opportunities that emerge.

☐ ☐ ☐

35. I have my own way of mobilising:

human resources,

☐ ☐ ☐

physical resources,

☐ ☐ ☐

capital resources …

☐ ☐ ☐

… when it is necessary to exploit an opportunity.

Appendix 5.3

Entrepreneurial Mindset Audit Instrument

Entrepreneurial Mindset Audit Instrument

We are interested in learning how you perceive your entrepreneurial behaviour in your workplace and organisation. Using the scales below, please indicate how much you agree or disagree with each of the characteristics applying to each primary dimension of your performance. It would be helpful you provided some explanation and examples of your performance. All responses will be kept confidential.

LEADERSHIP: **Collaborative**

Strongly Agree				Strongly Disagree
O	O	O	O	O

LEADERSHIP: **Directive:**

Strongly Agree				Strongly Disagree
O	O	O	O	O

List Examples...

DECISION-MAKING: **Intuitive:**

Strongly Agree				Strongly Disagree
O	O	O	O	O

DECISION-MAKING: **Analytical:**

Strongly Agree				Strongly Disagree
O	O	O	O	O

List Examples...

BEHAVIOUR: **Proactive:**

Strongly Agree				Strongly Disagree
O	O	O	O	O

BEHAVIOUR: **Reactive:**

Strongly Agree				Strongly Disagree
O	O	O	O	O

List Examples...

AWARENESS: **Spiritual:**

Strongly Agree				Strongly Disagree
O	O	O	O	O

AWARENESS: **Cognitive:**

Strongly Agree				Strongly Disagree
O	O	O	O	O

List Examples...

© Hazelton and Gillin 2019

Chapter 6: Jesus and the Leadership Team

The only definition of a leader
is someone who has followers.

—Peter Drucker

L eadership theory, concepts, and practice are currently discussed ad nauseum within academe, politics, churches, and business in what I define as a very linear mindset that focuses on right-or-wrong and black-or-white results, manipulation of outcomes, and measures of success or failure.

In the last chapter, we noted in the opportunity profile that Jesus was assessed as very high on the measures of the entrepreneurial team (Figure 5.8), life and spiritual expertise, integrity, and intellectual honesty. Also, using the entrepreneurial mindset audit (Figure 5.12), Jesus was assessed on the dimension of 'leadership' to have a maximum propensity for collaboration and a high propensity for directive leadership where and when required. This chapter will both review and compare Jesus' entrepreneurial style of leadership and particularly the focus on both His inspiration to, and management of, the discipleship team: in their selection, development, and collaboration practices as they participated in bringing the message and life changes to meet the needs of the community.

By way of contrast with general thinking in the community of today, a distinction is often made between the individual with the vision, skill, and mindset to start up a high-potential venture (thought of as the entrepreneur) and the typically more seasoned, risk-averse professional with the ability to scale the enterprise (referred to as the manager). But recent research has identified effective entrepreneurs as being internally motivated, high-energy leaders with a unique tolerance for ambiguity, a keen eye toward mitigating risk, and a passion for discovery and innovation.[117] Using this description, leaders create or identify and pursue opportunities by marshalling the diverse resources required to develop new markets focused on user needs and engage the inevitable competition. More than ever, it is found that the creation and liberation of human energy resulting from such entrepreneurial leadership is a major transformational force to developing a more just, loving, caring, and economically sustaining society. It was just such motivations and characteristics we observed in the ministry of Jesus. He was very much the social entrepreneur with an entrepreneur mindset focused on bringing a new relationship with God to the people of the first century CE in Judea and Galilee, but also in founding what is now a worldwide ministry to all in need and redemption.

Fundamentally, this concept of entrepreneur mindset, in contrast to linear and rational cognition, evokes the integration of the whole person in decision-making, actions, and values. As demonstrated in Chapter 5, the entrepreneur mindset is represented in the four dimensions: leadership, behaviour, decision-making, and awareness, which holistically influence the psychological, physiological, physical, emotional, and spiritual elements of the practising entrepreneur.

---

117 Jeffrey Timmons, Murray Gillin , Sam Burshtein and Stephen Spinelli. 2011 'New Venture Creation – Entrepreneurship for the 21st Century, McGraw-Hill, Australia (Pacific Edition).

Jesus and Entrepreneurial Leadership

In the words of Jesus in Mark 10: 42–45:

> *Jesus called them together and said, 'You know that those who are regarded as rulers of the Gentiles lord it over them, and their high officials exercise authority over them. Not so with you. Instead, whoever wants to become great among you must be your servant, and whoever wants to be first must be slave of all. For even the **Son of Man did not come to be served, but to serve** and to give his life as a ransom for many.*

Gene Wilkes commented that the essential lesson learned from Jesus on leadership was that:

> *He taught and embodied leadership as service. Jesus was a Servant Leader in every sense of the concept. I would describe him as one who served his mission (in biblical language, 'the will of [His] Father') and led by serving those he recruited to carry out that mission. This mission was everything for Jesus. It was his purpose and direction for all he did while on earth—including his death. [118]*

Table 6.1 compares the seven principles—identified by Wilkes—to describe how Jesus led and practised servant leadership with a set of seven principles listed by Phillip Kingston to describe business/enterprise entrepreneur leadership and practice.[119]

118 C. Gene Wilkes, 1998, 'Jesus on Leadership – timeless wisdom of servant leadership' LifeWay Press.
119 Phillip Kingston, 2016, '7 Ways to Lead Successful Entrepreneurial Teams' Entrepreneur – Asia Pacific, https://www.entrepreneur.com/article/279438.

Although the language descriptions differ, it is clear there exists a sense of commonality between these two expressions of entrepreneurial leadership. The difference reflects the specific emphasis each entrepreneur places on transforming the respective opportunity (business product/ mission message) into valued benefits which meet the user's needs.

Phillip Kingston— on Business leadership	C. Gene Wilkes— on Servant leadership
Leadership	Jesus humbled himself and allowed God to exalt him.
Willingness to Listen	Jesus followed his father's will rather than seeking a position.
People Management	Jesus defined greatness as being a servant.
Decision-making	Jesus took risks to serve others because he trusted he was God's son.
Articulating a Vision	Jesus built a team to carry out a vision worldwide.
Getting the Investors On-board	Jesus shared responsibility and authority with those he was called to lead.
Attracting Top Talent	Jesus left his place at the head table to serve the needs of others.

Table 6.1 Leadership Principles for Servant and Business-Entrepreneur Leadership Style

An interesting reflection on the differing foci and purpose of the leadership function is provided by Ethan Lin:

Sheep don't write history. Leaders do. Sheep are essentially followers. Leaders, through their actions, have changed the course of history. Military leaders have redefined borders of countries and defended their land against invaders.

Business leaders have built giant corporations that provide employment and income to thousands of people. Without these leaders, more people would be having trouble finding livelihood for their families.

Spiritual leaders have caused changes in thought and perspective, leading to new worldviews and culture, often adjusting the same story to a different context yet maintaining the principal. This has impacted everything from beliefs, values, fashion, behaviours . Mother Teresa changed history. She showed the world the true meaning of altruism. Having seen the poverty in the streets of Calcutta, she took the step to care for them. Did she need to? Nope. She could be like everyone else, living their own lives while the poor suffer and die. But she did something about it. She committed her life to ministering to the poor and needy and at the time of her death, her organisation Missionaries of Charity was operating 610 missions in 123 countries worldwide. She didn't just help poor people. She became a role model for many other great men and women. Her ideals and beliefs live long after she left us in 1997.[120]

To further appreciate the interrelationships within the leadership of a dynamic organisation/mission, we adapt Grant's concept for an entrepreneurial leadership paradigm.[121] Three clear areas

---

120 Ethan Lin, 2016, 'The Importance Of Leadership In Today's World', www. leadershipgeeks.com.

121 Alan Grant, 1992, 'The Development of an entrepreneurial Leadership Paradigm for Enhancing Venture Capital Success,' – as adapted by Jeffrey Timmons, Murray Gillin et al, 2011, 'New Venture Creation'.

evolved from his study: the lead entrepreneur, the venture team, and the external environment influences. Using these three elements, we have adapted a new version to reflect the leadership by Jesus of His first-century-CE mission. Table 6.2 reviews Jesus as the lead entrepreneur, the disciple team, and external environmental influences.

Jesus - Lead Entrepreneur	
Self-concept	Jesus has a realist's attitude rather than one of invincibility.
Intellectually honest	Trustworthy: His word is His contract. Admits what and when He does not know.
Pacemaker	Displays a high energy level and a sense of urgency.
Courage	Capable of making hard decisions: setting and beating high goals.
Communication skills	Maintains an effective dialogue with the disciple team as a 'servant' leader, in the needs based community, and with other follower constituents.
Team player	Outstanding in people management and team-building skills. Jesus 'did not come to be served, but to serve.'
The Disciple Team	
Organisational style	Jesus and the Disciple team blend their skills to operate in a collaborative manner and in a participative environment.
Ethical behaviour	Practices strong adherence to ethical mission practices.
Faithfulness	Stretched commitments are consistently met or bettered.

Focus Long-term	Mission strategies are kept in focus, but tactics are varied to achieve them.
Performance/reward	High standards of performance are created, and superior performance is rewarded fairly and equitably.
Adaptability	Responsive to rapid changes in human/ political/religious cycles.
External Environmental Influences	
Constituent needs	Mission needs are satisfied in parallel with those of the other publics the mission serves.
Prior experience	Extensive prior experiences are effectively applied.
Mentoring	The competencies of others are sought and used.
Problem resolution	New problems are immediately solved or prioritised.
Value creation	High commitment is placed on long-term value creation for sponsors, followers, mission staff and other stakeholders.
Skill emphasis	Communication skills are stressed over technical ones. Jesus left his place at the head table to serve the needs of others.

Table 6.2 The Jesus Entrepreneurial Leadership Paradigm (After Grant and Timmons et al.)[121]

This presentation of the paradigm is grounded in the fact that successful entrepreneurs possess a well-developed capacity to exert influence without formal power and is best understood as 'servant leadership' when considering Jesus as a social entrepreneurial leader. 'Servant leadership' has been described as the focus on the growth of the individual, that they might flourish and achieve their full potential and not primarily the growth and potential of the organisation, that distinguishes servant leadership from other leadership styles. The primary concern of the servant leader is service to their followers.

Such leaders are adept at conflict resolution. They know when to use logic and when to persuade, when to make a concession, and when to exact one. To run a successful venture/mission, the lead entrepreneur, Jesus, learns to manage with many different constituencies—the audience, the lead team, and the resource sponsors, as well as the disciples/followers and others on the inside—often with conflicting aims. Success comes when the entrepreneur is a mediator—by acting as a 'servant' of the team rather than as a dictator. The entrepreneur leader also knows how to deal with his/her own intuition.

From research into the behaviour of serial entrepreneurs,[122] with all demonstrating an entrepreneur mindset and leading growth ventures in the Cambridge Technopole (UK), we show the level each leader exhibits in a leadership profile. Significantly, they exhibit a high propensity for 'intuitive decision-making' and a deep 'desire to serve' or, as they express it, 'giving back' to the community (Figure 6.1).

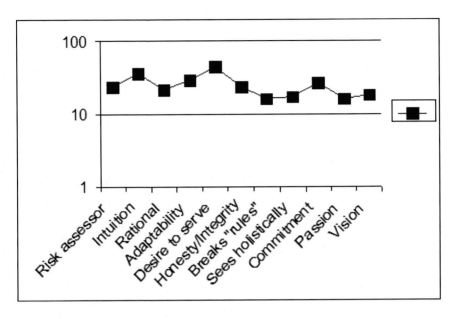

Figure 6.1 Contributions to Decision-making—Cambridge Serial
Entrepreneurs (LaPira and Gillin 2006)[122]

This strongly expressed 'desire to serve' (note log plot of data) is also at the core of Jesus' leadership in delivering and growing His mission and is also a major characteristic of entrepreneur mindset leaders in the society of today. Two examples from successful business entrepreneurs will suffice to illustrate this principle:

Bill & Melinda Gates Foundation (BMGF)

Bill Gates often tells the story of reading a newspaper article about the leading causes of childhood death, including rotavirus. How is it possible, he wondered, that

---

122 Frank LaPira and Murray Gillin, 2006, 'Non-local Intuition and the Performance of Serial Entrepreneurs', Journal of International Entrepreneurship and Small Business, Vol 3 #1, pp 17–35.

a disease that now kills 600,000 children per year is the focus of so little attention and investment?[123]

This realisation that children in developed countries had access to vaccines while children in developing countries were dying for lack of them prompted the Foundation to invest as a founding partner in Gavi. The primary goals of the foundation are, globally, to enhance healthcare and reduce extreme poverty, and, in the US, to expand educational opportunities and access to information technology and education developments, including the establishment of the Gates Cambridge Scholarships at Cambridge University.

This 'desire to serve' can be summarised as: treat others as you would want to be treated, share the wealth that is created with the creating team, and give back to the community.

Richard Pratt[124]

The core leadership principles practised by Richard Pratt in 'giving back to the community' were:

1. Philanthropy is good for business
2. Take philanthropy to the factory floor
3. Link it to your client base
4. Cast the charity net wide
5. Manage charity work on a professional basis
6. Decide charity priorities in advance.

---

123 Bill and Melinda Gates Foundation, https://www.gatesfoundation.org/.
124 J Kirby, 2004, 'Richard Pratt: Business Secrets of the Billionaire Behind Australia's Richest Private Company' Wiley & Sons.

'If you adopt my attitude to business, you cannot possibly fail', says Richard Pratt, founder and former owner of the Visy paper and packaging empire. An immigrant boy who grew up in rural Australia, he turned a small box-making business into the largest packaging and recycling company in the world. Visy employs more than 9,500 people in Australia and the United States (where it is known as Pratt Industries USA), with total sales exceeding more than $5 billion. Significantly, Visy has remained a private company, now led by Anthony Pratt after Richard's death in 2009. Richard Pratt was Australia's leading entrepreneur using all the dimensions that describe an entrepreneur mindset.

Richard Pratt practised philanthropy through the Pratt family's 'VisyCares', a non-profit foundation that began in 1995 and which promoted social responsibility at Visy through donations to establish community-based projects such as youth, immigrant, and learning centres. His principle is summed up by:

> it has taken the business sector a long time to realise that you can reverse the old slogan: what's good for the business is good for the community—to—what's good for the community is also good for business.[125]

From the example of Jesus and the two business entrepreneurs presented above, it is possible to conclude that great companies/missions can be built upon these simple yet elegant principles, but all the capital, technology, service management, and latest information available cannot substitute for these elegant principles, nor will they cause such an entrepreneurial culture to happen. These simple ideals are at the heart of the difference between good and great companies/missions.

---

125 Australian Financial Review, 15 February 2000.

Servant Leadership

To conclude this section, it is appropriate to define servant leadership as understood by the church leaders of today's missions as:

> *The focus on the growth of the individual, that they might flourish and achieve their full potential and not primarily the growth and potential of the organisation, that distinguishes servant leadership from other leadership styles. The primary concern of the servant leader is service to their followers.*[126]

Dr Thorsten Grahn, in his blog, comments such a focus on the growth of the individual provides the principles of servant leadership (SL), which were modelled by Jesus as he grew and developed the disciples into the leaders of his mission. As such, this is a model that should have primacy in Kingdom service.[126]

The concept of a servant leader is not such a modern concept but can be found in the biblical account of the life of Jesus Christ. Grahn comments as follows:

> *In John 13:1-17 Jesus gives a very practical example of what it means to serve others. He washes the feet of his followers, which was properly the responsibility of the house-servant. Examination of this passage shows that:*

> - *Jesus' basic motivation was love for his followers (v. 1).*
> - *Jesus was fully aware of his position as leader (v. 14).*

126 Thorsten Grahn, Blog, 'Jesus: The Role Model for Christian Leadership', http://christian-leadership.org/jesus-the-role-model-for-christian-leaders/.

- *Jesus voluntarily becomes a servant to his followers (v. 5–12).*
- *Jesus wants to set an example for his followers to follow (v. 14–15).*

Significantly, both Queen Elizabeth II (United Kingdom) and the Pope (head of the Catholic Church) celebrate the recognition of Jesus washing the disciple's feet, each on Holy Thursday—the Queen giving coins to individuals as she walked the street, and the Pope washing the feet of prisoners and homeless.

From the teaching and example of Jesus Christ, we learn that being a servant leader in the most general sense means being:

- 'A voluntary servant, who submits themselves to a higher purpose, which is beyond their personal interests or the interests of others,
- A leader who uses the power that is entrusted to them to serve others,
- A servant who, out of love, serves others needs before their own,
- A teacher who teaches their followers, in word and deed, how to become servant leaders themselves.'

However, such an entrepreneur mindset motivates entrepreneurs to create and build substantial enterprises/missions, but they are not 'lone wolves' and super-independent. They do not need to collect all the credit for the effort. They not only recognise the reality that it is rarely possible to build a substantial business working alone, they also actively build a team. They have an uncanny ability to make heroes out of the people they attract to the venture by giving responsibility and sharing credit for accomplishments. Jesus was the personification of this reality.

In summary, whether we focus on servant leadership or entrepreneur-minded leadership, we seek to endorse: 'Leadership is a mindset in action.' Leadership stems from social influence, not authority or power. Leadership, as practised by Jesus, requires others (Apostles) in the team to create the outcome, and that implies the team does not depend on responding to 'directive'-style commands (see Chapter 5) but embraces 'collaborative'-style behaviours to manage the team. This 'collaborative' style of leadership maximises the efforts of the team towards the achievement of the mission goals.

The Entrepreneurial Team

There is little dispute today that the entrepreneurial team is a key ingredient in the development and growth of a higher-potential venture/mission. Clearly, the new mission to Jews of Judea and Galilee in the first century CE required the lead social entrepreneur, Jesus, to demonstrate His physical, emotional, and spiritual characteristics (entrepreneur mindset) in presenting the message of a new relationship with God. In addition, His authority from God was central to the mission, but without a loyal, committed, sacrificing, and entrepreneurial team of apostles and extended follower disciples, the growth of the mission (locally and international) would have been severely limited.

Such a high-potential mission required more than evidence of His authority; it required Jesus to use His interpersonal skills and spiritual awareness (entrepreneur mindset) to foster communications with those chosen to be apostles/disciples for the mission, hence the importance of selecting the right team, practising team building, and securing team harmony.

High-performing teams are invariably formed around a very capable entrepreneurial leader who exhibits both mission accomplishments and articulates several non-negotiable qualities that His team must possess (Chapters 4 and 5).

These team qualities will include:

- Relevant formation, experience, and track record for the mission.
- Motivation to excel as a member of the team.
- Commitment, determination, and perseverance to Jesus and the mission.
- Tolerance of risk, ambiguity, and uncertainty.
- Creativity.
- Team locus of control.
- Adaptability to multiple challenges.
- Opportunity obsession.
- Leadership and courage.
- Communication with all members of the team.

The entrepreneurial leader is pivotal to such an entrepreneurial team as both a player and a coach. It is important to note that Jesus, like all outstanding entrepreneurs, act to some degree like a magnet in attracting motivated, quality individuals who passionately desire to be associated with the leader and His mission as a team player. This ability and skill in attracting key apostles to the mission and then building the team, is one of the most valued capabilities sponsors and followers look for in giving support to a new venture/mission. Indeed, venture capitalists investing in new ventures follow the truism.

I prefer a grade-A entrepreneur and team with a grade-B idea, over a grade-B team with a grade-A idea. In the world of today, there is plenty of technology, plenty of entrepreneurs, plenty of money, plenty of venture capital. What is in short supply is great teams. Your biggest challenge will be in building great teams.[127]

The founder, who subsequently leads the mission/enterprise, builds His 'A' team around outstanding 'players' from within the team in delivering the mission purpose and strategic goals. Such outstanding players like the apostles Peter, James, and John feature prominently in the success and international development of the mission. Also, in managing an A team, the leader adopts a philosophy that rewards success and supports honest failure, shares the 'wealth' with those who help create it, and sets high standards for both performance and personal conduct.

Such a team spirit involves 'the belief by everyone in the venture/mission that they are "in this thing together" and by working together, great things can be achieved.'[128] Small but important actions by the entrepreneur (leader) can create this team spirit—for example, Jesus sent Peter fishing so that they could pay the temple tax (Matthew 17:27), sent two of His apostles on a mundane job to fetch a colt (Matthew 21:1–2), and also sent His extended team of seventy disciples on a challenging excursion to preach the gospel and heal the sick (Luke 10:1–9). They weren't even allowed to take with them any money or supplies! Such actions by the entrepreneur leader seek to establish a 'we' spirit—not a 'me' spirit.

---

127 General Georges Doriot's dictum – quoted in Jeffrey Timmons, Murray Gillin , Sam Burshtein and Stephen Spinelli.. 2011 'New Venture Creation – Entrepreneurship for the 21st Century, McGraw-Hill, Australia (Pacific Edition).

128 Robert Hisrich, Michael Peters and Dean Shepherd, 2020, 'Entrepreneurship', McGraw Hill Education, New York.

In addition, Jesus recognised the importance of learning from 'battle scars' to enhance team quality and cohesion (Peter denying Jesus—Luke 22:54–62); appreciates the importance of the 'family atmosphere' to team members and Himself (Mark 3:33–35); and the incorporation of awareness of human values, the spiritual dimension of man, faith, compassion, and trust. Only by leading holistically with empathy and integrity can one expect to develop the complete team. A team motivated to achieve the common objective through faith, innovation, risk optimisation, taking advantage of opportunities, and managing the dynamic mission environment will be truly successful in the user marketplace.

Selection of Apostles and Disciples

In today's world of large corporations, dependence on technology, bureaucratic rules, media hype, and political influence, we tend to think that recruiting executives and staff is more a function of educational background, relevant degrees, or specialisations and the size of the remuneration package that will attract staff. Indeed, technician and trade qualifications or 'learned-on-the-job' experiences are often seen as second-rate in preparation for selection to executive and senior staff positions. Such a mindset is the very antithesis for selecting executive-level and team players for creative, dynamic, and fast-growing social entrepreneurial ventures. Of course, in the time of the first century CE, as reviewed in Chapter 1, tertiary education was not on the agenda and there was a big void between those of the ruling class and the peasant class in the community. Interestingly, not one of the chosen twelve Apostles was a scholar or rabbi. They had no extraordinary skills and were neither religious nor refined—they were ordinary people.

Jesus was not subject to such a class-focused mindset. He was committed to a higher spiritual value in meeting the personal needs of the community He came to serve.

> *For I have come down from heaven, not to do My own will, but to do the will of Him who sent Me. And this is the will of Him who sent Me, that I shall lose none of those He has given Me, but raise them up at the last day. For it is My Father's will that everyone who looks to the Son and believes in Him shall have eternal life, and I will raise him up at the last day.*
>
> —John 6:38 –40

Not only did Jesus 'come to serve' the community needs of the peoples of Judea and Galilee but, from Matthew 4:18–22, we see Jesus fully appreciated both the skills and mindset required of the team of twelve Apostles to deliver the mission message and strategy—in selecting Peter, Andrew, James and John, Jesus was seeking 'fishers for men'.

> *Jesus was walking by the Sea of Galilee. He saw two brothers. They were Simon (his other name was Peter) and Andrew, his brother. They were putting a net into the sea for they were fishermen. Jesus said to them, 'Follow Me. I will make you fishers for men!' At once they left their nets and followed Him. Going from there, Jesus saw two other brothers. They were James and John, the sons of Zebedee. They were sitting in a boat with their father, mending their nets. Jesus called them. At once they left the boat and their father and followed Jesus.*

Before seeking to identify the mindset and skills for the selected twelve Apostles, I propose to summarise my assessment of the principles used by Jesus in the selection process for the Apostles. We concluded in Chapter 5 that Jesus was a social entrepreneur exercising a well-formed entrepreneur mindset. As such, He was aware that the mission needed a team to facilitate His vision of a mission to 'change societal values and behaviours through a new relationship with God' and exhibited the following behaviours in selecting the team:

- **Understanding Himself:**
  A formidable team begins with Jesus the founder and social entrepreneur.
- **Focus on understanding potential mission users:**
  Has a holistic understanding of first-century-CE society and class structure.
- **Recruit action-takers who can get the job done:**
  No business/mission has ever taken off based simply on an idea.
- **Build for the long term:**
  Jesus built the team with the entire mission's structure in mind, including growth internationally.
- **Personalities matter:**
  Jesus understood constant friction gets in the way of the work.
- **Avoid homogeneity in your team:**
  If everyone conforms to the same identity, there will be no new ideas.
- **Get the team members to buy into your vision:**
  An essential part of success in any business/mission is crafting a vision. Sell your team on that big picture.

As an effective social entrepreneur, Jesus fully understood the need to select the right team members. At thirty years of age, He recognised that not all needed to be 'called' at the start of the mission in 29 CE. Selection was completed over about six months (see Fig. 5.2 for timeline). We note that John the Baptist had many followers committed to his message, but when Jesus came down to the Jordan River to be baptised by John, John immediately proclaimed that Jesus was the Lamb of God who takes away the sin of the world. He also recognised Jesus as the Son of God (John 1:29–34). Significantly, two of John's disciples immediately left to follow after Jesus and see where He was staying. Over a couple of days, the group attracted to Jesus grew to four: Andrew, the brother of Simon Peter; Peter (who was recruited to this group by Andrew); Phillip; and Nathanael. Importantly, Jesus recognised in Nathanael a prospective, valuable team member by saying, 'Behold, an Israelite in whom there is no guile.' At this stage, these men can be described as believing followers but not yet full disciples (John 1: 35–51).

Some four months later, we read of Jesus walking alongside Lake Galilee (see Matthew 4:18–22, above) and seeing Peter and Andrew tending their fishing nets. He calls to them to follow Him and promises the two they will become 'fishers for men'. Close by, He sees two brothers, James and John, also mending nets with their father. Again, He calls them to follow and immediately they jump out of their boat to follow Jesus, leaving their livelihood and father behind. Clearly, Jesus saw in each of these four successful fishermen a quality character, not afraid of hard work, persistent in seeking to catch many fish, and, above all, committed to Jesus the Son of God. Matthew, the tax collector, while sitting in his custom collector's booth, was called a month or two later. Matthew 9:9 records that Matthew immediately left his booth and followed Jesus. This response caused many tax collectors to sit down with Jesus and His existing disciples for a discussion. This result shows how Jesus sought communication with business/bureaucrats in the community. However, this caused a stir with the Pharisees (religious representatives), asking of the disciples, 'Why does your teacher eat with tax collectors and sinners?'

Jesus responded, 'Those who are well have no need of a physician, but those who are sick.' He continues with a challenge to His disciples—'Go and learn what this means, I desire mercy, and not sacrifice. For I came not to call the righteous but sinners to repentance' (Matt. 9:10–13).

During this period, Jesus was calling potential disciples, teaching them, and evaluating their readiness for full-time service in support of the mission. Around the early winter, when Jesus was thirty-one years of age, He appointed twelve disciples and renamed them Apostles (Luke 6:12–13):

Jesus went up on a mountainside and called to him those he wanted , and they came to him. He appointed twelve that they might be with him and that he might send them out to preach and to have authority to drive out demons.

—Mark 3:13–15

The names of the twelve apostles are these: first, Simon, who is called Peter, and Andrew his brother; James the son of Zebedee, and John his brother; Philip and Bartholomew [Nathanael]*; Thomas and Matthew the tax collector; James the son of Alphaeus* [James the less]*, and Thaddaeus* [Judas, son of James]*; Simon the Cananaean* [Zealot]*, and Judas Iscariot, who betrayed him.*

—Matthew 10:2–4 (Bracketed info my additions)

The Mission of the Twelve (Matthew 10:5–15)

As the founding entrepreneur and leader of the mission, Jesus has a clear understanding of the vision for the mission, the strategic direction and goals (verses 5–7), and the plans and processes to be used by the team (v. 8–12) in turning the opportunity—'change societal values and behaviours through a new relationship with God'—into outcomes that are both valued and meet the need of peoples of the region. This understanding is best stated in Matthew's Gospel:

> These twelve Jesus sent out, charging them, 'Go nowhere among the Gentiles, and enter no town of the Samaritans, but go rather to the lost sheep of the house of Israel. And preach as you go, saying, 'The kingdom of heaven is at hand.' Heal the sick, raise the dead, cleanse lepers, cast out demons. You received without paying, give without pay. Take no gold, nor silver, nor copper in your belts, no bag for your journey, nor two tunics, nor sandals, nor a staff; for the labourer deserves his food. And whatever town or village you enter, find out who is worthy in it, and stay with him until you depart. As you enter the house, salute it. And if the house is worthy, let your peace come upon it; but if it is not worthy, let your peace return to you. And if anyone will not receive you or listen to your words, shake off the dust from your feet as you leave that house or town. Truly, I say to you, it shall be more tolerable on the day of judgment for the land of Sodom and Gomorrah than for that town.

The Mission of the Seventy Disciples (Luke 10:1–20)

About six months before the crucifixion of Jesus, and just after Jesus, the Apostles and the disciples celebrated the Festival of Tabernacles in Jerusalem (John 7 and 8), Jesus initiated another strategic initiative designed to prepare the people of Judea for His forthcoming visit to preach the Kingdom of Heaven is at hand, heal the sick, bring hope to the needy, and seek 'believers'. It is likely this campaign was in preparation for His final journey and entry into Jerusalem.

To start this campaign, Jesus chose seventy disciples (most likely from amongst the followers present with Jesus and the Apostles at the Feast of Tabernacles) and sent them out two by two. Thus, there were thirty-five teams of Kingdom preachers in the territory, where 'the harvest is great, but the workers are few' (v. 2). As the leader of the mission, Jesus commissioned the seventy, giving them these instructions:

- **Go** (v. 3). Visit all the places where Jesus was about to go.
- **Be wary** (v. 3). The seventy were like lambs among wolves, surrounded by danger.
- **Live by faith** (v. 4). Carry no extra provisions. Carry the message of Jesus.
- **Be focused** (v. 4). Greet no-one along the road and do not allow yourself to be sidetracked.
- **Extend your blessing** (v. 5–6). Whoever housed the seventy were to be blessed.
- **Be content** (v. 7). The seventy were told not to seek better accommodations.

- **Receive your due** (v. 7). The labourer is worthy of his wages.
- **Be flexible** (v. 7–8). The seventy were to eat whatever their hosts served.
- **Heal the sick** (v. 9). Jesus gave the seventy disciples specific authority to heal diseases.
- **Proclaim the Kingdom** (v. 9). The message of the seventy disciples was simple.[129]

Jesus warned the seventy disciples they might expect rejection in some villages (v. 10) and advised them to publicly wipe the dust of that town from their feet (v. 11), proclaim the Kingdom one more time, and warn them of coming judgment (v. 12). By way of comparison, Jesus had told the Twelve Apostles that they were to preach in Galilee, avoiding Gentile areas and Samaria, but the seventy were given no such restriction. Interestingly, these seventy disciples were to focus on going to people's homes to teach rather than teaching in synagogues. From a management perspective, Jesus has laid out clear instructions or rules to guide the disciples in fulfilling His campaign plans. This campaign management bears some resemblance to the strategy and planning for the 'Billy Graham' evangelical missions in the 1960s and 70s.

Behaviour and skills for the selected twelve apostles

The following skills and behaviours attributed to the twelve Apostles, are provided in point form. A full analysis of each Apostle is provided in Appendix 6.1. This list is to highlight some of the characteristics Jesus identified in members of His

---

129 https://www.gotquestions.org/70-or-72-disciples.html.

chosen team to share in the mission to 'change societal values and behaviours through a new relationship with God.'[130]

Central to this is the focus on relationships: with Jesus, God, each other in the team, and with the followers in the community.

- Peter was a gregarious, natural leader and an obvious spokesperson for the twelve.
- Peter was known for being bold, confident, courageous, frank, impulsive, energetic.
- Andrew was not a dominant person next to his outspoken brother.
- James was the elder brother of John. He was a rather quiet part of the team.
- John wrote more about love than any other New Testament author.
- Philip, of whom we know almost nothing.
- Nathanael was recognised by Jesus as having a sincere love for God.
- Matthew was a tax collector—the most despised people in all of Israel.
- Thomas was an outspoken sceptic to the point of being known as a pessimist.
- James the Less—James was somewhat in the background but was chosen by Jesus.
- Simon the Zealot was a man of fierce loyalties, amazing passion, courage, and zeal.
- Judas, son of James, lived in obscurity as one of the Twelve.
- Judas Iscariot betrayed Jesus for thirty pieces of silver.

---

130 Robert R. McLaughlin, 'The Twelve Apostles', https://gbible.org/doctrines-post/the-12-apostles/.

These twelve men responded to the call of Jesus to be 'Fishers for Men'. They were Jews, uneducated commoners, and simple men of faith who gave up everything to be followers of Christ, yet we see from the summary of their skillsets and behaviours that they provided the necessary human, spiritual, and loyal resources to grow the vision with Jesus for His mission on earth. Jesus spent three years training these men to be leaders. Jesus' plan was to eventually have the disciples take over and carry on the work He had started.

By recognising the social and entrepreneurial behaviours practised by Jesus and the Apostles as a team in delivering the mission to the community, and comparing these with the Enablement Effectiveness Model[131] presented in Figure 3.4, there is confirmation of the need for 'team compatibility' amongst leader, mission staff, and volunteer resources. In particular, the model confirms the primary requirement for the team to 'connect with the cause' and facilitate the 'social network resources.' Some comments from the research study for the model[131] are eerily appropriate and analogous to the behaviours observed in the Apostle team; e.g., for 'connect to cause', comments such as, 'I did not think first about the inconvenience', 'the opportunity was greater than the cost of personal inconvenience', 'I felt enthused by the opportunity to serve.' For the 'social network resources' challenge, comments included, 'a large or small team did not matter', 'Interconnectedness with others was satisfying', 'Interconnectedness with others who share values inspires me.' This comparison confirms the value of the close-knit team in achieving the desired and effective outcomes.

---

131 Loris Gillin, 2006, 'Social Value Creation as a Core Determinant from the Impact of Social Entrepreneurship', Thesis, Swinburne University of Technology, Hawthorn, Australia.

In summary, we confirmed in Chapter 5 that Jesus exhibited a strong and forthright social entrepreneur mindset determined to lead the God-given mission in Judea, Galilee, and the outermost parts of the earth. To achieve such a result, it was necessary to have an 'A' class team. This is exactly the calibre of the team of Apostles and disciples Jesus assembled in around 29–33 CE in the region. It is important to note that such a dynamic team was not dependent on status, an education level (both Matthew and John were clearly literate), or monetary wealth, but on spiritual values: faith, passion, energy, and loyalty to both the leader and the cause.

It is significant that Jesus fully commissioned this team of Apostles (Matthew 28:16–2, Mark 16:15) to advance God's Kingdom and carry the gospel message to the world. History and tradition suggest this commission was both acted on and had worldwide ramifications for civilisation. The following briefly lists some of these achievements:

- Peter's call was to those of the 'circumcision'. He ended up in Rome, witnessed to many, and was crucified in Rome.
- John spent time witnessing in Ephesus, where he died.
- Philip witnessed in Asia Minor and was stoned and crucified in Hierapolis, Phrygia.
- Nathanael died as a martyr while serving the people of Albinopolis, Armenia.
- Matthew brought the gospel to Ethiopia and Egypt.
- Tradition strongly suggests that Thomas started the Christian church in India.

- Tradition says that Simon the Zealot, after preaching on the west coast of Africa, went to England, where he ended up being crucified in 74 CE.
- Judas, son of James, a few years after Pentecost, took the gospel north to Edessa (today the Southeast Anatolia region of Turkey).
- Tradition identifies Thaddeus (Jude) as ministering in Armenia.

Significantly, the activities of the Apostles listed above followed the ascension of Jesus (Acts 1:9) at the Feast of Weeks (fifty days) after the resurrection Sunday. The events of Pentecost released amazing energy amongst the Apostle team, disciples, and followers to evangelise well beyond Judea and Galilee. Together with Paul and others, the mission was extended to Gentiles and all parts of the Roman Empire. Indeed, the selection and training of the Apostle team by Jesus provided both the structure and mindset for the team to fulfil His strategy and mission to 'change societal values and behaviours through a new relationship with God'.

Appendix 6.1

With the permission of Pastor Robert R. McLaughlin, I append his expansive and insightful review of the twelve apostles and their team contributions to the Jesus' mission.

The Twelve Apostles

Robert R. McLaughlin

Peter—(Simon Peter)

Let's look at the type of people our Lord chose as his disciples. Let's begin in Luke 6:14 *'Simon, whom He also named Peter.'* The character of Peter is transparent and easily analysed. He appears to have been the leader of the apostles on every occasion. He is named first in every list of them and was their common spokesman. Peter was known for being bold, confident, courageous, frank, impulsive, energetic, vigorous, strong, loving and faithful to his Master in spite of his defection prior to the crucifixion. It is true that he was liable to change, and inconsistency prevailed at times. Because of his peculiar temperament, Peter sometimes appeared forward and rash. Yet, his virtues and faults had their common root in his enthusiastic disposition. Such was Peter's makeup, his nature, and his personality traits. Peter was not a phony. However, at times, he was the type of individual who did not think before acting. He apparently had the strongest character in the group, and he frequently served as a spokesman for the disciples. He was their recognised leader. Mark 1:35-36 *'And in the early morning, while it was still dark, He arose and went out and departed to a lonely place, and was praying there. And Simon and his companions hunted for Him.'*

An inner circle of three apostles existed among the Twelve. Peter was also the leader of this small group. This trio—Peter, James, and John—was present with Jesus on a number of occasions. These three witnessed the raising of a young girl from the dead, Mark 5:37; Luke8:51. They were present at Jesus' transfiguration, Matthew 17:1-2. And they were present during Jesus' agony in Gethsemane, Matthew 26:37, MAR 14:33.

Andrew

Luke 6:14 *'Simon, whom He also named Peter, and Andrew his brother;'*

Andreas means 'manly,' and has also been interpreted as 'the mighty one' or 'conqueror.' Andrew was the first called of the Twelve Apostles, which is significant. The choice was an important one, for Andrew's influence on the remaining followers of Christ would be one of searching and desiring higher things and a deeper knowledge of God. These character traits are what encouraged Andrew to first follow John the Baptist and then the Lamb of God to whom John pointed Andrew. Along with a keenness of perception regarding spiritual truths, Andrew also had a strong sense of personal conviction which enabled him not only to accept Jesus as the Messiah, but to win his brother Peter also as a disciple of Christ. Andrew was not the greatest of the apostles, yet he is typical of those men of open-minded understanding and sound common sense without whom the success of any great movement cannot be assured. Void of the boldness and ruggedness of Peter's character, to which only a few can aspire, Andrew had that feature which makes him a pattern within the reach of all—a simple, earnest determination in carrying out the dictates of his personal convictions. Another feature in Andrew was his eagerness to win souls in private to Jesus. Andrew was not a powerful public speaker. He was a low-keyed individual who was very trustworthy.

While we admire Peter as the foremost apostle through whom 3,000 were added to the church on the day of Pentecost, let us not forget that without Andrew, 'Simon' would never have become 'Peter.' So well known was his love for souls, that when certain Greeks desired to see Jesus, Andrew was the person to whom Philip brought them.

John 12:20-22 'Now there were certain Greeks among those who were going up to worship at the feast; these therefore came to Philip, who was from Bethsaida of Galilee, and began to ask him, saying, 'Sir, we wish to see Jesus.' Philip came and told Andrew; Andrew and Philip came, and they told Jesus.'

However, Andrew had his faults; in John 6:8-9 he shared in the disciples' unbelief when Jesus tested their faith.

John 6:8-9 'One of His disciples, Andrew, Simon Peter's brother, said to Him, 'There is a lad here who has five barley loaves and two fish, but what are these for so many people?''

Luke 6:12-16 'And it was at this time that He went off to the mountain to pray, He spent the whole night in prayer to God. And when day came, He called His disciples to Him; and chose twelve of them, whom He also named as apostles: Simon, whom He also named Peter, and Andrew his brother; and James and John; and Philip and Bartholomew; and Matthew and Thomas; James the son of Alphaeus, and Simon [not Peter] who was called the Zealot; Judas the son of James, and Judas Iscariot, who became a traitor.'

James

The next Apostle we will look at is James, the son of Zebedee and the older brother of John. From the time he was ordained an apostle, James occupied a prominent place among the apostles, and, along with Peter and John, became the special confidant of Jesus. These three apostles alone were present at the raising of Jairus' daughter (Luke 8:51), at the Transfiguration (Matthew 17:1-8), and at the Agony in the Garden of Gethsemane, Matthew 26:36-46.

Shortly after the Transfiguration, when Jesus was determined to go to Jerusalem, in Luke 9:51, they were passing through Samaria, the fury of James and John was kindled by the unkind reception given to our Lord by the crowd, Luke 9:53.

Luke 9:51-56 'And it came about, when the days were approaching for His ascension, that He resolutely set His face to go to Jerusalem; and He sent messengers on ahead of Him. And they went, and entered a village of the Samaritans, to make arrangements for Him. And they did not receive Him, because He was journeying with His face toward Jerusalem. And when His disciples James and John saw this, they said, 'Lord, do You want us to command fire to come down from heaven and consume them?' But He turned and rebuked them, and said, 'You do not know what kind of spirit you are of; for the Son of Man did not come to destroy men's lives, but to save them.''

It was probably for this type of hotheaded rashness and fanaticism that the surname 'Boanerges,' which means 'Sons of Thunder,' was bestowed on them when they were ordained to the Twelve, Mark 3:17. Note, however, that there was some excuse for their action. The impression left by the Transfiguration was still greatly upon them. They felt strongly that their Lord, whom they had just beheld 'in His glory' with 'His countenance altered' and 'shining garments,' should not be subjected to such indignities by the Samaritans. Upon the occasion of our Lord's last journey to Jerusalem, Mark 10:32, the two brothers gave expression to this presumptuous rashness in a more selfish manner, Mark 10:35-45. They presumed upon their intimacy with Jesus and made the following request.

Mark 10:35-40 'And James and John, the two sons of Zebedee, came up to Him, saying to Him, 'Teacher, we want You to do for us whatever we ask of You.' And He said to them, 'What do you want Me to do for you?' And they said to Him, 'Grant that we may sit in Your glory, one on Your right, and one on Your left.' But Jesus said to them, 'You do not know what you are asking for. Are you able to drink the cup that I drink, or to be baptised with the baptism with which I am baptised?' And they said to Him, 'We are able.' And Jesus said to them, 'The cup that I drink you shall drink; and you shall be baptised with the baptism with which I am baptised. But to sit on My right or on My left, this is not Mine to give; but it is for those for whom it has been prepared."

In Matthew 20:20-28, these words are put in the mouth of their mother, not directly from James and John. However, this request drew forth the rebuke of Jesus and moved the other ten with indignation, MAR 10:40-45 *'And hearing this, the ten began to feel indignant with James and John. And calling them to Himself, Jesus said to them, 'You know that those who are recognised as rulers of the Gentiles lord it over them; and their great men exercise authority over them. But it is not so among you, but whoever wishes to become great among you shall be your servant; and whoever wishes to be first among you shall be slave of all. For even the Son of Man did not come to be served, but to serve, and to give His life a ransom for many."*

James was the first of the twelve apostles to be put to death. Herod Agrippa I, the grandson of Herod the Great, killed James sometime between AD 42-44. His death is the only martyrdom mentioned in the New Testament, Acts 12:2.

John

Luke 6:14 *'Simon, whom He also named Peter, and Andrew his brother; and James and John;'*
Both John and James were men of considerable wealth, assumed from the fact that they had 'hired servants' with them, and John's wife was one of those women who ministered of their substance to Jesus and His disciples, Matthew 27:55-56. A comparison of Mark 15:40-41 identifies the wife of Zebedee, John's mother, with Salome. It seems a fair inference from John 19:25, though all do not accept it, that Mary, the mother of Jesus, and Salome, the wife of Zebedee, were sisters. If true, James and John were cousins of Jesus, and were also related to the family of John the Baptist.

John also held an intimate connection with the Lord. He was a young man of fiery zeal and a tendency toward intolerance and exclusiveness, evident in his desire to call down fire upon the Samaritan village. His tendency toward exclusiveness is manifested in the request of his mother as to the place her sons were to occupy in the kingdom—the highest positions. Jesus did not encourage this and rebuked these tendencies, but the tendencies reveal the man. John was in the inner circle of the disciples. Indeed, nearest of all to Jesus, he was called, *'the disciple whom Jesus loved'* (John 13:23; 19:26; 20:2; 21:7,20). Because of that love, John became the apostle of love. Interestingly enough, he is the only one who wrote that he was the disciple that Jesus loved.

John was the kind of man who could profit by the rebuke of Jesus. John's passionate disposition was held in check and under control and was allowed to vent only on occasions when it was permissible, and even necessary. In John's gospel writings, note the intensity that he had displayed, but directed only against those who refused to believe in, and to acknowledge, Jesus as the Christ.

John 13:21-23 When Jesus had said this, He became troubled in spirit, and testified, and said, 'Truly, truly, I say to you, that one of you will betray Me.' The disciples began looking at one another, at a loss to know of which one He was speaking. There was reclining on Jesus' breast one of His disciples, whom Jesus loved.'

Did Jesus love all the disciples? According to John 13:1, *'having loved His own who were in the world, He loved them to the end.'* However, John calls himself, the disciple whom Jesus loved. Note John 19:26 *'When Jesus therefore saw His mother, and the disciple whom He loved standing nearby, He said to His mother, Woman, behold, your son!'*

John 20:1-8 'Now on the first day of the week Mary Magdalene came early to the tomb, while it was still dark, and saw the stone already taken away from the tomb. And so she ran and came to Simon Peter, and to the other disciple whom Jesus loved, and said to them, 'They have taken away the Lord out of the tomb, and we do not know where they have laid Him.' Peter, therefore, went forth, and the other disciple and they were going to the tomb. And the two were running together; and the other disciple ran ahead faster than Peter, and came to the tomb first; and stooping and looking in, he saw the linen wrappings lying there; but he did not go in. Simon Peter, therefore also came, following him, and entered the tomb; and he beheld the linen wrappings lying there, and the face-cloth, which had been on His head, not lying with the linen wrappings, but rolled up in a place by itself. So the other disciple who had first come to the tomb entered then also, and he saw and believed.'

In John 21:7 'That disciple therefore whom Jesus loved said to Peter, 'It is the Lord.' And so when Simon Peter heard that it was the Lord, he put his outer garment on for he was stripped for work, and threw himself into the sea.'

In John 21:20 'Peter, turning around, saw the disciple whom Jesus loved following them; the one who also had leaned back on His breast at the supper, and said, 'Lord, who is the one who betrays You?''

John had 'a quiet and thoughtful temperament' which is not inconsistent with a certain fierceness. It is not without significance that in the three narratives which are cited from the gospels to prove the overbearing temper of John, we are told that Jesus corrected him all three times. Are we to suppose that these rebukes made no impression? Is it more likely that they sank deep into his heart, and that the agony of beholding his Master's crucifixion made them impossible to forget and reject? And as he grew older and wiser, he began that long development which changed that youthful 'son of thunder' into the 'aged apostle of love.' Never forget that love itself has its side of vehemence and passion, and the intensity of love toward a person or a cause may be measured by the intensity of antagonism and of disdain toward those who oppose and contradict that which they love. There are many reflections in the gospel of John and in his epistles, which display this energy of hatred toward the work of the devil and toward those dispositions under the influence of the father of lies. John, as a fervent youth devoted to his Master, carried with him to the end this same disposition which was characteristic. The power options—namely the filling of the Spirit and Bible doctrine— caused him to redirect that energy, fervency and passion toward the things of God.

Philip

Philip was one of the first followers of Jesus Christ, and he wasted no time calling others, like Nathanael, to do the same. Although little is known about him after the ascension of Christ, Bible historians believe Philip preached the gospel in Phrygia, in Asia Minor, and died a martyr there at Hierapolis. Learn how Philip's search for the truth led him directly to the promised Messiah.

Nathanael or Bartholomew

Nathanael, believed to be the disciple Bartholomew, experienced a jarring first encounter with Jesus. When the apostle Philip called him to come and meet the Messiah, Nathanael was sceptical, but he followed along anyway. As Philip introduced him to Jesus, the Lord declared, 'Here is a true Israelite, in whom there is nothing false.' Immediately Nathanael wanted to know, 'How do you know me?'

Jesus got his attention when he answered, 'I saw you while you were still under the fig tree before Philip called you.' Well, that stopped Nathanael in his tracks. Shocked and surprised, he declared, 'Rabbi, you are the Son of God; you are the King of Israel.'

Nathanael garnered only a few lines in the Gospels, nevertheless, in that instant, he became a loyal follower of Jesus Christ.

Matthew

Levi, who became the apostle Matthew, was a customs official in Capernaum who taxed imports and exports based on his own judgment. The Jews hated him because he worked for Rome and betrayed his countrymen.

But when Matthew the dishonest tax collector heard two words from Jesus, 'Follow me,' he left everything and obeyed. Like us, he longed to be accepted and loved. Matthew recognised Jesus as someone worth sacrificing for.

Thomas

The apostle Thomas is often referred to as 'Doubting Thomas' because he refused to believe that Jesus had risen from the dead until he saw and touched Christ's physical wounds. As far as disciples go, however, history has dealt Thomas a bum rap. After all, each of the twelve apostles, except John, abandoned Jesus during his trial and death at Calvary.

Thomas was prone to extremes. Earlier, he had demonstrated courageous faith, willing to risk his own life to follow Jesus into Judea. There is an important lesson to be gained from studying Thomas: If we're truly seeking to know the truth, and we're honest with ourselves and others about our struggles and doubts, God will faithfully meet us and reveal himself to us, just as he did for Thomas.

James the Less

James the Less is one of the most obscure apostles in the Bible. The only things we know for certain are his name and that he was present in the upper room of Jerusalem after Christ ascended to heaven.

In *Twelve Ordinary Men*, John MacArthur suggests that his obscurity may have been the distinguishing mark of his life. Discover why James the Less' complete anonymity may reveal something profound about his character.

Simon the Zealot

Who doesn't like a good mystery? One puzzling question in the Bible is the exact identity of Simon the Zealot, the Bible's own mystery apostle.

Scripture tells us almost nothing about Simon. In the Gospels, he is mentioned in three places, but only to list his name. In Acts 1:13 we learn that he was present with the apostles in the upper room of Jerusalem after Christ had ascended to heaven. Beyond those few details, we can only speculate about Simon and his designation as a Zealot.

Thaddeus or Jude

Listed together with Simon the Zealot and James the Less, the apostle Thaddeus completes a grouping of the least known disciples. In *Twelve Ordinary Men*, John MacArthur's book about the apostles, Thaddeus is characterised as a tender-hearted gentleman who displayed childlike humility.

Judas Iscariot

Judas Iscariot is the apostle who betrayed Jesus with a kiss. For this supreme act of treachery, some would say Judas Iscariot made the greatest error in history.

Down through time, people have had mixed feelings about Judas. Some experience a sense of hatred toward him, others feel pity, and some have even considered him a hero. No matter how you react to Judas, one thing is certain, believers can benefit greatly by taking a serious look at his life.[132]

---

132 Robert R. McLaughlin, 'The Twelve Apostles', https://gbible.org/doctrines-post/the-12-apostles/.

Part 2

Chapter 7: Entrepreneur Mindset and the Reality of Spirit Power

The dual nature of the quantum objects which are the building blocks of nature show that it is not unreasonable to assume the biblical monist interpretation of a person.

—Ranjit Thuraisingham[133]

Jesus' Preparation to Exercise Spiritual Power

Within Part 1 and the first four chapters of this book, we focused our consideration of Jesus during His development and formation and exposure to extant Jewish culture in first-century-CE Judea and Galilee. Up to the age of thirty, we studied Jesus as 'fully man' and how such experiences of life, emotions, challenges, and career options influenced His understanding of 'being about His Father's business'. Importantly, we recognised the development of His IQ, EI, and SI, and that all were integrated into the whole person of Jesus. We noted that intuition was an important dimension in considering the spiritual aspects of decision-making.

Chapter 5 developed our understanding of entrepreneur mindset (EM) and the reality and significance of EM in Jesus' passion, commitment, compassion, and energy to 'make it happen'

---

133 Ranjit A. Thuraisingham, 2019, 'Prayer and Entangled Quantum States' http://iscast.org/articles/Thuraisingham_Prayer_and_Entanglement_Opinion_Published_Jan_2019.pdf.

by delivering a true mission that changed both an individual's relationship with God but also influenced the development of the world as we know it some 2,000 years later. Jesus was a pre-eminent example of what it means to be a social entrepreneur that brings real value to His followers. Chapter 6 reviewed the leadership of Jesus in selecting and managing His team of Disciples, their passion, commitment and loyalty to the mission, and the strategic principles the team delivered on.

The remainder of this book (Part 2, Chapters 7–11) is designed to examine selected case studies in Jesus' ministry. The purpose is to gain a fuller understanding of how non-local intuition, prayer, meditation, and human intention could be associated with the spiritual dimension of Jesus' entrepreneur mindset and help explain how spiritual connectivity (between God, Jesus, and follower) could contribute extra power and energy to facilitating changes in a follower's personal wellbeing and control of nature. These cases are not examples of Jesus being a 'magician' or a 'sorcerer', but seek to demonstrate the application of the Creation principles of physics, chemistry, prayer, non-local intuition, and human intention to bring about real and observable change.

Such miracles (transfiguration, turning water into wine, walking on water, stilling the storm) are difficult for modern man to accept in an unqualified manner simply as faith. It was noted in Chapter 5, Jesus' entrepreneurial mission (ministry) commenced at His baptism in the Jordan River with the 'descent' of the Spirit, as observed by John the Baptist. It was immediately after this event that Jesus was led into the desert for forty days (Matthew 4:1–11; Luke 4:1–12).

Significantly, it is recorded that after forty days, Jesus returned to Galilee in 'the power of the spirit'. It is, therefore, appropriate we consider possible developments within Jesus the man as a result of this wilderness experience, impacting His entrepreneurial mission and development of an entrepreneur mindset, and bringing great benefits to many in need.

Specific details are minimal, but we do know Jesus fasted, was hungry, and experienced severe temptation—functions that are experienced by a human being. Indeed, Paul says, 'Jesus was tempted in all points as we' (Hebrews 4: 15). It is suggested that what happened during these forty days of isolation was accompanied by prayer, meditation, fasting and deep reflection, ministering angels, and examination of the mission ahead.

We might well ask—what do prayer, meditation, and fasting provide for our human and spiritual development? They were of such significance to Jesus that He spent forty days in isolation, or rather, it may be better described as spending forty days seeking deep connectivity with the Creator.

Wilson, (2020) in an online sermon, comments that in Luke 4:1:

> *Jesus was led by the Spirit' into the wilderness—or, in the Greek text it means 'allowed oneself to be led.' But importantly, using 'The imperfect tense of the verb suggests that Jesus was continuously led by the Spirit during these 40 days. But the preposition found in this verse is Greek 'ἐν', which has the idea of 'in, within.' In other words, the text indicates that the Spirit did not just send Jesus off into the desert and deposit him there to struggle with the devil. Rather the Spirit continuously led Jesus in the desert area for the 40 days. He was not left alone. The Spirit went with him throughout the entire time.*[134]

---

134 Ralph Wilson, 2020-http://www.jesuswalk.com/lessons/4_1-13.htm.

From our information about Jesus, and up to this time when He was led into the wilderness, we are not aware of His performing any miracles or healings but, on emerging from this period of forty days of isolation, He demonstrated an ability to use miracles and healing that added 'authority' to His mission. So, what changed? He certainly went into the wilderness experience as 'fully man' and He emerged still as 'fully man' but with the capacity to interact with humans and nature in a way that facilitated observable change. Tiller comments:

> Humans are a mix. They have a physical body—the stuff of flesh and bones and matter—which medicine pays attention to. Mostly. When we think in terms of a substance or a physical body constructed of atoms and molecules, we also must think about an energy part, an information part, and a consciousness part. They are all part of us. [135]

How does this awareness affect our understanding of connecting with the power source—God the Creator?

It is appropriate, therefore, to ponder the basic essence of Creation, as recorded in Genesis 1:27, 'So God created man in his own image, in the image of God he created him; male and female he created them.' It is generally acknowledged that we are made in God's image, which implies we are not simply made from the dust of the earth (chemicals) but also with the spirit that connects us to the energy/power which gives us life.

These immaterial aspects—the spirit, soul, heart, conscience, mind, and emotions—make up the whole personality. The Bible makes it clear that the soul and spirit are the primary immaterial aspects of humanity, while the body is the physical container that

---

135 William Tiller, 2019, Quoted in Nisha Manek, Bridging Science and Spirit, pp. 63.

holds them on this earth. The material aspects are obviously those that are tangible and only exist as long as the person is alive. The immaterial aspects of man are those which are intangible: soul, spirit, intellect, will, conscience, etc. These characteristics exist beyond the physical lifespan of the individual. Human beings *have* a spirit, but we are *not* spirits.

Man, in his immaterial nature, reflects his Creator (1 Colossians 1: 15–18):

> *Do not misunderstand. This is not saying that man in his body reflects the Creator, but in his immaterial nature. The immaterial part of man reflects God, and it is going to be housed in a material body that has to be the best possible expression of that which is the representative and the reflection of God. We are to represent God and reflect His character in ruling the creation.*[136]

It is this perspective we see in Jesus after the forty days in the wilderness. Indeed, this reference to 'image' in Gen. 1:27,

> *does not imply that God is in human form, but that humans are in the image of God in their moral, spiritual, and intellectual essence. Thus, humans reflect God's divine nature in their ability to achieve the unique characteristics with which they have been endowed. These unique qualities make humans different from all other creatures: rational understanding, creative liberty, the capacity for self-actualisation, and the potential for self-transcendence.*[137]

---

136 Robert L. Dean, Jr, 2003, http://www.divineviewpoint.com/sane/dbm/setup/Genesis/Gen022.html.

137 Editorial staff, Christianity Today 2019, www.christianity.com/wiki/bible/image-of-god-meaning-imago-dei-in-the-bible.html.

The Catholic catechism (item 1705) says, 'By virtue of his soul and his spiritual powers of intellect and will, man is endowed with freedom, an 'outstanding manifestation of the divine image.'[138]

With this background, we can be assured Jesus emerged from the wilderness still 'fully man' and with the added realisation of full access to the immaterial aspects of being created in the Image of God. He was no 'magician' or 'sorcerer'. So, what is special about prayer, meditation, and fasting that can facilitate such access to the image of God? A few definitions of these practices will act as a foundation to help in our consideration of quantum entanglement, human intention, and non-local intuition.

What is prayer?

The most basic definition of prayer is 'talking to God'. Prayer is not meditation or passive reflection; it is a direct address to God. It is the communication of the human soul/spirit with the Lord who created the soul and spirit. Prayer is the primary way for the believer in Jesus Christ to communicate his emotions and desires with God and to fellowship with God. Prayer can be audible or silent, private, or public, formal or informal. All prayer must be offered in faith (James 1:6), in the name of the Lord Jesus (John 16:23), and in the power of the Holy Spirit (Romans 8:26). As the *International Standard Bible Encyclopedia* puts it, 'Christian prayer in its full New Testament meaning is a prayer addressed to God as Father, in the name of Christ as Mediator, and through the enabling grace of the indwelling Spirit'.

---

138 Catechism of the Catholic Church, (1705) https://www.vatican.va/archive/ccc_css/ archive/catechism/p3s1c1a1.htm.

What is Meditation?

Meditation (the psychological definition) is the practice of turning your attention to a single point of reference. It can involve focusing on the breath, on bodily sensations, or on a word or phrase known as a mantra. In other words, meditation means turning your attention away from distracting thoughts and focusing on the present moment. Meditation (the Eastern definition) is a practice where an individual uses a technique—such as mindfulness or focusing the mind on a particular object, thought, or activity—to train attention and awareness, and achieve a mentally clear and emotionally calm and stable state. Meditation (the Christian, Biblical definition) is focusing 'attention beyond thought and imagination' and leading to a 'still, wakeful presence to the reality of God'. Biblical meditation is *focused thinking* about a Bible verse that speaks to you so that you can more effectively apply its truth to the thinker/meditator.

Meditation is not relaxation, although it may lead to a sense of peace and calm. Meditation is about praying with our whole being. It is about gathering oneself in the centre of one's being in order to be attentive to the presence of God. It is a way of simplicity where 'we allow God's mysterious and silent presence within us to become more and more … *the reality* in our lives'.[139]

What is Fasting?

Fasting is essentially giving up food (or something else) for a period of time in order to focus your thoughts on God. While fasting, many people read the Bible, pray, or worship. Fasting is found throughout the Old and New Testaments of the Bible.

---

139 John Main, 1987, The Inner Christ. (London: Darton, Longman & Todd, 1987), 15.

What is non-local intuition?

The *Concise Oxford Dictionary* (1964, p. 639) defines intuition as 'immediate apprehension by the mind without reasoning, immediate apprehension by a sense, and immediate insight,' and generally associated in the literature with cognitive perception that is largely the result of past experience—a function of the unconscious mind accessing existing information within the brain from prior experience, pattern recognition, or memory retrieval.

Significantly, while there is little doubt that prior experience—both conscious and unconscious knowledge—plays an important role in informing entrepreneurial decisions and actions, there are many instances when accurate 'gut feelings' or 'intuitive insights' about distant or future—non-local—events are found to be scientifically valid and occur under controlled experimental conditions that preclude information from past experience. Taking this information processing perspective and a series of experiments to measure heart rate variability of serial entrepreneurs making intuitive decisions, we define non-local intuition as:

> *A process by which implicit information normally outside the range of cognitive processes is sensed and perceived by the body's psychophysiological systems as certainty of knowledge or feeling (positive or negative) about the totality of a thing distant or yet to happen.*[140]

It is clear from the definitions of fasting and prayer that such practice helped Jesus to focus solely on God. Jesus was thus

---

140 Ray Bradley, Murray Gillin, Rolin McCraty, and Mike Atkinson, 2011, 'Nonlocal Intuition in Entrepreneurs and Nonentrepreneurs: Results of Two Experiments Using Electrophysiological Measures,' International Journal of Entrepreneurship and Small Business. vol 12 (3): 343–372et al., 2011).

more sensitive to the 'voice' of God and more attuned to hearing what God had to reveal to Him. As discussed earlier, Jesus' time of prayer, meditation, and fasting during His forty days in the wilderness was crucial to Jesus the man becoming fully aware of His mission (his Father's business). Importantly, this enhanced 'connectivity', based as it was on a close intimacy and persistent sharing of identity, vulnerability, and with radical transparency, between Jesus and God, enabled Jesus to fully understand the immaterial reality of what it means to be 'in the image of God' and to express its importance during His public ministry.

This is in contrast to our living in the 'Age of Connectivity' where we are all linked with each other through email, social media, and a dozen other programs running on this mysterious web that envelops the world—maybe we have become a 'networked species' and lost the value of spiritual connectivity.

However, the 'spiritual connectivity' experience with God in the wilderness validated Jesus' ministry to mankind of personal salvation, and delivered added authority to Jesus as He demonstrated the full potential of the energy/power applied to performing miracles and healing.

With this understanding of the context for the observed miracles and healings associated with the ministry of Jesus, it is appropriate to evaluate a selection of the recorded nature miracles in the natural world of first-century-CE Judea and Galilee.

Science and Explaining Nature Miracles

We might ask, 'Do present-day science and physics provide an important contribution to our understanding of the nature miracles performed by Jesus?'

Such an evaluation of these selected events, and particularly if the principles of physics provide an enhanced understanding of the integrity within the nature miracle, then understanding the psychoenergetic factors (i.e., purported links between the human psyche and mystical forms of energy) *will not* make them any less miraculous. Indeed, any such finding will show Jesus and His message as even more relevant and truthful by demonstrating Jesus' control of the natural processes and, significantly, the timing of the events.

Bridging Science and Spirit

For over one hundred years, and generally ignored by the scientific establishment, psychics, healers, meditators, and their associated experiments and observations have suggested that human intervention as human intention can influence physical reality. This apparent blindness to potential new knowledge is not a recent phenomenon. The findings of Sir Isaac Newton (1642–1727), a mathematician, physicist, astronomer, and theologian (described in his time as a 'natural philosopher'), brought a new and greater understanding of the universe at that time, which challenged the traditionalists of the day. Significantly, such discoveries were not accepted universally and were ignored or argued over for many decades. Again, following Albert Einstein's (1879–1955) development of the theory of relativity and important contributions to the theory of quantum mechanics, these contributed directly to the current understanding of our universe and physical reality and enabled dramatic progress in human control of the lived environment and universe. But, as in Newton's time, it took decades for Einstein's theories and mathematics to be fully accepted by the scientific community and applied universally. Significantly, and not surprisingly, the groundbreaking, fundamental, theoretical, and experimental work of Emeritus Professor William Tiller (from 1970 to now) to understand human consciousness and its relationship to the discovered psychoenergetic factors is the next step towards a fuller understanding of the spiritual dimension of our beings. During this period, using the power of mathematics, physics, and simple, independent, and replicated experiments, as reported in his many books, Tiller and his team have demonstrated unequivocally that in inanimate material, in-vitro biological matter, and in-vivo living systems, human intention can indeed affect physical measurements and reality.[141, 142, 143]

In support of the research of Tiller is that of Dr Francis Collins, a leading geneticist and long-time head of the Human Genome Project. He is a world-respected and distinguished scientist who has reviewed the scientific evidence that is compatible with the belief that the God of Creation cares about us humans and 'can interfere in human affairs—and on rare occasions, even miraculously.' This relates directly to the deeper considerations of a spiritual relationship with God.[144]

This fruitful approach of extending the science of human behaviour is based on observation of the external world and theoretical models of how these observations can be accounted for, as every observation is always dependent on a theoretical model we have of our world and the predictions such a model makes. This approach is reflected in the work of Tiller.

141 William Tiller, William Dibble and Michael Kohane, 2001, 'Conscious Acts of Creation : The Emergence of a New Physics,' Pavior Publishing.

142 William Tiller, 2007, Psychoenergetic Science: A Second Copernican-Scale Revolution, Pavior Publishers, ISBN 978-1-4243-3863-4.

143 Kinney Douglas, 2014, Framework of Reality: Understanding Our Subtle Spiritual Nature, Mira Digital Publishing.

144 Collins Francis, 2006, The Language of God, Free Press, New York, NY.

Building on the work of philosopher Thomas Nagel, Robert Pepperell claims one of our greatest intellectual challenges is how to explain mental processes as physical processes, using the principle that consciousness can be explained as a physical process which can be explicable in terms of energy, forces, and work. Energy is a physical property of nature that is causally efficacious and, like forces and work, can be conceived as actualised differences of motion and tension. This organisation results in a pattern of energetic activity Tiller calls 'human intention' that blossoms to a degree of complexity sufficient for consciousness.[145]

> *Men ought to know that from the brain, and from the brain only, arise our pleasures, joys, laughter and jests, as well as our sorrows, pains, griefs and tears. Through it, in particular, we think, see, hear, and distinguish the ugly from the beautiful, the bad from the good, the pleasant from the unpleasant.*
>
> —Hippocrates, fifth century BCE.

However, in a recent article, Graziano and Kastner hypothesise that human consciousness is more than an emergent property of information processing in the brain. They say,

> *When we introspect about our own awareness, or make decisions about the presence or absence of our own awareness of this or that item, we rely on the same circuitry whose expertise is to compute information about other people's awareness. Awareness is best described as a perceptual model. It is not merely a cognitive*

---

145 Pepperell Robert, 2018, Consciousness as a Physical Process Caused by the Organization of Energy in the Brain, Fronter Psychology, 9: 2091.

or semantic proposition about ourselves that we can verbalise. Instead it is a rich informational model that includes, among other computed properties, a spatial structure, with spatial localisation.[146]

Such a model fits well with Tiller's mathematical model for human intention.

Before leaving this short review, it is opportune to introduce the concepts of ontology and epistemology as they relate to our concepts of reality and distinguish between them. In an extensive examination, Walach first describes epistemology as our understanding of how we arrive at knowledge about the world, and ontology as our understanding of what the world consists of, and they are intimately tied together. He goes on to say,

Our scientific model of understanding the world has been very successful if we consider the progress we have made in understanding our natural world around us. This is partly due to the fact that this scientific model has originally restricted itself to understanding the material world. In order to arrive at reliable knowledge, the scientific epistemological model has started from the assumption that the material world consists of material particles only and has restricted itself to discovering the forces that act on these and the laws that govern these forces.

This was, by and large, the success of the approach used by the research theorists over the past three centuries and now followed in Tiller's published works.

---

146 Graziano Michael and Kastner Sabine, 2011, Human consciousness and its relationship to social neuroscience: A novel hypothesis, Cognitive Neuroscience, Jan 1; 2(2): 98–113.

However, if a researcher directs observations to purposeful outcomes, this is called an experiment. Such purposeful experiments are the hallmark of Tiller's research. Wallach continues:

> *The ontological assumption behind this experimental approach is quite clear: What we observe is the material world outside, in contrast to the inner world of our dreams and phantasies. Thus, our observations refer to objects in the world, the nature outside. Therefore, the subject matter of science or the object of interest is nature, the world outside, and its constituents. There might have been invisible things out there as well, such as spirits, ghosts, or suchlike things. But the progress of science and its associated program of ontological reduction has led us to believe that invisible things, if they exist, can always be traced and reduced to material objects or their reverberations. Electromagnetic radiation is a pertinent example. We cannot see electromagnetic radiation, except within the small window of visible light. If the wavelength is too long, there is only a small window where we can feel it as infrared radiation or warmth. If the wavelength is too short, we cannot even feel it, let alone see it. We, at most, feel the distant effects, when we suffer from sunburns, or even more distant effects such as genetic deviations that manifest as skin cancer.* [147]

This review supports the importance of Tiller's research to open up a type of ontology that sees consciousness and matter as two

---

147 Walach Harald, 2020, Inner Experience – Direct Access to Reality: A Complementarist Ontology and Dual Aspect Monism Support a Broader Epistemology, Frontier Psychology, 11: 640.

complementary aspects of one reality and our fuller understanding of human intention.

In the same way, a team of researchers from the Australian Graduate School of Entrepreneurship (AGSE) and the Institute of HeartMath (IHM) in the USA collaborated to develop a theoretical framework and experimental tests that identify an additional source of intuitive information that enables the entrepreneur to access information regarding future opportunities. This information about future events is received and processed by the brain, heart, and autonomic nervous system (ANS). Moreover, this tacit and ontological information is not accessed by the dispassionate cognitive processing that underlies reason and logic. Rather, it is the entrepreneur's passionate focus on his mission to deliver the opportunity that attunes his body's psychophysiological systems, by process of energetic resonance, to intuitive information from non-local sources.[148] This 'passionate focus' is at the core of applied spiritual intelligence and the significant spiritual characteristic identified with an entrepreneur's mindset.

In seeking to 'build a reliable bridge of understanding for humans that seamlessly joins the foundations of traditional science on one end, extends through the domains of psyche, emotion, and mind and is firmly planted in the bedrock of Spirit at the other end,' we will review the findings of William Tiller through his many publications. Tiller is acknowledged as at 'the forefront in the field of consciousness studies.'[149] In addition, Tiller's extensive research is groundbreaking in that he both theorises and experimentally demonstrates that 'magnetic

---

148 Ray Bradley, Murray Gillin, Rolin McCraty, and Mike Atkinson, 2011, 'Nonlocal Intuition in Entrepreneurs and Nonentrepreneurs: Results of Two Experiments Using Electrophysiological Measures,' International Journal of Entrepreneurship and Small Business. vol 12 (3): 343–372et al., 2011).

149 Hope Umansky, Academic Dean of the California Institute for Human Science.

vector potential appears to play the role of 'bridge' between the subtle, unobservable energies and physically observable energies associated with electric and magnetic fields.'[150]

Personal Associations with Psychoenergetic Study

During my career, Bill Tiller has been a direct and lasting influence in my seeking to better understand 'being made in the image of God' and how such insight impacts the integration of IQ, EI, and SI into a recognisable and practised entrepreneur mindset (EM). I first met Bill at a materials science conference in late 1968 in Melbourne, Australia. As a co-organiser, I was given the honour of entertaining Bill, who was then Head of the Department of Materials Science and Engineering at Stanford University in California, USA.

During our drive through the Victorian countryside, I found Bill was considering researching the possibility that human consciousness might meaningfully influence physical matter. This exciting discussion was truly a challenge to better inform my understanding of spirituality. From 1971 to 1974, I was the Defence Science Research Attaché in the Australian Embassy in Washington, DC and visited Bill at Stanford a number of times. I was excited by his findings on the role of human intention on physical reality and we discussed a number of possible applications of the theory to defence research.

Interestingly, after reporting these discussions to my superior in the Defence Science and Technology Organisation in Canberra, I never received a request to explore opportunities further. Subsequently, I changed my work activity and we lost contact.

---

150 Manek Nisha, 2019, Bridging Science and Spirit, Coscious Creation LLC, USA.

As chair of a Christian Counselling Service in Melbourne, I was made aware that a client was experiencing severe 'mind control through an elaborate system of brain-washing programming, indoctrination hypnosis, and the use of various mind-altering drugs.' A corollary of this abuse and mind control in the abused person is the process of dissociation, a condition related to the creation of multiple personalities and known as dissociative identity disorder (DID) and described in DSM-IV. Such traumatic abuse practices are usually deliberate and can be shown to evolve over time in both intensity and technical sophistication.[151] From discussion with the therapist, it was concluded that the client was, as a result of family and institutional abuse, fully conditioned in the psychological sense to respond to traumatic and electromagnetic triggers to achieve control of her persona, behaviour, and loyalty.[152] Being aware that 'human intention' was an important dimension to facilitating spiritual healing in the client, I visited Bill Tiller in San Francisco in 1998, to discuss a way forward.

From that discussion, and based on Tiller's frequency-based theory for the integration of physical reality with reciprocal space, a paradigm was available to show that human intention can interact with and influence physical processes and properties. Tiller explained how the human body has the capacity to sense the presence and the information within the frequencies of these subtle energy waves and feed them to the brain for processing with subsequent effects within body organs and consciousness.

151 Van der Kolk Bessel, McFarlane Alexander and Weiseth, 1996, Traumatic Stress – The Effects of Overwhelming Experiences on Mind, Body and Society, The Guilford Press, New York.

152 Gillin Murray and Gillin Loris, 2003, Subtle Energies, Intentionality and the Healing of Traumatically Abused Persons September, International Conference on Trauma, Attachment and Dissociation, Melbourne, Australia.

With this knowledge, an effective intervention was developed that brought healing to the client.

Subsequent research into the behaviours, intuition, and decision-making styles of serial entrepreneurs led to the formulation of the concept of entrepreneur mindset as the primary reality in effective entrepreneurship and innovation. Again, I sought discussion with Bill Tiller by visiting him at his laboratory in Payson, Arizona, USA, during visits in 2002, 2006, and 2007. These discussions brought an introduction to Rollin McCraty, Ray Bradley, and Mike Atkinson, all members of the Institute for HeartMath, an institute with world standing in the area of non-linear intuition and relationship to measures of heart rate variability in entrepreneurs, children, defence force personnel, and corporate staff. Bill Tiller co-founded the Institute and was a board member for many years. As evident from the discussion in Chapter 5, a number of joint papers[153] and experiments were initiated from the ongoing joint research on non-local intuition in serial entrepreneur decision-making. By understanding the reality of subtle energies, as discussed with Bill Tiller, our team was better able to interpret the role of passion and intention to the observed entrepreneur. This understanding formed the basis for my entrepreneurial teaching both within the university classroom and, importantly, to in-house teaching courses with corporate staff seeking to use entrepreneurship orientation and entrepreneur mindset to create new value.

Importantly, Bill Tiller's spiritual contribution to this book is best described using a statement from Nisha Manek:

---

153 Ray Bradley, Murray Gillin, Rollin McCraty, and Mike Atkinson, 2011, 'Nonlocal Intuition in Entrepreneurs and Nonentrepreneurs: Results of Two Experiments Using Electrophysiological Measures,' International Journal of Entrepreneurship and Small Business. vol 12 (3): 343–372.

Tiller often talks about 'the bridge of understanding.' The main emphasis is on the general unifying principles that emerge from the great mass of detailed observations. A bridge does not 'solve' a problem or 'explain' mysteries; a bridge merely helps us to locate them, identify them, and get across to the other side of greater understanding and coherence. In his imagination, a bridge is an edifice constructed to hold the weight of evidence together, with the invisible wonder of faith acting as cables and his inner vision as the structure's towers. This all rests on a hidden foundation buried deep inside. You can't see what underlies the structure, but it is there and everything else depends upon the strength of the inner structure. [154]

An amazing example of such a hidden foundation can be observed in the experiences of Srinivasa Ramanujan FRS, an Indian mathematician who lived during the British rule of India. Though he had almost no formal training in pure mathematics, his time at Trinity College, Cambridge with Prof G H Hardy amazed the world of pure mathematics by his ability to intuit complete solutions but without using formal proofs.

A devoted Hindu and deeply religious, Ramanujan said that whole formulas and theorems came to him from God. He was deeply intuitive and credited his substantial mathematical capacities to a divine source. He said, 'An equation for me has no meaning, unless it expresses a thought of God.'[155] Ramanujan's method of intuition was hotly contested, but in the end, Hardy reasoned, 'They must be true because, if not, no-one would have

---

154 Nisha Manek, 2019 'Bridging Science and Spirit' Conscious Creation LLC.

155 Robert Kanigel. 1991, 'The Man who Knew Infinity', illustrated. 438 pp. New York: Charles Scribner's Sons.

had the imagination to invent them.' Ramanujan died in 1920 at the age of thirty-two, but his notebooks and work opened new avenues of inquiry and his calculations are still being proved as true to this day—he considered that 'intuition is a state in which the soul is being enlightened directly by the Super-soul (spirit)) on a particular subject matter.'

With this insight, and before examining the four 'case studies' relating to Jesus' nature miracles (Chapters 8–11), five appendices are attached to provide full explanations by the contributing authors on psychoenergetic science. A summary for each contribution follows:

a) Appendix 7.1 on 'Consciousness' by William Tiller. From the author's experimental work, a form of consciousness can be activated seemingly anywhere in D-space (spacetime) and intentionally tuned to materialise a particular property change (e.g., pH of water) via the use of an intention-host device demonstrating that psychoenergetic phenomena were real in nature. Such consciousness-related phenomena involve new categories of energies (subtle energies) beyond those of the four fundamental forces of traditional science. The term consciousness, here, is used by Tiller to mean a unique quality of nature that is ultimately convertible to energy, although it also conforms to the typical dictionary usage of being awake, aware, etc.;

b) Appendix 7.2 on 'Human Intention' by William Tiller. For the past thirty-five to forty years, and in parallel with Tiller's traditional science research and teaching at Stanford University, Bill has seriously investigated the effects of human intention on both the properties of materials (inorganic and organic; non-living and living) and on what we call physical reality. This research demonstrated that it is possible to make a significant change in the properties of a material substance by *consciously holding a clear intention to do so*. For example, the Tiller team have repeatedly been able to change the acid/alkaline balance (pH) in a vessel of water either up or down, without adding chemicals to the water, by creating an intention to do so. Pivotally, this effect has been shown to be transferrable across thousands of kilometres and between the USA and Europe. Such results are consistently reproducible. 'How is it possible for something like this to occur in the physical reality with which we are all so familiar?' The answer is that, from our experimental work of the past ten years, we have discovered that there are actually two levels of physical reality and not just the one with which we are all familiar. It is this new level of physical reality that can be significantly influenced by human intention—not our familiar electric atom/ molecule level.'

c) Appendix 7.3 on 'Subtle Energies', reviewed by Murray Gillin, considers the use of mathematical equations (tools in physics research) that predict behaviours and phenomena in nature. When considering the effect of subtle energies that have been loosely described as paranormal capabilities, which include healing hands, remote viewing, precognition, telepathy, homeopathy, etc., Tiller, using differential equations of the Schrödinger type, shows a strong correlation with magnetic energies as distinct from electric energies. Subtle energies are all those beyond the ones generated by the four fundamental forces of gravity, electromagnetism (EM), the weak nuclear force, and the strong nuclear force.[156] Tiller hypothesises subtle energies reside in the space (vacuum)—also called reciprocal space or mirror image of physical space—that is between the fundamental particles comprising atoms and molecules. They are not weak energies—they are merely elusive to our present-day measurement systems. In accord with making observations in physics, Tiller creates reproducible experiments that can and do reveal the effect of subtle energies in human intention. Using the concept of over-the-horizon radar and its associated signal processing algorithms of distant information received at a large array of single dipoles, it is possible to conceive an analogous reception and analysis of received subtle energies from the vacuum (reciprocal space) by the human body. In this analogous case, the 'aerial arrays comprise the body's hundreds of acupoints (energy sensors) along the underlying meridians that form the energy network distributed throughout the body. These meridian lines are the channels by which our energy flows, thus transporting the received subtle energy throughout the body for processing. Importantly, this received energy and information is processed in the autonomic nervous system where the heart acts as a

---

156 Tiller William, 1997, Science and Human Transformation: Subtle Energies, Intentionality, and Consciousness. Walnut Creek, CA, Pavior.

central processor before transmitting the information to the brain for final decision-making. This understanding underpins the importance of the 'spirit' characteristic to exercising an entrepreneur mindset.

d) Appendix 7.4 on 'Quantum Entanglement' by Ranjit Thuraisingham. The Christian believes that though separate, God the Father, Son Jesus, and the Holy Spirit are one. Focusing now on the quantum world, two quantum objects which have interacted with each other at one time but are now separated by large distances from each other cannot be described in the same way they were characterised before the interaction. This is different from what is observed in classical physics as based on Newtonian mechanics and Maxwell's electromagnetic theory which can explain a wide range of macroscopic phenomena but fails spectacularly when applied to microscopic phenomena such as proton-atom scattering or the flow of electrons in a semiconductor. In the quantum world, the two quantum objects have become correlated or entangled due to the interaction, even though they are at present separated by such long distances as to consider them as separate. For such entangled states, communication between them is instantaneous. Such a result from quantum physics with instant communication between entangled states indicates that an analogous situation can exist during Christian prayer, where the Spirit within us makes instant contact with God through Jesus, all of whom form part of the Trinity. The presence of such an instant communication channel between entangled states provides a scientific counterargument to the sceptic who denies the possibility of any known outside communication routes during prayer.

e) Appendix 7.5 on 'Interconnectivity and Coherence' by Raymond Bradley. Rather than human perception being limited to the five senses, research shows the human psychophysiological systems can unconsciously respond to randomly selected future emotional stimuli. This received and associated positive emotional attention is directed to the object body's psychophysiological systems where we perceive the information as a quantum-hologram so giving increased depth of meaning.[157] We can then perceive this space/time experience as an intuition: importantly, when the entrepreneur calms his mind and feelings and adopts a heart-focused state of positive emotion concentrating on the object, the entrepreneur mindset intuitive capacity is enhanced.

These contributions (appendices 7.1–7.5) are gratefully acknowledged. Adding this detail will help the reader better understand these physics-based insights into Creation and human behaviour that enables greater exploration into the relationship between the immaterial part of man, as it reflects God, and the availability of energy to human intention and life's potential. Perhaps we will agree that Jesus, post-wilderness communing with God, and expressing the entrepreneur mindset dimensions of collaborative leadership, intuitive decision-making, proactive

---

157 Bradley, R. T. (2007). The psychophysiology of intuition: A quantum-holographic theory of nonlocal communication. World Futures: The Journal of General Evolution, 63: 61–97.

behaviour, and spiritual awareness (Chapter 5), is indeed the appropriate reality in relating the immaterial and spiritual dimensions of being Jesus 'fully man', to demonstrate what it means to be 'made in the Image of God.'

In summary, the foregoing strongly suggests that our human capacity to receive and process information about nonlocal events appears to be a property of all physical and biological organisation and is likely due to the inherent interconnectedness of everything in the universe. During His early years, Jesus would have been aware of this human and spiritual capability to process such information from without himself. It is emphasised such information processing is not a 'magical'-type event.

We, as humans, are constructed totally of energy and matter and all communication and power transfer is by energy wave transmission, whether locally or even from within the universe. With this physics understanding of the created universe, it can be suggested that the same physics principles apply to the communication between God and Jesus for the 'voice' of the Spirit of God at Jesus' baptism. These insights will be applied to the following miracles as case studies in the remaining chapters.

Appendix 7.1

Consciousness: With permission, William Tiller explains:

'A long, long time ago in human history, there were two accepted and compatible pathways to the acquisition of knowledge. This applies not only to the historically well-known cultures but also to the not so well-documented indigenous cultures of the world. These two pathways were designated as the human inner path of revelation and the latter the human outer path of logic applied to external observations of Nature.

Humankind has always been concerned with scientific enquiry because we really want to understand the milieu in which we find ourselves. Our mindset is that we also want to engineer and modulate as much of our environment as possible to sustain, feed, enrich and propagate our lives. Following this path, the goal of science has been to gain a reliable description of natural phenomena which eventually allows accurate quantitative prediction within certain error-bar limits of Nature's behaviour as a function of an ever-changing environment. As such, past and present science is incapable of providing us with absolute truth. Rather, it seeks to provide us with relative knowledge, but internally self-consistent knowledge, about the relationships between different phenomena and between different things.

In the first half of the 17th century, Rene Descartes, a great philosopher of the new science, realized that a clear division between matter and mind or between body and soul was needed in order to gain a system of fundamental knowledge about the outer world. Thus, he proposed a real compartmentalization of thought between natural philosophy; wherein human consciousness was not an experimental variable of relevance, and theology where it was! Over time, this became an unstated assumption of science that 'no human qualities of consciousness, intention, emotion, mind or spirit can significantly influence a well-designed target experiment in physical reality.' Thus, consciousness has not been allowed as a significant experimental variable, even though the experimental data leading would indicate otherwise

However, one of the downsides of almost total acceptance of this assumption by scientists is that their philosophical worldview has generally become very reductionistic and materialistic. The basic equation needs an additional term for 'consciousness'

Mass Ä Energy Ä Information Ä Consciousness

The term consciousness, here, is used by this author to mean a unique quality of nature that is ultimately convertible to energy, although it also conforms to the typical dictionary usage of being awake, aware, etc. Today, there is no adequate and generally accepted definition of the word consciousness. However; if instead of asking what consciousness means, one asks what consciousness does, we almost immediately see that consciousness manipulates information in the form of numbers, alphabet letters, jigsaw puzzle pieces and , most generally, symbols

Over the past four decades, Tiller has shown unequivocally, to anyone who wished to look, that:

1. Psychoenergetic phenomena were real in nature,
2. Such consciousness-related phenomena involved new categories of energies (subtle energies) beyond those of the four fundamental forces of traditional science,

3. A simple, low-tech, electronic device had been invented that could be imprinted from a deep meditative state with a specific intention and shipped to a distant site such that, when plugged into an electric power source and switched on, it was able to both (a) lift the fundamental symmetry state of the space by activating the indwelling-consciousness of that space to a higher level of physical reality(4-6)†b and (b) tune that intention-host device-conditioned space to manifest the material property changes consistent with that specific intention,

4. We have designed and conducted four unique and successful intention-modulated target experiments, which prove to the world that human consciousness can significantly influence physical reality,

5. we have successfully replicated one of these four experiments in ten laboratories located in both the U.S. and Europe.

From the foregoing points, our last decade of experiments have revealed that there are two unique levels of physical reality, not just the one associated with our normal, electric atom/molecule level of substance. The second level consists of information wave substance occupying the highest band of energy states in the physical vacuum. However, under normal, everyday conditions, these two very different kinds of substances occupy the same general space but do not interact with each other. We label this the uncoupled state of physical reality. In this state, our traditional measurement instruments are unable to directly detect the information wave substance.'[158]

---

158 William Tiller, 2009, 'It Is Time for a Consciousness-Inclusive Science' White Paper #4, The William A Tiller Foundation.

Appendix 7.2

Human Intention: With permission, William Tiller explains:

The Webster dictionary defines 'intention' as the determination to do a specific thing or act in a specified manner; having something in mind as a plan, design, purpose, or goal.

'I and my colleagues have discovered that it is possible to make a significant change in the properties of a material substance by consciously holding a clear intention to do so. For example, we have repeatedly been able to change the acid/alkaline balance (pH) in a vessel of water either up or down, without adding chemicals to the water, by creating an intention to do so. This is very exciting—but even more exciting is the fact that we have been able to use a simple electronic device and actually 'store' a specific intention within its electric circuit. This is important because now, this intention-host device can be placed next to a vessel of water at any physical location and one can expect to obtain the same results. In this way, we have had others replicate these water results at multiple locations around the world; such results are consistently reproducible! So, one might ask, 'How is it possible for something like this to occur in the physical reality with which we are all so familiar?' The answer is that, from our experimental work of the past ten years, we have discovered that there are actually two levels of physical reality and not just the one with which we are all familiar. It is this new level of physical reality that can be significantly influenced by human intention—not our familiar electric atom/molecule level! The two basic kinds of unique substances inhabiting these two levels of physical reality appear to interpenetrate each other but, normally, they do not interact with each other. We label this state as the uncoupled state of physical reality. In the uncoupled state, with one's five physical senses, we can detect our normal physical environment all around us. This new level of substance, because it appears to function in the physical vacuum (the empty space between the fundamental electric particles that make up our normal electric atoms and molecules), is currently invisible to us and to our traditional measurement instruments. It also appears to be of a magnetic information-wave nature.

Phase 1 Experiments: The first phase of our intention-host device experiments involved designing four separate target experiments. Each was to be influenced by an appropriate, separate intention-host device that would be plugged into a wall outlet of the experimental space, placed within a few feet of the target experiment apparatus and switched on. Our novel procedure for introducing a specific intention into a host device was to do it mentally and emotionally from a deep meditative state. For the first target experiment, the intention was to increase the pH of a vessel of water in equilibrium with air at room temperature by +1.0 pH units with no chemical additions. Our measurement accuracy was ±0.02 pH units. Figure 7.1 shows a sample result for this target experiment.

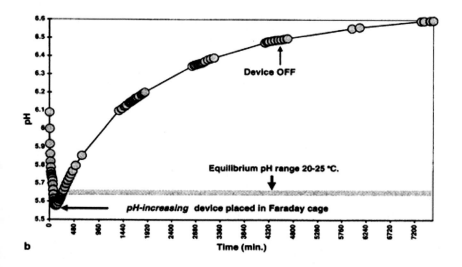

Figure 7.1. Plot of pH rising one full pH unit due to exposure to a pH-increasing intention-host device.

One can readily see that it was robustly successful in producing the intended result (which was 100 times larger than the noise level). The second target experiment was with water in equilibrium with air at room temperature, but the intention was to decrease the pH by ~1.0 pH units, again with no chemical additions. Once again, this experiment was successful. Similar successful results have been obtained for a variety of water types. For the third target experiment, the material medium was an in vitro biological molecule, alkaline phosphatase (ALP), a liver enzyme. The intention was to increase the chemical activity of ALP by a significant amount via just exposing the ALP for a period of 30 minutes to its intention-host device 'conditioned' space that had been brought to the coupled state. Once again, the experimental results were remarkably successful compared to the built-in controls. About a 25%–30% increase in ALP chemical activity was achieved at $p < 0.001$.

In the fourth target experiment, the material medium was an in vivo living system, fruit fly larvae. Here, the intention was to significantly increase the ratio of the cell's energy storage molecule, ATP, to its chemical precursor, ADP, so as to make the larvae more physically fit and thus have a greatly reduced larval development time, τ, to the adult fly stage. Again, with built-in controls, this living system was exposed to its intention-host device-'conditioned' space for the entire period, $\tau \sim 28$ days. We found that the ratio [ATP/ADP] increased by ~15%–20% with $p<0.001$

An overview perspective on the time-dependence of these remarkably successful experimental results is schematically illustrated in Figure 7.2

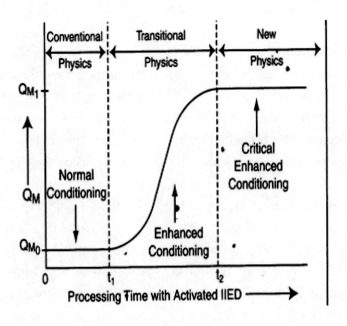

Figure 7.2 Degree of Conditioning Using Intention,

Q = Coupling Effect

Here, one sees that nothing much happens to Q_M, the magnitude of the material property under consideration, during exposure of the experimental space to the particular intention-host device for time, t, until a threshold time t_1 ~1 month has been passed. Then Q_M begins to change from Q_{M0}, the uncoupled state value, always in the direction of the particular intention before it begins to level off and plateau at time t_2~3 months, when $Q_{M1}-Q_{M0}=\Delta Q$ ~ the magnitude of the intention imprint. Put into equation form, the results of Figure 2 can be represented by

$$Q_M(t) = Q_e + \alpha_{eff}(t)Q_m \ (1)$$

where Q_e is our normal electric atom/molecule value, Q_{M0}, of the uncoupled state, Q_m is the vacuum level value and α_{eff} is the time-dependent coupling coefficient between these two types of substance due to use of the intention-host device as the space transitions from the uncoupled state to the coupled state of physical reality.

These experimental results have been published in over a dozen scientific papers and three seminal books. Experiment 1 has been replicated by others in ten US and European laboratories.

Phase 2 Experiments:

The second phase of our experimental research began with the performance of a replication study for experiment #1 because of its simplicity. The study was conducted at ten sites in the U.S. and Europe. Three of the intention-host sites, in Arizona, Missouri and Kansas, had control sites 2 to 20 miles distant. These control sites had exactly the same type of equipment and water but never an intention-host device. Excellent experimental replication occurred at all three intention-host device sites with the pH(t) rising exponentially with time in the following fashion:

$$pH(t) = pH_{th} + \Delta pH(1- e^{-\beta t}) \ (2)$$

Here, pH_{th} is the theoretically predicted value for an uncoupled state space at room temperature, ΔpH is the total magnitude of pH change and is usually quite close to the intended value, while β determines how rapidly the exponential function, e, decays. Both ΔpH and β are site-specific. Surprisingly, at the nearby control sites, very similar pH(t)-behaviour was observed. This behaviour strongly suggested that room temperature, information entanglement was occurring between the intention-host device sites and their control sites 2 to 20 miles away. To test this hypothesis, we utilised the Baltimore and Bethesda sites as control sites for the Arizona, Missouri, and Kansas intention-host device-sites. We found that within one to two months, the pH(t) was increasing exponentially by ~0.8 pH units. Thus, the room temperature information entanglement was both found to exist and now had been extended to ~1500 miles. Next, we decided to use the London-site, and ~3 months later the Milan site as control sites for the (AZ, MO, and KS) intention-host device sites. Within 3 weeks the ΔpH had increased by ~1 pH unit at the London-site and, 3 months later the Milan site went online and within 1 week the ΔpH at that site had increased exponentially to ~1 pH unit. Thus, this information entanglement phenomenon had now been proved to extend at least 6000 miles. Switching gears now, during this replication experiment, we invented a new and novel procedure for actually measuring, for the aqueous H^+-ion, the excess thermodynamic free energy change, δGH^{+*}, of the coupled state relative to the uncoupled state for an experimental space. Values of δGH^{+*} were measured for all ten sites involved in the replication experiment. The fact that all of the control sites exhibited non-zero values for δG^*H^+ demonstrates very clearly that the control sites are informationally connected to the intention-host device sites even over such huge distances.

In energetic terms, the magnitude of the $\delta G*H^+$-values can be quite large, equivalent thermal energy changes for an uncoupled-state space of ~150 °C. to ~500 °C. even though there was no significant change in the measured temperature at these sites.

As we reflect upon our world and upon the humankind that populates its surface, one soon perceives that there are several categories of phenomena and information wherein we need to gain reliable understanding in order to understand our life's journey. These might be classified as (1) things of the physical, (2) things of the psyche, (3) things of emotion, (4) things of the mind and (5) things of the spirit. In addition, we need a meaningful perspective or reference frame (RF) from which to view these different categories of phenomena and information. Ultimately, our understanding of all these phenomena must be internally self-consistent.' [159]

---

[159] William Tiller, 2009, 'A Brief Introduction to Intention-Host Device Research', White Paper #1, The William A Tiller Foundation.

Appendix 7.3

Subtle Energies: Murray Gillin reviews:

The pioneering work of Professor William Tiller to mathematically model this multi-dimensional reality has been called by Gerber 'The Tiller-Einstein Model of Positive-Negative Spacetime'—the next physics paradigm, and capable of incorporating the effect of human intention on physical matter through behaviour of etheric matter and emotional matter.[160] At the emotional level, certain thoughts, either conscious or unconscious, may exist as distinct energy fields or thought forms, with unique shapes, colours, and characteristics. Some thoughts, especially those that are charged with emotional intensity, can have a separate identity apart from their creator. Certain thoughts may actually be charged with subtle energetic substance and exist (unconsciously) as thought forms in the energetic fields of their creators.[161] (These thought-forms can frequently be seen by clairvoyant individuals who are very sensitive to higher energetic phenomena). The fact that human consciousness can influence the energy fields of subtle energetic anatomy has important implications for both medicine and psychology—including conditioning and control (trigger). Chalmers argues that no physical theory alone can explain why cognitive brain functions such as perception, memory, and decision-making are accompanied by conscious sensations.[162]

160 R. Gerber, 2001, Vibrational Medicine, Bear & Coy., Rochester, Vermont.

161 William Tiller, 1997, Science and Human Transformation, Pavior, California.

162 D. Chalmers, 1996, The Conscious Mind, Oxford University Press, New York.

Based on well-documented evidence for subtle energies and what have been loosely described as paranormal capabilities which include healing hands, remote viewing, precognition, telepathy, homeopathy, etc. Tiller shows a strong correlation with magnetic energies as distinct from electric energies. Subtle energies are all those beyond the ones generated by the four fundamental forces of gravity, electromagnetism (EM), the weak nuclear force and the strong nuclear force. They are thought to reside in the space between the fundamental particles comprising atoms and molecules and thus in the physical vacuum. They are not weak energies—they are merely elusive to our present-day measurement systems. Based on the theory of Barrett, Tiller concludes that when one considers phenomena where magnetic charge is important, as in the examples above, one must focus on another or higher level of reality than that of the coarse, physical level of reality.[163] This is referred to as the 'etheric' level of energy. Also, using quantum theory and explanations for the photons that can be seen and not seen, Deutsch 'rules out the possibility that the universe we physically see around us constitutes the 'whole of reality.'[164] Bohmconstructed a theory of reality 'with predictions identical to those of quantum theory' and such that his enfolding and unfolding 'does not change the fact that, in this theory reality consists of large sets of complex entities, each of which can perceive other entities in its own set but can only indirectly perceive entities in other sets.'[165] To help understand this condition and drawing freely from his books, Tiller et al. extends the work of Nobel prize winner deBroglie on wave/particle duality in which every particle in matter has a

163 T. W.Barrett, 1988, Comments in the Harmuth Ansatz, IEEE Transactions of Electromagnetic Capability, 30 , 419.

164 D. Deutsch, 1997, The Fabric of Reality, Penguin Books, New York.

165 D. Bohm, 1980 Wholeness and the Implicate Order, Routledge & Kegan Paul. London.

pilot-wave envelope enclosing it and moving at the velocity of the particle.[166] The faster moving information waves enter and leave this envelope as it moves along with the particle. Based on Quantum Mechanics and Einstein's relativity theory,

Particle Velocity V_p x Information Wave Velocity $V_w = c^2$

Since V_p is always less than c, then V_w must always be greater than c.

Tiller[143] shows that the deBroglie type particle coordinate is best described in D (direct)- space coordinates (x, y, z, t) while the information wave coordinate is an R (reciprocal)-space system $(x^{-1}, y^{-1}, z^{-1}, t^{-1})$. Following this approach, any formal description of substance or 'material' behaviour would involve at least eight coordinates. These two space systems clearly interact in the particle/wave picture, but relativity theory precludes the two-space systems from directly interacting with each other. Tiller invents the presence of an additional coupling substance that is not constrained by relativity theory.

The moieties of this coupling substance are thought to be from the domain of emotion and have been labelled 'deltrons.'[16] This means that any formal description of substance behaviour in nature, without any human intervention, involves at least nine coordinates (x, y, z, t), $C_{\delta 0}$, $(x-1, y-1, z-1, t-1)$ where $C_{\delta 0}$ is the cosmic background-activated deltron concentration. When human intervention, via human consciousness in the form of the application of human intentionality acts on nature, one must add at least 'one' more coordinate, (I^*) to any meaningful description of nature. Thus, formal descriptions of nature, which includes human intention, involves at least ten coordinates (x, y, z, t), $C_{\delta 0}$, $(x-1, y-1, z-1, t-1)$, I^*. I^* represents the intensity of human intention and it

166 William Tiller, W.E. Dibble and M. J. Kohane, 2001, Conscious Acts of Creation, Pavior, California.

influences the magnitude of C_δ. A diagrammatic representation of the functionality is given in Fig. 7.3.

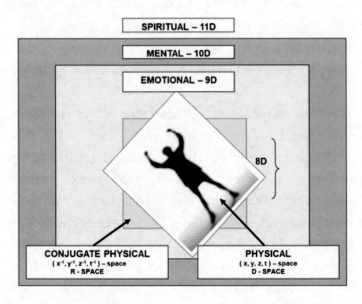

Figure 7.3 A visualisation of dual four-space frames embedded in three higher dimensional frames (Tiller et al 2001)

Here, the cognitive domain or physical reality is shown in the centre and a dual or conjugate 4-space reality is connected to it. Tiller makes the additional postulate that the moieties that write the waves in this etheric or R-space are the magnetic monopoles. Thus, the electric monopoles operate in direct-space while the magnetic monopoles operate in reciprocal space with a very special type of 'mirror' relationship (not a reflection mirror but an inversion mirror) functioning between them. Via this unique mirror, the magnetic monopoles (ie. particles charged either north or south) of R-space generate magnetic dipole images in D-space while the electric monopoles of D-space generate electric dipole images in R-space. This leads to the normal Maxwell equations for electromagnetism functioning in D-space and another set of analogous equations for magnetoelectrism functioning in R-space. What we have for the first time in this frequency-based theory is a means to test and understand the reality and behaviour of other levels of reality which are not based on myth, personal visions (even though they may be real), but can be tested against observable research.

So how does the human being sense/receive or radiate information/energy from exposure to subtle energies?

Modern quantum science, as well as the ancient teachings of Chinese medicine, is based on the reality that everything is energy, whether identified with D-space or R-space. According to our understanding of matter, physics and chemistry, the universal energy field comprises all matter and psychological processes—thoughts, emotions, beliefs, and attitudes—we are composed of energy. When applied to the human body, every atom, molecule, cell, tissue, and body system is composed of energy that, when superimposed on each other, create what is known as the human energy field.

Indeed, as human beings, created in the 'Image of God', our elements of mind-body-spirit are indivisibly interconnected with the universal energy source that both regulates and makes possible us as living beings.

A corollary of the above is the necessity for the human body to have 'receptors' that can sense the energy realities described above. These receptors can be described as biological transducers that convert energy from both external and internal environments into electrical impulses. They may be massed together to form a sense organ, such as the eye or ear, or they may be scattered, as are those of the skin and viscera. Significantly, there are hundreds of acupoints (energy sensors/receptors) along the underlying meridian's that form the energy network distributed throughout the body. These meridian lines are the channels by which our energy flows, thus transporting the received subtle energy throughout the body for processing and effecting change. Receptors are connected to the central nervous system by afferent nerve fibres. The region or area in the periphery from which a neuron within the central nervous system receives input is called its receptive field.

Receptors are of many kinds and are classified in many ways. Steady-state receptors, for example, generate impulses as long as a particular state such as temperature remains constant. Changing-state receptors, on the other hand, respond to variation in the intensity or position of a stimulus (e.g. subtle energies). Receptors are also classified as exteroceptive (reporting the external environment), interoceptive (sampling the environment of the body itself), and proprioceptive (sensing the posture and movements of the body). Exteroceptors are the likely interface with external subtle energies.

Cell membrane receptor proteins help cells communicate with their external environment through the use of hormones, neurotransmitters, and other signalling molecules and are remarkably flexible. Significantly, these exteroceptors are distributed over the surface of the body and, as such, form an array where received information at each receptor point will be slightly out of phase with the others. This provides the foundation for the central nervous system to apply an antenna array (often called a 'phased array') concept to processing the signal information from the receptors. The signals from the 'antennas', receptors are thus combined or processed in order to achieve improved performance over that of a single receptor.

An analogous example is that of the Jindalee Operational Radar Network (JORN), an over-the-horizon radar (OTHR) network that can monitor air and sea movements across 37,000 km^2 (14,285 sq miles). It has a normal operating range of 1,000 km (621 mi) to 3,000 km (1,863 mi). It is used in the defence of Australia, and can also monitor maritime operations, wave heights and wind directions. Over-the-horizon radar and its associated signal processing algorithms can interpret distant information received at a large, phased-array of single dipoles. Using two transmitting/receiving sites provides the triangulation necessary to locate target position. Such transmission and reception are facilitated by a small asymmetry in Maxwell's equations, which triggers an electromagnetic wave to decouple from (transmission) and couple into(reception) a medium carrying free electric charges (antenna). The application of Maxwell's equations to the most fundamental radiation element, the Hertzian dipole, is then explained.

Indeed, just as Jindalee transmits and receives energy from/to distant parts so we can infer that human intention and its associated energy (explained by Tiller using modified Maxwell equations to allow for monopoles to operate in R-space)[167] is transmitted from the human body's exteroceptors to effect the change associated with the intention. Also, the distributed exteroceptors over the human body allow for triangulation in locating the focus of human intention, and together with the meridian network the human being can incorporate emotion and spirit with the heart and brain in decision-making processes.

This understanding and physics-based explanation underpin both the reality and importance of the 'spirit' characteristic

---

167 William Tiller, 1999, 'Towards a Predictive Model of Subtle Domain Connections to the Physical Domain Aspect of Reality: The Origins of Wave-Particle Duality, Electric-Magnetic Monopoles and the Mirror Principle' Journal of Scientific Exploration, Vol 13 No 1, pp41–67.

in exercising an entrepreneur mindset. Furthermore, this explanation underpins the demonstrated behaviour of serial entrepreneurs to incorporate non-local intuition in their decision-making processes.[168]

168 Murray Gillin & Loris Gillin, 2003, 'Subtle Energies, Intentionality and the Healing of Traumatically Abused Persons,' International Conference on Trauma, Attachment and Dissociation. Melbourne, Australia.

Appendix 7.4

Quantum Entanglement and Prayer: With permission Dr. Ranjit A. Thuraisingham.

Dr Thuraisingham recently published an article seeking to discuss the reality of prayer from a spiritual understanding with full appreciation of quantum physics:

'Prayer is an important aspect of the Christian spiritual life. Prayer, for the faithful, is a way to come into a deeper relationship with God and to seek his help and guidance not only for them but also for others. The Catholic Encyclopedia defines prayer as 'the raising of the mind and soul to God.'[169] When an attempt is made to understand prayer, many questions arise in the mind of a person. A sceptic can view prayer as talking to someone at a distance without any apparent mechanism or communication between the person and God, thus degenerating prayer to talking to oneself, wishful thinking or as an escape from reality. To understand this communication at a distance, this article looks at Christian prayer and the concept of entangled states from quantum mechanics where a physical mechanism is used to explain the interaction between quantum objects separated by large distances. It is suggested here that Christian prayer has an analogy in quantum entanglement, providing an argument that counteracts the criticism that there are no known scientific

169 R. C. Broderick, Catholic Encyclopedia (New York: Thomas Nelson Publishers, 1976), 485–487.

269

channels of communication in prayer. Often science and theology are put in separate compartments. In contrast to the mechanical view of the universe, presented by classical physics, the advent of quantum mechanics has produced a paradigm shift, replacing the logical processes observed in the macroscopic world with processes that obey a different physics in the quantum world. One of them is entanglement, a characteristic trait of quantum physics. It is a physical phenomenon that occurs when a pair or groups of independent particles enter into a temporary physical interaction due to known forces between them, so they can no longer be described independently of the others; and then after a time of mutual influence they separate, where even at large distances, they can no longer be described separately; instead, they must be described as a whole. Christian Prayer: In Genesis 2:7 the account of the creation of humanity is described as follows: 'Then the Lord God formed man of dust from the ground and breathed into his nostrils the breath of life; and the man became a living being.'[170] This brief description of the Genesis account of the creation of humanity implies that the human being is made up of matter and a life-giving spirit. However, due to the disobedience of humanity, this spirit lost its relationship with God. The redemption of this spirit back to God is the message of Christianity. For Christians, the saving grace of Jesus, made possible by his death on the cross, restored the fallen spirit of humans to union with the Spirit of God. Thus, in baptism when the Christian accepts Jesus as their saviour by faith, they receive the Holy Spirit. Paul in his letter to the Corinthians reminds them of this redeemed spirit in them: 'Do you not know that you are the temple of God and that the Spirit of God dwells in you' (1 Cor 3:16). Further in Romans we read:

---

170 The quotes from the Bible were taken from the New American Standard Bible, Reference Edition (1973), Foundation Press, CA, USA.

'And in the same way the Spirit also helps our weakness; for we do not know how to pray as we should, but the Spirit Himself intercedes for us with groaning too deep for words; and He who searches the hearts, knows what the mind of the Spirit is; because He intercedes for the saints according to the will of God' (Rom 8:26–27). Thus, it is the Holy Spirit who enables us to pray. The Holy Spirit is part of the Trinity, which comprises God the Father, Son, and the Holy Spirit. The Holy Spirit is in total 'entanglement' with God. Though separate, they act together. When our minds and souls reach out in humble dependence to God in prayer through Jesus, our faith dictates that the Holy Spirit transfers our pleas and supplications to God's presence. This transmission is instantaneous. However, what is being transferred is what the Holy Spirit communicates. The result is that the Holy Spirit receives back power to act according to God's will in our lives but also in the lives of others. Such a belief in the Trinity and instantaneous transmission in prayer cannot be dismissed as irrational or unscientific since a similar physical phenomenon exists in the quantum world. This phenomenon is referred to as quantum entanglement which will be examined next section.

Quantum Entanglement: The concept of quantum entanglement arose as a result of the argument put forward by Einstein, Podolsky and Rosen (EPR) questioning the validity of quantum mechanics as a complete physical theory.[171] Schrödinger described this concept in the following manner:

When two quantum systems of which we know by their respective representatives, enter into a temporary physical interaction due to known forces between them, and when after

171 A. Einstein, B. Podolsky, and N. Rosen, 'Can Quantum–Mechanical Description of Physical Reality Be Considered Complete? Phys. Rev. 47 (1935): 777.

a time of mutual influence the systems separate again, then they can no longer be described in the same way as before: viz. by endowing each of them with a representative of its own. I would not call that one but rather the characteristic trait of quantum mechanics, the one that enforces its entire departure from classical lines of thought.[172]

What this says is that two quantum objects which have interacted with each other at one time but are now separated by large distances from each other cannot be described in the same way they were characterised before the interaction. This is different from what is observed in classical physics. In other words, the two quantum objects have become correlated or entangled due to the interaction, even though they are at present separated by such long distances as to consider them as separate. Thus, quantum entanglement is a physical resource, like energy, associated with the peculiar non-classical correlations that are possible between separated quantum systems. Entanglement can be measured and transformed.[173]

A pair of quantum systems in an entangled state can be used as a quantum information channel to perform tasks that are impossible in classical systems. Thus, entanglement is a strange feature of quantum physics, the science of the very small. What it tells us is that if it is possible to link together two quantum particles, photons of light or atoms in a special way that makes them effectively two parts of the same entity and then separate them as far as you like, then a change in one is instantly reflected in the other. It is as if two particles act together. They behave like one object but remain as two separate objects. A good analogy is

172 E. Schrödinger, 'Discussion of Probability Relations Between Separated Systems.' Proceedings of the Cambridge Philosophical Society 31 (1935): 555–563.

173 5 Bub, Jeffrey, 'Quantum Entanglement and Information,' The Stanford Encyclopedia of Philosophy (Spring 2017 Edition), Edward N. Zalta (ed.), https://plato.stanford.edu/archives/spr2017/entries/qt-entangle/.

two people seated on a seesaw. No matter how long the sea saw is, if one end is down, the other end must be up. This happens instantaneously. There are no messages between the two people saying, 'I'm going down, therefore, you must go up' and waiting for the person to receive the message. Yet, the two people are always connected and behave as one. This physical phenomenon of entangled particles though separate but behaving as one with instant communication between them, throws some light on Christian prayer. The existence of quantum entangled states is evidence that a corresponding situation can exist during Christian prayer dismissing the sceptical view that it is talking to someone at a distance with no channels of communication.

Conclusion

To the sceptic, prayer can be viewed as talking to someone at a distance with no scientific mechanism to link them, akin to talking to oneself. To overcome this scepticism, this article first examined Christian prayer, which is understood as the indwelling Holy Spirit in the believer's heart interceding to God the Father through Jesus. The Christian believes that though separate God the Father, Son Jesus, and the Holy Spirit are one. Focusing now on the quantum world, one finds that objects which have interacted before but are now separated by large distances, though separate, behave as one. Such objects are termed entangled states. For such entangled states, communication between them is instantaneous.

Such a result from quantum physics with instant communication between entangled states indicates that an analogous situation can exist during Christian prayer, where the Spirit within us makes instant contact with God through Jesus, all of whom form part of the Trinity. The presence of such an instant communication channel between entangled states provides a scientific counterargument to the skeptic who denies the possibility of any known outside communication routes during prayer. For millions of Christians all over the world, prayer is a source of power and solace. They do not analyse how their prayers are communicated because prayer is real to them. They do not require any convincing of its veracity because of their experience in answered prayers. Prayer forms the backbone of their faith. To the sceptic, on the other hand, who requires scientific proof for everything, what is put forward here is that in the quantum realm, within the class of entangled particles, communication takes place instantly. Such a result dismisses the claim of the skeptic that there are no known communication channels in science between a person and God during prayer.'[174]

---

174 Ranjit A. Thuraisingham, 2019, 'Prayer and Entangled Quantum States' http://iscast.org/articles/Thuraisingham_Prayer_and_Entanglement_Opinion_Published_Jan_2019.pdf.

Appendix 7.5

Intuition, Interconnectivity and Coherence: With permission.

Ray Bradley writes:

Recent theories that explain the space/time-defying phenomena of nonlocal interaction build upon three scientific developments[175]. The first is the discovery of the *hologram*—specifically, the principle of distributed organization by which information about an object is spectrally encoded throughout a field of potential energy by the radiating oscillations of energy waveforms, such that an image of the object can be retrieved from any location[176]. The second is the discovery of quantum entanglement or *nonlocality*—that everything in the universe at the subatomic level is inter-connected. The third is the discovery of *quantum coherence*—that subatomic emissions from macro-scale objects are not random but exhibit coherence at the quantum level, reflective of an object's material organization and event history[177].

A Quantum-Holographic Theory of Entrepreneurial Intuition

Coupling these developments in physics with the psycho-physiological evidence mentioned above on the involvement of

---

175 Bradley, R. T. (2007). The psychophysiology of intuition: A quantum-holographic theory of nonlocal communication. World Futures: The Journal of General Evolution, 63: 61–97.

176 Gabor, D. (1946). Theory of communication, J. of Inst. Electrical Engineers, 93: 439–457.

177 Schempp, W. (1992). Quantum holography and neurocomputer architectures, J. of Mathematical Imaging and Vision, 2: 109–164.

mental attention and positive emotions in nonlocal interaction, Bradley has developed a quantum-holographic theory to explain entrepreneurial nonlocal intuition.

A key concept in this theory is the notion of the spectral encoding of information in the radiating oscillations of energy, as used in quantum holography[178]. Quantum holography is based on Gabor's energy-based concept of information, the *logon* (Figure 7.4a), and it provides the foundation for a non-determinist kind of holographic organization. Gabor's concept of information—the encoding of information in energy oscillations at *any* frequency— is a general concept that applies to energetic information communication at *both* the 4-dimensional macro-scale world and the micro-scale of quantum reality. Logons are not discrete units of information but overlap with each other and occur as a modularized series of space-time-constrained sinusoids in which the data in each module are spectrally enfolded, to some degree, into the data of adjoining logons (Figure 7.4b). This overlap among logons has a significant implication for information communication from the future, in that each logon, in Gabor's words, contains an '*overlap [with] the future*'[29]. This means, in effect, that each unit of information, by virtue of its spectral enfoldment with adjoining units, contains information about the future order energetically encoded in the unit that succeeds it.[179]

178 Pribram, K. H. (1991). Brain and Perception: Holonomy and Structure in Figural Processing, Lawrence Erlbaum Associates, Hillsdale, NJ.

179 Bradley, R. T., & K. H. Pribram (1998). Communication and stability in social collectives, J. of Social and Evolutionary Systems, Vol. 21, 1: 29–81.

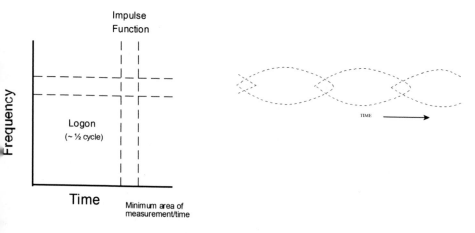

Figure 7.4a (left). An idealised graph of a Hilbert Space showing a logon in terms of limits of measurement[30]. Figure 7.4b (right). A representation of the overlap among logons

Building on HeartMath's core proposition of the key role of the heart and positive emotions in creating a channel for intuition, the quantum-holographic theory provides an understanding of the physical and psychophysiological processes by which entrepreneurial intuition occurs. The perception of things remote in space or ahead in time—*nonlocal communication*—is viewed as involving processes of energetic resonance connecting the body's psychophysiological systems to the quantum level of the object of interest. The theory explains how positive emotional attention directed to the object attunes the bio-emotional energy generated by the body's psychophysiological systems to a domain of quantum-holographical information, which contains implicit, energetically encoded information about the object. The body's perception of such implicit information about things distant in space/time is experienced as an intuition:

'The entrepreneur's passionate attention—that is, the biological energy activated in his emotional connection to the object of interest (e.g., the quest for future opportunities in a certain field of business)—attunes him to the object's unfolding pattern of activity and to the implicit order of its future potential. Both the pattern of activity and the potential future order are spectrally encoded as a quantum hologram in a field of potential energy as implicit information in a domain apart from space and time. At a biological level, the body's psychophysiological systems generate numerous fields of energy at various frequencies that interpenetrate the field of potential energy. Of these, the heart generates the most powerful rhythmic electromagnetic field, which radiates out from the body in all directions.

When the entrepreneur calms his mind and feelings and adopts a heart-focused state of positive emotion directed to the object, a global shift to psychophysiological coherence is induced which optimizes attentional resonance with the incoming quantum level information from the object of interest. Such attunement brings the outgoing wave field of attentional energy from the entrepreneur's psychophysiological systems into harmonic resonance with the incoming wave field of energy from the object [see Figure 7.5]. The harmonic resonance between the two wavefields of energy creates an optimal channel for communication of nonlocal information.'[180]

---

180 Bradley, R. T. (2006). The psychophysiology of entrepreneurial intuition: A quantum-holographic theory. 3rd AGSERE, UNITEC, Auckland, NZ.

Figure 7.5. A channel of coherent interaction is created between a percipient (P) and an object (O) when their two interpenetrating wavefields are radiating synchronised oscillations at the same energy frequency (top). However, this does not hold for interaction between wavefields radiating energy oscillations at different frequencies (bottom).

To the degree that a coherent relationship of energetic resonance between the object of interest and the percipient entrepreneur is maintained—that the object's quantum wave field and the attentional wave field of the percipient locked in a resonant feedback loop[181]—the entrepreneur's psychophysiological system (the heart, brain, and body as a whole) can receive and process

---

181 Marcer, P., & W. Schempp (1998). The brain as a conscious system, Int. J. General Systems, 27: 231–248.

nonlocal information as quantum holograms. Once received, such quantum-holographic information about distant objects is decoded and converted by the psychophysiological systems, through a reverse Fourier transform process, into mental imagery, feelings, and other sensations.

The theory leads to the following hypothesis: The more the entrepreneur maintains coherent, passionate attentional interest directed to the object of interest, the greater the psychophysiological systems' access to an implicit field of quantum-holographic information and the greater the intuitive foreknowledge about the object of interest.[182]

182 Raymond Bradley, Murray Gillin, Mike Atkinson, Frank LaPira, and Rollin McCraty, 'Intuitive perception: As measured on repeat entrepreneurs in the Cambridge Technopol using electrophysiological instrumentation'; 2007, Frontiers of Entrepreneurship Research, Babson College, Boston.

Introduction to Case Study Chapters

The experience of God, or in any case the possibility of experiencing God, is innate.

—Alice Walker, novelist

In Chapter 7, we reviewed the significance of the work by Emeritus Professor William Tiller, along with a number of independent researchers, that both theorised and demonstrated that 'focused human intention', along with 'quantum mechanics', can explain the true created nature of the universe—one based on energy, frequency, and waves (Appendices 7.1–7.5).

Indeed, there are actually two levels of reality and not just the one which is the most familiar. There is the well-known physical reality including the five senses, but also another level or ethereal reality that can be significantly influenced by human intention— consciousness, meditation, emotion, mind, and focused prayer. Indeed, we have presented what might be called unequivocal experimental evidence that it is possible to make a significant change in the properties of water, a liver enzyme, and an in-vivo living system (fruit-fly) by consciously holding a clear intention to do so. Such an intention is defined as 'the determination to do a specific thing or act in a specified manner; having something in mind as a plan, design, purpose, or goal.' William Tiller referred to these measured effects as psychoenergetic phenomena, or consciousness-related phenomena involving new categories of energies (subtle energies) beyond those generated by the four fundamental forces: gravity, electromagnetism (EM), the weak nuclear force, and the strong nuclear force. The subtle energies are thought to reside in the space between the fundamental particles of matter comprising atoms and molecules and thus are found in the physical vacuum. These subtle energies are not weak forces.[183]

The significance of these realities is that they can be experienced and practised by human beings with appropriate meditation, prayer and other consciousness-raising actions. Importantly for our study of Jesus and understanding the so-called 'nature miracles', we are reminded that 'Jesus is fully man', as established in Chapter 2. The Bible record is clear that Jesus was born with a human body, into a human community and experienced all the personal realities of living. There was no special treatment given to Jesus while here on earth. He felt the same things that every other human being feels. Also reviewed was His personality, creativity, intuition, emotions, awareness, authenticity, and love, with the conclusion that Jesus exhibited all the characteristics of a man in terms of body, soul, and spirit.

Important to understanding the following case studies is the fundamental reality that Jesus experienced the full realisation of access to and empowerment by the Holy Spirit through the fundamental relationship established with God from His baptism and wilderness experience (Chapter 5). In addition, we note that Jesus' ministry and authority were fully endorsed by the Apostle Peter before a multitude, following Jesus' ascension, by saying:

---

183 William Tiller, 2009, 'A Brief Introduction to Intention-Host Device Research', White Paper #1, The William A Tiller Foundation.

Fellow Israelites, listen to this: Jesus of Nazareth was a man accredited by God to you by miracles, wonders and signs, which God did among you through him, as you yourselves know.

—Acts 2: 22

Clearly, man's physical body functions together with the five senses and enables us to observe the facts and gather the data necessary for living. But there is more, much more that complements our perception and reality of what it is to be a human being (body, soul, and spirit). Significantly, when non-local intuition and mindfulness—expressed as intention, attention, and attitude—are coupled with spirit, we become aware of our deep inner values that give meaning and purpose to life. In the models of Daniel A Helminiak and Bernard Lonergan, the human spirit is considered to be the mental functions of awareness, insight, understanding, judgment, and other intention-driven powers compared to the separate component of the psyche, which comprises the entities of emotion, images, memory, and personality.[184,185] In each of the four cases studied—so-called 'nature miracles'—the hypothesis examined is that:

Jesus used His enhanced powers of human intention, interconnectedness, and close personal relationship with God the Holy Spirit to affect the observed 'miracle' using the natural mechanisms of physics and science.' This description of a 'miracle' concords with Augustine (Bishop of Hippo) who said,

184 William Tiller, 2009, 'A Brief Introduction to Intention-Host Device Research', White Paper #1, The William A Tiller Foundation.
185 Daniel A. Helminiak, 2014, More than awareness: Bernard Lonergan's multi-faceted account of consciousness. Journal of Theoretical and Philosophical Psychology 34(2):116–132.

'Miracles are not contrary to nature, but only contrary of what we know about nature.'

Humphreys, in commenting on the language of Aristotle to understand miracles: identified the efficient cause as 'a natural agent'; the final cause as 'the will of God'; and the revelation of the miracle by the extraordinary timing of the event. Put another way, in considering the relationship between science and religion there must be the reality of consonance, i.e. of compatibility, as the existence of any contradiction would violate this relation. Using the analogy of a music composer, Humphreys comments, 'the composer uses the key signature relevant to his composition but is free to introduce 'accidentals' when considered necessary or appropriate. The composer is in control and the resultant insertion is okay, but in so doing adds to the beauty and wonder of the finished composition.'[186]

The emphasis in this consideration of a 'miracle' is focused on 'what is true'—the facts reinforcing the principle that God works through natural resources to effect change.[187] 'It may be thought that such a science-based explanation will destroy the wonder and awe of the observed event. I refute this supposition and emphasise that it is God using His creation to effect change—the wonder and awe is in the timing of the event so that the 'miraculous' observation occurs at exactly the time and place it is required. We can rejoice in the reality of God exercising His authority over the created universe.'

186 Colin Humphreys, 2016, https://www.cis.org.uk/ireland/walton/documents/Colin-Humphreys-3-Nov-2016-slides.pdf.
187 Colin Humphreys, 2018, https://www.premierchristianradio.com/Shows/Saturday/Unbelievable/Episodes/Unbelievable-Is-there-scientific-evidence-for-Old-Testament-miracles-Colin-Humphreys-Bob-Price.

In relationship to the ministry of Jesus, it is totally understandable that such 'good news' is communicated more effectively to those who do not believe it when accompanied by such manifestations of signs and wonders delivered by Jesus the man in collaboration with the Holy Spirit.

Chapter 8: Case #1—Jesus and His Transfiguration

If you want to find the secrets of the universe, think in terms of energy, frequency, and vibration.

—Nikola Tesla

The transfiguration is one of the miracles of Jesus in the Gospels. This miracle is unique among others that appear in the canonical gospels in that the miracle happens to Jesus himself. Thomas Aquinas considered the transfiguration 'the greatest miracle' in that it complemented baptism and showed the perfection of life in Heaven. 'The transfiguration is one of the five major milestones in the gospel narrative of the life of Jesus, the others being baptism, crucifixion, resurrection, and ascension.'

As a demonstration of Jesus' spiritual awareness and obedience to His mission of preaching access to a new and personal relationship with God, I want to take you on a journey that will demonstrate the transfiguration of Jesus on Mt Tabor was no 'trick of magic' or 'sorcery', nor is it unexplainable. We will also see that deep focused prayer can and does lead to an enlivening communion with God and awareness of the power we have within our beings.

Text and Analysis

Matt 17.1-9	Mark 9.2-9	Luke 9.28-36
1. Six days later, Jesus took with him Peter and James and his brother John and led them up a high mountain, by themselves.	2. Six days later, Jesus took with him Peter and James and John, and led them up a high mountain apart, by themselves. And *he was transfig- ured* before them,	28. Now about eight days after these sayings Jesus took with him Peter and John and James, and went up on the mountain to pray.
2. And *he was transfigured* before them, and his face shone like the sun, and his clothes became dazzling white.	3. *and his clothes became dazzling white,* such as no-one on earth could bleach them.	29. And while he was praying, the appearance of his face changed, and his clothes became dazzling white.
3. Suddenly there appeared to them Moses and Elijah, talking with him	4. And there appeared to them Elijah with Moses, who were talking with Jesus.	30. Suddenly they saw two men, Moses and Elijah, talking to him.
4. Then Peter said to Jesus, 'Lord, it is good for us to be here; if you wish, I will make three dwellings here, one for you, one for Moses, and one for Elijah.'	5. Then Peter said to Jesus, 'Rabbi, it is good for us to be here; let us make three dwellings, one for you, one for Moses, and one for Elijah.'	31. They appeared in glory and were speaking of his departure, which he was about to accomplish at Jerusalem.

5. While he was still speaking, suddenly *a bright cloud overshadowed them,* and from the cloud a voice said, This is my beloved Son; with him I am well pleased; listen to him!'	6. He did not know what to say, for they were terrified.	32. Now Peter and his companions were weighed down with sleep; but since they had stayed awake, they saw his glory and the two men who stood with him.
6. When the disciples heard this, they fell to the ground and were overcome by fear	7. Then a cloud over-shadowed them, and from the cloud there came a voice, *'This is my beloved Son*; listen to him!'	33. Just as they were leaving him, Peter said to Jesus, 'Master, it is good for us to be here; let us make three dwellings, one for you, one for Moses, and one for Elijah'—not knowing what he said.
7. But Jesus came and touched them, saying, 'Get up and do not be afraid.'	8. Suddenly when they looked around, they saw no-one with them any more, but only Jesus.	34. While he was say-ing this, a *cloud came and overshadowed them*; and they were terrified as they entered the cloud.

8. And when they looked up, they saw no-one except Jesus himself alone.	9. As they were coming down the mountain, *he ordered them to tell no-one* about what they had seen, until after the Son of Man had risen from the dead.	35. Then from the cloud came a voice that said, *'This is my Son, my Chosen;* listen to him!'
9. As they were coming down the mountain, *Jesus ordered them, 'Tell no-one* about the vision until after the Son of Man has been raised from the dead.'	10. So they kept the matter to themselves, questioning what this rising from the dead could mean.	36. When the voice had spoken, Jesus was found alone. And they kept silent and in those days told no-one any of the things they had seen.

In the days leading up to the transfiguration, Jesus tells His Apostles that he is going to die, be buried, and rise again (Mark 8:31). Peter is shocked and rebukes Jesus (8:32–33). It is clear from the context of these interchanges between Jesus and His Apostles they did not fully grasp the reality of His coming death, only months away. Indeed this struggle continued for them for the most part until the day of Pentecost. From that point on, their sermons make it clear that they fully understand what Jesus had been trying to tell them.

Undoubtedly, the purpose of the transfiguration of Christ into at least a part of His heavenly glory was so that the 'inner circle' of His Apostles could gain a greater understanding of who Jesus was. Christ underwent a dramatic change in appearance so that the Apostles could behold Him in His glory. The Apostles, who had only known Him in His human body, now had a greater realisation of the deity of Christ, though they could not fully comprehend it. Also, this experience gave them the reassurance they needed after hearing the shocking news of His coming death.

Symbolically, the appearance of Moses and Elijah represented the Law and the Prophets. But God's voice from heaven—'Listen to Him!'—clearly showed that the Law and the prophets must give way to Jesus. The one who is the new and living way is replacing the old—He is the fulfilment of the Law and the countless prophecies in the Old Testament. Also, in His glorified form, they saw a preview of His coming glorification and enthronement as King of kings and Lord of lords. This experience has been the subject of many artists, an example by Alexander Ivanov is shown in Figure 8.1[188]

Figure 8.1. The Transfiguration—Alexander Andreyevich Ivanov—1824

---

188 Alexander Ivanov, 1824, http://nnm.ru/blogs/hhnu/ivanov_aleksandr_andreev-ich_1806_1858/, Public Domain, https://commons.wikimedia.org/w/index.php?curid=9086637.

But it was this experience that caused Peter, James, and John to fully recognise the reality of Jesus as both 'fully man' and 'fully God'. The disciples never forgot what happened that day on the mountain and no doubt this was intended. John wrote in his gospel, 'We have seen His glory, the glory of the one and only' (John 1:14). Peter also wrote of it, 'We did not follow cleverly invented stories when we told you about the power and coming of our Lord Jesus Christ, but we were eyewitnesses of His Majesty.'

1. Miracle Elements and 'Science' Theories Luke 9:29—'And while he was praying, the appearance of his face changed'

In this account of the transfiguration, it is noted that 'prayer' is central to the exchange between Jesus and God the Holy Spirit. Given the intensity of the action, it is reasonable to conclude this was an act of great 'human intention' on the part of Jesus and can be called 'focused prayer.' Importantly, this interchange with God in prayer (communication) was not His first occurrence, given the intensity of such action during Jesus' wilderness experience.

Given that man, along with the universe, is composed of particles such as atoms and molecules, it is reasonable to describe Jesus, and all human beings, as exhibiting a 'quantum object' signature along with God. In the case being considered, we can conclude the two quantum objects (Jesus and God the Holy Spirit) have become correlated or entangled due to the interaction (prayer), even though they are separated by such long physical distances as to consider them as being separate.

Quantum mechanics (Appendix 7.4) shows these two quantum particles (objects), photons of light or atoms or magnetic monopoles, to be fully correlated or entangled in a physical interaction due to known forces in a special way that makes them effectively two parts of the same entity. As such, they can no longer be described independently of each other, and if after a time of mutual influence, they separate, even at large distances (earth and heaven), they can no longer be described separately. Instead, they must be described as a whole.

Thuraisingham provides a good analogy of this 'lock-step' relationship between Jesus the man and God the Holy Spirit following the initial communion.[189] With each seated on an end of a see-saw (figuratively), we observe no matter how long the see-saw is, if one end is down, the other end must be up. This happens under all circumstances. There are no messages between the two people saying, 'I'm going down, therefore, you must go up' and waiting for the person to receive the message. Yet, the two people are always connected and behave as one.[190]

This physical phenomenon of entangled particles but behaving as one though separate, with instant communication between them, throws some light on Christian prayer. This is an amazing, indeed awesome, way to see Jesus in prayer with God. The existence of quantum entangled states is evidence that a corresponding situation can exist during Christian prayer dismissing the sceptical view that prayer is talking to someone at a distance with no channels of communication. The most basic definition of prayer is 'talking to God.' Prayer is not meditation or passive reflection; it is a direct address to God. It is the communication of the human soul/spirit with the Lord who created the soul and spirit. Prayer is the primary way for the believer in Jesus Christ to communicate his emotions and desires with God and to fellowship with God. Surely our faith is enhanced by this understanding.

189 Ranjit A. Thuraisingham, 2019, 'Prayer and Entangled Quantum States' http://iscast.org/articles/Thuraisingham_Prayer_and_Entanglement_Opinion_Published_Jan_2019.pdf.
190 Bradley, R. T. (2007). The psychophysiology of intuition: A quantum-holographic theory of nonlocal communication. World Futures: The Journal of General Evolution, 63: 61–97.

2. Luke 9: 29—'And his clothes became dazzling white'

When we think in terms of a substance or a physical body constructed of atoms and molecules, we also must think about an energy part, an information part, and a consciousness part. They are all part of us human beings. How does this awareness affect our understanding of connecting with the power source—God the Creator?

During prayer, Jesus was in a high spiritual communion and personal communication with God. Basically, He had an open channel to God, the source of power and energy. We know from our experience of switching on lights in our homes and offices that to transform a dull/dark globe to a dazzling white light, it is necessary to flick the switch and connect to the power or energy source. Without energy, there is no light.

From each of the three accounts of this miracle, we have a common observation that the Apostles saw Jesus 'and his clothes became dazzling white … and they saw His glory.' In our home light example, there is a need for a power cable from the energy source to the light bulb. So where is the 'energy cable' on Mt Tabor? Indeed, the energy to change the clothes to 'dazzling white' was not delivered through a cable carrying electromagnetic form of energy transference but, by making a significant change in the properties of the material fabric through Jesus consciously holding a clear intention to receive this power from God—the source of the power (see appendix 7.1). With the 'link' established, as described for prayer above, the energy was literally 'pumped' or flowed as correlated/entangled magnetic monopoles down the channel into the garment, changing its state to a dazzling light so bright that the Apostles cannot see for a short time after looking at Jesus. Indeed, the principle of entrepreneur 'intention' is a conscious mental state that precedes the action and directs attention towards the goal of establishing the desired outcome. As discussed in Chapter 5, we demonstrated that intention is part of the 'awareness' dimension in an entrepreneur mindset and is a fundamental spiritual behaviour. Therefore, it is not surprising that Jesus could have applied His entrepreneur mindset to delivering spiritual outcomes through 'intention' based practices.

To understand a mechanism that can explain the property change in the clothing fabric using an 'intention' based energy source, I refer to the critical experiment of Tiller.[191] In his experiment, the material medium on which to effect change was a biological molecule, alkaline phosphatase (ALP). The specific intention, generated by the experienced meditators, was to increase the chemical activity of ALP by a significant amount via just exposing the ALP for a period of 30 minutes to its intention-host device 'conditioned' space, and in such relationship that the material molecule formed a coupled state (quantum relationship) with the host device. The experimental results were remarkably successful compared to the built-in controls. About a 25%–30% increase in ALP chemical activity was achieved at $p < 0.001$. In the case of Jesus' cotton clothing, it is 99% cellulose. Cellulose is a macromolecule—a polymer made up of a long chain of glucose molecules. Investigation shows the lustre of the cotton is enhanced the more circular the cross-section of the cotton hairs is. Also, when exposed to light radiation, the cotton increases the energy content of its molecules and may appear to 'glow'.

For this to occur, much energy was needed to be 'pumped' into the clothes Jesus was wearing for the material to appear 'dazzling white.' To help understand a possible mechanism for

---

191 William Tiller, 2009, 'A Brief Introduction to Intention-Host Device Research', White Paper #1, The William A Tiller Foundation.

such high-power transmission, I introduce the observation by Leonardo da Vinci. Standing by a still pond of water, he took two pebbles of equal mass, one in each hand, and held them at the same height before dropping them at exactly the same instant into the water. He observed two sets of ripples, one set of concentric waves emanating from each pebble impact with the water. Significantly, the ripple interactions, as they crossed into each other, produced reinforcement and smooth flow in the space between the two impact points. Repeating the experiment with pebbles with non-equal mass and from different arm heights, he noticed the intersecting waves produced turbulence between the impact points.

Using quantum holography (see appendix 7.5) to replicate the same experience observed by da Vinci, we find the resulting hologram (Fig. 8.2) based on two interpenetrating wave fields and radiating synchronised oscillations at the same energy frequency and amplitude can interpenetrate each other and produce an enhanced tunnel effect that facilitates very increased flows of information.

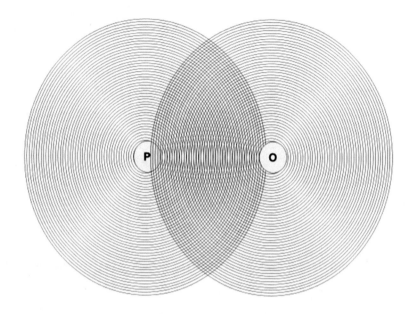

Figure 8.2. A channel of coherent interaction is created between a percipient
(P) and an object (O) when their two interpenetrating wavefields are
radiating synchronised oscillations at the same energy frequency

In addition, associated, 'quantum coherence' occurs when the
subatomic emissions from macro-scale objects are not random,
but exhibit coherence at the quantum level, reflective of an
object's material organisation and event history.[192,193]

This finding provides confirmation that when two 'intention'-
linked sources are in a coherent relationship of energetic
resonance between themselves—that the source quantum wave
field (here God the Holy Spirit) and the attentional wave field of

192 Bradley, R. T. (2006). The psychophysiology of entrepreneurial intuition: A quantum-
holographic theory. 3rd AGSERE, UNITEC, Auckland, NZ.
193 Schempp, W. (1992). Quantum holography and neurocomputer architectures, J. of
Mathematical Imaging and Vision, 2: 109–164.

the receiver (Jesus the man) are locked in a resonant feedback loop with Jesus able to receive and process both the nonlocal information and power transfer, possibly through a reverse Fourier transform process. Indeed, the process of transfiguration is central to spirituality. It is one thing to believe in the power of love, another to feel it in one's body as one gets caught up in the worship of the God of love. When we invite these energies to become present in our bodies, they subtly alter the way we habitually respond in the world. This is the power of spiritual practice; it is the journey of moving our lofty spiritual ideals from our imaginations into our everyday body experiences.

3. Luke 9:29—'The appearance of his face changed'; Matthew 17:2—'And his face shone like the sun'

Specifically, the glory of Jesus was observed by His very face shining like the sun. The Apostles clearly recognised Jesus in a way they had not seen before. Shining like the sun implies His face was glowing strongly with a golden hue in keeping with the concept of 'glory'. But can humans glow like the sun? Research shows biophoton emission or ultra-weak photon emission (UPE) is the spontaneous emission generated by all living systems without an external excitation.[194] Indeed, we are more than the atoms and molecules that make up our bodies, but human beings in which light, as well as biophotons, are emitted by the human body. The body emits visible light, but it is 1,000 times less intense than the levels to which our naked eyes are sensitive. This is why we do not see this photon emission. Recently, Kobayashi has actually managed to photograph the dim glow of humans using an incredibly sensitive camera by detecting light at the level of a

---

194 Fernando Ortega-Ojeda, Matías Calcerrada, Alejandro Ferrero, Joaquín Campos, and Carmen Garcia-Ruiz1, 2018, https://www.ncbi.nlm.nih.gov/pmc/articles/PMC5948505/.

single photon. These reactions involve fluorophores—molecules that give off photons when they shift from a high-energy 'excited state' to a low-energy 'ground state'. His photos reveal that our faces are the shiniest parts of our bodies, with our mouths and cheeks glowing particularly brightly.[195]

We also know that in earlier and less sophisticated times, Jesus, saints, and spiritual people were depicted with an aura around them. It is possible, artists, being more sensitive to sensing human 'vibes', used to paint them into their religious works. Also, the Kirlian photographic process (invented in 1939 by Semyon Davidovitch Kirlian), is a technique that involves shooting a high voltage charge through an object that is connected to a photographic plate that records (captures) the phenomenon of electrical coronal discharges around living and inanimate objects.[196] The resulting image typically includes a coloured 'aura' around the object and was claimed to represent the 'life force' of the object being photographed. Scientists today generally believe that these observed physical phenomena are of the corona plasma discharge rather than showing life forces. They point out that even inanimate objects appear to have 'auras' and point to methodological errors in the 'torn leaf' experiment showing the pre-existing half of the leaf before being torn off. No-one denies that these auras really do appear, but scientists believe that they reveal water molecules surrounding the object. This explains the diminishing aura as the leaf dries out in the first experiment. Significantly, the Kirlian effect is not observed when

195 Kobayashi, M., Kikuchi, D., & Okamura, H. (2009). Imaging of Ultraweak Spontaneous Photon Emission from Human Body Displaying Diurnal Rhythm PLoS ONE, 4 (7) DOI: 10.1371/journal.pone.0006256.

196 Rachael Towne, 2020, 'What is Kirlian Photography? Aura Photography Revealed', https://www.lightstalking.com/what-is-kirlian-photography-the-science-and-the-myth-revealed/.

performed in a vacuum with no water vapour present to be ionised in the high-voltage discharge of the Kirlian photo process.

As established in the text (Luke 9:28), Jesus was in direct communion (focused human intention) with God the Holy Spirit and, as demonstrated above, real quantum energy was available from the Spirit. This extra energy would be available to boost the energetic chemical reactions involving fluorophores—the molecules that give off biophoton emission within Jesus the man so His face would 'shine like the sun' and demonstrate His glory. Kobayashi observed that our faces are the shiniest parts of our bodies, with our mouths and cheeks glowing particularly brightly.

Significantly, from appendix 7.2 and based on the experiments of William Tiller, we showed that focused human intention could affect an increase in the energy levels of a living system. For this experiment, Tiller used the fruit fly (*Drosophila*) to prove that intention could benefit a living system, under laboratory conditions, and with controls. Tiller's intention read 'To increase the ratio of the cell's energy storage molecule, adenosine triphosphate (ATP), to its chemical precursor, adenosine diphosphate (ADP), such that the larval developmental time to adult is twenty-five percent shorter or better' when compared to standard developmental times. After 28 days of exposure to the 'intention', Tiller found that the ratio [ATP/ADP] increased by ~20% with $p < 0.001$.

This experiment on a living system, with a fruit-fly sharing an astounding sixty percent of human DNA, gives real confidence in understanding both the role and the capacity for application of 'focused intention' to massively increase energy production in biophoton excitation such that Jesus truly glowed and for the disciples 'to see His glory.'

Conclusion

From the observations reported in the Gospels of the transfiguration of Jesus on Mt Tabor, where Jesus was in deep prayer, and the theory of quantum entanglement can explain the reality of 'talking with God', we can confidently conclude Jesus the man and God the Spirit were in lock-step during the communication, talking together, yet totally independent of the distance separating them. This understanding is in itself a 'miracle' as it confirms how we as Christians can 'talk with God' or commune together in spirit independent of any physical or celestial distance, time or place. However, the research identified above indicates that such communion is not 'hit-or-miss' or 'when I get the urge', but dependent on establishing a sincere, purposeful, and persistent 'intention' that I call 'focused prayer'.

The wonder in these teachings from the Gospels is that the transfiguration is a pivotal moment, at a specific time in Jesus' ministry, and the setting on the mountain is identified as the point where human nature meets God: the meeting place of the temporal and the eternal, with Jesus himself as the connecting point, demonstrating His glory and acting as the bridge between heaven and earth. The transfiguration not only supports the identity of Jesus as the Son of God (as in his baptism), but the statement 'listen to him' identifies him as the messenger and mouthpiece of God. The significance of this identification is enhanced by the presence of Elijah and Moses, for it indicates to the apostles that Jesus is the voice of God 'par excellence', and instead of Moses or Elijah representing the Law and the prophets, He should be listened to, surpassing the laws of Moses by virtue of his divinity and filial relationship with God. God assigns to Jesus a special 'honour and glory' and it is the turning point at which God exalts Jesus above all other powers in creation, and positions Him for eternal leadership.

With this understanding of the meaning and timing of the Transfiguration, or 'miracle', it is not inappropriate to ask, 'how was such a glorious change in Jesus' being and dress possible?' Extending the reality (based on quantum mechanics and subtle energies discussed in Chapter 7) that human beings have both the capacity and means to enter into a spiritually based 'focused intention' to effect a change in matter around us, we can conclude the following:

Focused intention

It is both possible and probable that Jesus, whilst on the mountain with His Apostles, used a time of deep prayer to establish a 'focused intention' to commune with God the Holy Spirit. In this state, an 'information' channel (conduit) was created with God the Spirit and the subtle energies 'flowed' (independent of distance, time or place) such that the material molecules of the fabric were excited to the point where they 'dazzled white'.

Information Channel

Similarly, in this state of 'focused intention', an 'information' channel (conduit) was created with God the Spirit and the subtle energies 'flowed' (independent of distance, time or place) such that the biophotons in the face of Jesus were further energised to a level where His face shone to demonstrate His glory.

Interfacing with God

This explanation preserves the fact that Jesus remains fully man, yet with the capacity and relationship to interface with God the Holy Spirit and so access all the elements of creation. Significantly, this 'miracle' experience is available to all in a relationship with God through Jesus, even if more weakly. Importantly, this conclusion helps us to understand the true worth of those saints that exercised and those still exercising this relationship today including the blessings and power from a close and personal relationship with God.

This example of Jesus using the principles of physics and chemistry in no way minimises faith but rather engenders a response of worship and attitude of awe at the amazing spiritual heritage available to spiritually enlivened humans.

Chapter 9: Case #2—Jesus Turning Water into Wine

The fairest thing we can experience is the mysterious. It is the fundamental emotion which stands at the cradle of true art and true science. Whoever knows it not and can no longer feel amazement, is as good as dead, a snuffed-out candle.[197]

—Albert Einstein

I am encouraged in this review of miracle case studies by the argument of CS Lewis and presented in his book *God in the Dock*.

The experience of a miracle in fact requires two conditions. First we must believe in normal stability of nature, which means we must recognise the data offered by our senses recur in regular patterns. Secondly, we must believe in some reality beyond Nature. When both beliefs are held, and not till then, we can approach with an open mind the various reports that this super- or extra- natural reality has sometimes invaded and disturbed the sensuous content of space-time which make our natural world.[198]

---

197 A Einstein, *The World As I See It*, translated from *Mein Weldbilt* by Alan Harris, Philosophical Library, 2011 (originally published 1934).

198 C. S. Lewis, 1970, 'God in the Dock', William B Eerdmans Publishing, Cambridge, UK.

Indeed, the concepts discussed in Chapter 7, 'Entrepreneur mindset and the Reality of Spirit Power', provide an insight into 'ethereal' reality (reciprocal space), in parallel with physical reality, as a basis for reality beyond the senses-driven physical reality.

Significantly, Lewis[198] reminds us that in the natural world of grapevine horticulture, we observe the vine does turn water into wine. A literal grapevine takes water from beneath the ground and as the water goes up the vine, it is transformed. It then spreads out into the branches and the branches burst forth with the fruit (grapes). When the grapes are cared for and aged properly, they are used to make sweet wine. But Jesus is not a literal grapevine, is he?[199] So, when at the Cana wedding, Jesus turns water into wine, the mask is off. The miracle has only half its effect if it only convinces us that Jesus the man is God: it will have its full effect if whenever we see a vineyard or drink a glass of wine, we remember that it was Jesus who sat at the wedding party in Cana and showed His full authority over nature.

So, to seek understanding of this first amazing sign and wonder, performed by Jesus in the presence of wedding guests, the disciples and perhaps extended family members, I propose we take you on a journey to Cana in Galilee and, in spirit, to 'observe' the progress of this event.

---

199 Chris Kidd, 2015, 'The True Meaning of Turning Water into Wine', http://madeworthy. com/jesus-turns-water-into-wine/.

Text and Analysis

John 2: 1-11
1. On the third day there was a marriage at Cana in Galilee, and the mother of Jesus was there;
2. *Jesus also was invited to the marriage, with his disciples.*
3. When the wine gave out, *the mother of Jesus said to him, 'They have no wine.'*
4. And Jesus said to her, *'O woman, what have you to do with me? My hour has not yet come.'*
5. His mother said to the servants, *'Do whatever he tells you.'*
6. Now *six stone jars were standing there, for the Jewish rites of purification,* each holding twenty or thirty gallons.
7. Jesus said to them, *'Fill the jars with water.'* And they filled them up to the brim.
8. He said to them, *'Now draw some out, and take it to the steward of the feast.'* So they took it.
9. When the *steward of the feast tasted the water now become wine, and did not know where it came from* (though the servants who had drawn the water knew), the *steward of the feast called the bridegroom*
10. and said to him, *'Every man serves the good wine first; and when men have drunk freely, then the poor wine; but you have kept the good wine until now.'*
11. This, the first of his signs, Jesus did at Cana in Galilee, *and manifested his glory; and his disciples believed in him.*

There is little doubt that the story of Jesus, as told by John, was the first miracle performed by Him after His baptism by John the Baptist. We can also note that the disciples attending the wedding with Jesus numbered five: Andrew, Simon Peter, Phillip, Nathanael, with one anonymous disciple. From John 1:39, we note that the next day after the baptism, two of John the Baptist's disciples went to see where Jesus was staying. One was Andrew, and the second of these disciples, most likely John, transferred from being disciples of John the Baptist to be disciples of Jesus Christ. This helps to explain how the author (John the Apostle) knows all the details of what is going on here. He is an eyewitness to these things.

Where did Jesus turn water into wine?

The town of 'Cana' in our story has been identified as Khirbet Cana, nine miles from Nazareth, in the Lower Galilee, not far from the Jordan River, and also the hometown of Nathanael (John 21:2). According to archaeologist Tom McCollough, this site offers the most compelling evidence that the Cana of Galilee is indeed Khirbet Cana.[200] Khirbet Cana was a modest, well-connected Jewish village in the Hellenistic and Roman periods (323 BCE–324 CE). Archaeology has confirmed the presence of a Roman-period synagogue, several Jewish ritual baths and stone purification jars, and six Maccabean coins and an ostracon incised with Hebrew letters.

Invitation to the wedding: verses 1–3
Indeed, wedding ceremonies at the time of Jesus were always accompanied by celebratory feasts and were important in Jewish culture.[201]

According to the custom, wedding celebrations normally lasted seven days [...] Although wine was a standard part of daily life in the ancient Mediterranean world,

200 Robin Ngo, 2020, 'Where Did Jesus Turn Water into Wine?', https://www. biblicalarchaeology.org/daily/biblical-sites-places/biblical-archaeology-places/where-did-jesus-turn-water-into-wine/.
201 Edward W. Klink III, 2017, 'An Exegetical Reading of the Wedding at Cana (John 2:1-11)', https://zondervanacademic.com/blog/an-exegetical-reading-of-the-wedding-at-cana-john-21-11-an-excerpt-from-john.

Jewish literature makes clear that wine was an important part of festive occasions, especially at weddings. Since weddings in the first century were not about two people but about two families, the social dynamics were more comprehensive and intense. For this reason, to run out of wine during the wedding celebration was likely to have caused a loss of family honor and status.[201]

It has been suggested that Jesus and His mother were most likely present because of family connections to either the bride or groom (a sister or a brother). The attendance of the disciples is more problematical, but they may have been included along with their 'teacher' or one regarded as a scholar/rabbi in the community.

Jesus, His mother, and shortage of wine: verse 4

For the Jews, wine was a symbol of God's blessing and was part of any joyous celebration, particularly a wedding feast. To run out of wine would be a supreme embarrassment to family honour but also considered rude to the guests. Clearly, Mary, referred to in verse 3 as the mother of Jesus, as she is throughout John's gospel, seeks to find a solution to the problem. Again, we do not know her exact role in the wedding, but she has some role in helping in the feast, as seen in her action to resolve this problem of running out of wine and her authority over the servants in verse 5. When she becomes aware that there is no more wine, she goes to Jesus to inform Him. Her statement is straightforward and factual. They have no wine. She does not tell Jesus what to do, nor does she even ask Him to do something. She simply informs Him of the problem. Jesus is her son, but He is an adult, not a child. Mary treats Him with respect due to Him being an adult and in this case, also a respected rabbi.

From purification water to celebratory wine: verses 5–8

The jars described here are not pottery but stone. They were most likely the storage jars and not the smaller pottery types used for carrying water from the well to the home. Such stone jars have been found in Capernaum within the synagogue (around 3 CE), and in the old city of Jerusalem (1 CE). They held about twenty gallons (US) (seventy-five litres) and were covered by a flat piece of stone. Clearly, the servants would require a number of trips to the water source to fill these jars. John notes that such jars were used to hold water for ceremonial washing or purification. Before a meal, servants (or perhaps the host) would pour water over the hands of each of the guests. Such custom is confirmed in Mark 7:3: 'the Pharisees and all the Jews do not eat unless they give their hands a ceremonial washing, holding to the tradition of the elders.' Much water would already have been drawn from the jars to rinse the hands of guests at the wedding feast. This suggests there was some time between when Jesus told them 'to fill the jars' and when wine was brought to the steward.

From first sign of Jesus' glory: verses 9–11

It is clear that the new wine brought to the 'MC' or 'toastmaster' of the feast was of amazing quality, bouquet, and taste, and certainly not 'fruit juice', for he comments to the bridegroom 'you have kept the good wine until now' (verse 10). The point, of course, is that the wine Jesus has created is not only abundant—120 gallons or so—but the finest of wine! A real miracle. Figure 9.1 displays the significant elements of this 'miracle.'[202]

The ending of this story is well expressed by Twelftree as saying it reveals more than 'this sign revealed Jesus' glory and that His disciples believed in Him (verse 11)' when note is taken

202 Giotto di Bondone, 14th Century, Marriage at Cana - Wikipedia.

of John's reference to this being the first of His signs to reveal His glory.

> *As we have noted, for John the suffering, death, and resurrection reveal Jesus' glory most clearly. However, this is one of a number of clear statements in John that show he saw the miracles pointing to the glory of Jesus, no less than the suffering, death, resurrection and Parousia. The believing response of the disciples to the miracle is an echo of the response of the disciples to the sign of the resurrection (John 28: 8, 29, 31), reinforcing the importance of the miracles, alongside the resurrection, as a legitimate basis for faith. They are a legitimate basis of faith because the signs show that 'all previous religious institutions, customs, and feasts lose meaning in His presence'.* [203]

---

203 Graham Twelftree, 1999, 'Jesus the Miracle Worker' pp 196. Intervarsity Press, IL. USA.

Figure 9.1. Marriage at Cana by Giotto di Bondone, 14th century

Miracle Elements and Scientific Explanation

During our review of Jesus (Chapter 5), we concluded He exhibited an outstanding social entrepreneur mindset. We also noted that such a mindset was characterised by a strong propensity for spiritual behaviour within the dimension of 'awareness'. Subsequent to His baptism, descent of the Holy Spirit, and forty days in communion with God (in focused intention) through prayer, fasting, and deep communion, it can be reasonably asserted Jesus had established his commitment to and outworking of the 'intention' concept (understanding explained in Chapter 7) as, in this case, practised at the wedding feast in Cana. At the feast, we note 'Jesus completed the first of His signs [...] and manifested His glory' (John 2:11) and, significantly, 'His disciples believed in Him.'

Twelftree affirms

> *the nature miracles point beyond themselves to the true identity or glory of Jesus and His filial relationship, or even identify, with the Father—and also in the various expressions of the salvific gift He brings. For the Fourth Gospel (John) the signs, including the nature miracles are a basis of faith.*[204]

From the mathematics and experiments of Tiller, as reported in his book *Conscious Acts of Creation*,[205] we note that, in the development of the 'focused human intention state', 'there is a fundamental change in the electromagnetic nature of the space associated with the conditioning process—due to a DC magnetic field polarity effect.' Tiller is talking about a monopole effect, a singular signature of conditioned space. This conditioned space (i.e., space surrounding where the focused human intention was created) is different from ordinary space.

Tiller, and his fellow experimenters, conclusively report that when standing in 'conditioned space' (space used previously to develop 'intention') 'there seems to be a vibrancy, a certain aliveness, and a warmth [...] the feeling is like *you are standing in hallowed space.*'[206] Importantly, their experiments also show

---

204 Graham Twelftree, 2017, 'The Nature Miracles of Jesus', Cascade Books, Wipf and stock Publishers, Eugene, Oregon, USA.

205 William Tiller, Walter Dibble, and Michael Kohane, 2001, 'Conscious Acts of Creation: The Emergence of a New Physics', Pavior.

206 Nisha Manek, 2019, 'Bridging Science and Spirit' pp. 211 Conscious Creation LLC.

that when the 'intention creator' moves to another space to apply the intention, the 'conditioned space' reality is established within the new space instantaneously. With this understanding, it is reasonable to claim that Jesus (already holding a focused intention), and on entering the wedding feast, brought with His presence the very means to create 'conditioned space' and thus provide the environment in which to demonstrate a 'sign' in turning water into quality wine.

Important to our seeking to understand the energy and chemical processes involved in this 'sign', we need, firstly, to stand back in awe at the reality of Jesus producing this dramatic change, on command, and at the very time it was needed—the wine supply had run out. As noted in the comments on the text, 'to run out of wine' would cause a loss of honour for the bride's family. Clearly, Jesus' mother, aware of the situation, did not command Jesus to overcome the problem but instructed the servants, 'Do whatever he tells you.' Indeed, this filling of the stone jars with water and then pouring out high-quality wine was a true 'sign and wonder'. In attempting to review the possible energy and chemical processes associated with this 'wonder', I propose to look at the underlying physics concerning three aspects of the story:

Ordinary and conditioned space

In this description, 'ordinary space' (which we are all familiar with) is the familiar four-dimension world of matter (all elementary particles). Its governing forces, such as electromagnetism and gravity, complete the standard model. Tiller's research has found and proved that when an 'intention' (initially to change pH of water by more than 1 pH unit) is repeated numerous times in this same 'ordinary' space, eventually the intention becomes a 'permanent' feature of the space which is then called 'conditioned' space. When that happens, the laws of physics in that conditioned space no longer operate as they did before! This result points to a new dimension of reality having magnetic wave information characteristics, but not material (elementary particle) stuff. Tiller calls this new expression of 'gauge symmetry' to that in ordinary space 'reciprocal' space. In technical terms, the reciprocal space pilot waves guide the ordinary space particles and matter such as electrons. The waves in this Tiller model are superluminal, faster than the speed of light, and have a magnetic nature.

An illustration of this relationship between ordinary and reciprocal space is found in a mirror image.

> *If you reflect, say. Your home in a mirror, you can plot each point from its original ordinary space location to its matching mirror-image location in reciprocal space. The twist here is that reciprocal space is a reciprocal variation of ordinary space. By plotting the ordinary space data points - height, depth, and length on a graph—and apply a reciprocal function—1/height, 1/depth, and 1/length, you will get a mirror-like symmetry.[206]*

Significantly, we can see that as measurements in the denominator of reciprocal space increase, the reciprocal space becomes smaller, and in the extreme, reaches infinity. The bridge between the subtle energies of reciprocal space and the ordinary (physical) space is the magnetic vector potential.

Tiller's mathematics and experiments demonstrate the conditioning results from producing domains of order in the vacuum! This is not an 'empty' vacuum but contains dense energy potential. In ordinary space, that potential is chaotic and amorphous. But, in the ordered reciprocal space, a change takes place in which the symmetry actually changes the state of the particles that make up ordinary (physical) reality. And since Tiller has shown that the order thus created in the vacuum is based upon human intent, this shows that we can actually harness the power of the vacuum through our consciousness. This theory and related experiments provide a physics understanding of the created principles to exercises Jesus' 'intention' to deliver signs and wonders.

From such experiments, we can see that energy is transferred during the intention creation to effect produced processes of change in matter. But how large is this potential energy within the 'vacuum stuff' from the underlying background energy that exists in space throughout the entire Universe? They are connected. The answer to this begins with the understanding that the vacuum is not empty or void. It's empty only of physical matter (particles) but, the vacuum contains 'energy density'. Theoretical measures of these energies range from 'near to zero', 'indeterminate', or 'enormous but finite'. It is noted that for quantum mechanics and relativity theory to be internally self-consistent, the calculations require that the vacuum must contain an enormous but finite energy density.

If human consciousness, and in our study Jesus, can interact with this large energy reservoir around us, then even a little bit of that is energy quanta can be intentionally directed to bring about change in matter and nature.

Acidity level of water and wine

From the science discussed above, we have discovered that there are actually two levels of physical reality (ordinary and reciprocal) and not just the one with which we are all familiar (ordinary). It is this new level of physical reality (reciprocal) that can be significantly influenced by human intention—not the familiar electric atom/molecule level! The two basic kinds of unique substances (particles and waves) inhabiting these two levels of physical reality appear to interpenetrate each other but, normally, they do not interact with each other. Tiller (appendix 7.2) labels this state as the 'uncoupled state' of physical reality. In the uncoupled state, with one's five physical senses, we can detect our normal physical environment all around us. However, this new level of substance, because it appears to function in the physical vacuum (the empty space between the fundamental electric particles that make up our normal electric atoms and molecules), is currently invisible to us and to our traditional measurement instruments. As noted above, this substance appears to be of a magnetic information-wave nature.

In John 2:7, Jesus instructed the servants to fill the jars with water. In this miracle, the starting point is water, and for the springs of Cana with a pH, it is assumed, to be around 6.8 (allowing for some salinity). For winemakers, the pH of wine is critical not only to its flavour but to nearly every aspect of the wine and they seek to achieve a pH of around 3.4 for quality wines. This standard would suggest the wine created by Jesus' miracle would be in the range of 3.4, requiring a significant change in pH units of around 3 units: a very significant change.

In Tiller's first target experiment (appendix 7.2), the intention was 'to increase the pH of a vessel of water in equilibrium with air at room temperature by +1.0 pH units' with no chemical additions and the measurement accuracy of ±0.02 pH units. This is a massive change in internal energy. Within three days, the increase had been successfully achieved—a result which was 100 times larger than the noise level. The second target experiment was with water in equilibrium with air at room temperature, but the intention was to decrease the pH by ~1.0 pH units, again with no chemical additions. Once again, this experiment was successful. Similar successful results have been obtained for a variety of water types. Clearly, 'intention' can play a very significant role in changing the pH of water by at least two pH units both to alkaline and acid outcomes. Fluctuations in pH could mean the difference between a wine going down the sink and one you hang a double gold medal on.

Enzymes that catalyse molecular change

Sugars in wine are at the heart of what makes winemaking possible. During the process of fermentation, sugars from wine grapes are broken down and converted by yeast into alcohol (ethanol) and carbon dioxide. Grapes accumulate sugars as they grow on the grapevine through the translocation of sucrose molecules that are produced by photosynthesis from the leaves. During ripening, the sucrose molecules are hydrolysed (separated) by the enzyme invertase into glucose and fructose. Invertase is the enzyme that catalyses the hydrolysis of sucrose with a resulting mixture of fructose and glucose, which is called invert sugar.

Significantly, an enzyme is a complex protein produced by living cells that promotes specific biochemical reactions by acting as a catalyst. For the case of the Tiller experiment on enzymes, we refer to the experiment using the material medium of an in-vitro biological molecule: alkaline phosphatase (ALP), a liver enzyme. The intention was to increase the chemical activity of ALP by a significant amount via just exposing the ALP for a period of thirty minutes to its intention-host within the 'conditioned' space that had been brought to the coupled state. Once again, the experimental results were remarkably successful compared to the built-in controls. About a 25%–30% increase in ALP chemical activity was achieved at $p<0.001$.

These two experiments—changing the pH of water and enhancing the chemical activity of an enzyme, which have been replicated in other laboratories both in the USA and Europe—spectacularly confirm not simply the creation of an 'intention', but the fact that such changes included in the intention can produce outcomes equal to that specified in the intention. It is reasonable to conclude that Jesus used His conscious powers to effect the turning of water into wine miracle through the created principles of the natural world. That Jesus was able to achieve this miracle to meet a social need, and at the time required, only enhances our belief and wonder in Jesus as both fully man and fully God.

In summary, C S Lewis says:

If we open such books as Grimm's Fairy Tales, or the Italian Epics, we find ourselves in a world of miracles so diverse that they can hardly be classified. Beasts turn into men and men into beasts, or trees. Trees talk, ships become goddesses, and a magic ring can cause tables richly to spread with food to appear in solitary places... If such things really happen, they would, I suppose, show that nature was being invaded. But they would show she was being invaded by an alien power. The fitness of the Christian miracles, and their difference from those mythological miracles, lies in the fact that they show invasion by a power which is not alien. They are what might be expected to happen when she is invaded not simply by a god, but by the God of nature; by a power which is outside her jurisdiction; not as a foreigner but as a Sovereign. They proclaim that he who has come is not merely a king, but the King, and the King of nature, her King and ours.[207]

---

207 C. S. Lewis, 2001, 'Miracles' Zondervan.

Chapter 10: Case #3—Jesus Walking on Water

In God's eyes, walking on water is no more miraculous
than the ability of haemoglobin to bond with oxygen
inside a red blood corpuscle.

—Deepak Chopra

This nature miracle, 'Jesus walking on water' is perhaps the most challenged as to its authenticity because it goes totally against our own experience of gravity and implausibility for a human to defy the 'pull of gravity'. Perhaps, it is generally accepted that human levitation is untrue because such action defies common sense and contradicts the laws of physics. But this can be argued as unreasonable because common sense is historically and culturally dependent, and the current understanding of science does not know everything there is to learn about physics or human consciousness.

In early Christian writings from the middle of the second century CE to the middle of the third century, the writers assumed these nature miracles to be historical and significant both in terms of who Jesus was but also in meaning and purpose. For Tertullian (160–225 CE), the miracles of nature and the healings were of a piece, part of the picture of Jesus' power. He said, 'Jesus reduced to obedience the very elements of nature, calming storms, walking upon the waters.'[208]

During the period of the Medieval Church, Bonaventure (1221–1274 CE) stressed the spiritual meaning of Jesus walking on water in terms of 'the destination of the boat as *heavenly homeland*; disciples travelled in the *boat of penance* through the bitter sea of tribulation, buffeted by the *winds of temptation*,' whereas Thomas Aquinas (1224–1274) followed Augustine, in 'describing a miracle as an exciting wonder, not because it is contrary to nature, but because it was beyond our knowledge of nature.'[209] Aquinas considered the miracles to be historical.

The reformers (the Reformation: sixteenth to seventeenth century CE) emphasised their understanding to be that the nature miracles reflected the divinity of Jesus. Calvin (1509–1564 CE) highlighted 'that the disciples believed in Jesus as a result of turning water into wine shows that the miracle was intended for the confirmation and progress of the faith.'[210]

During the eighteenth and nineteenth centuries CE, theological and philosophical views on the reality and or meaning of the nature miracles were based on one's opinions and actions concerning reason and knowledge rather than on religious belief or emotional response. The dispute between rationalism and empiricism takes place within epistemology, the branch of philosophy devoted to studying the nature, sources, and limits of knowledge. Rationalists claim that there are significant ways in which our concepts and knowledge are gained independently of

---

208 Graham Twelftree, 2017, quoted in 'The Nature Miracles of Jesus' pp. 15, Cascade Books, Eugene, OR.

209 Graham Twelftree, 2017, quoted in 'The Nature Miracles of Jesus' pp. 20–21, Cascade Books, Eugene, OR.

210 Graham Twelftree, 2017, quoted in 'The Nature Miracles of Jesus' pp. 23, Cascade Books, Eugene, OR.

sensory experience. Empiricists claim that sensory experience is the ultimate source of all our concepts and knowledge. During this period, Paulus (1761–1851 CE), when commenting on the historicity of Jesus, demonstrated strong rationalist arguments.

> *In the case of the story of Jesus walking on the water, the disciples had a vision. For Jesus was walking alone on the shore. Through the mist Jesus was taken for a ghost. However, when Jesus called him, Peter jumped into the water. Just as he was sinking Jesus dragged him into the shore.*[211]

Strauss (1808–1874 CE), a German theologian, 'set aside the rationalism of Paulus as a half-measure that did not take the text seriously.'[212] Strauss applied a mythological explanation to the miracle stories. Regarding Peter 'walking on water', Strauss called it 'an allegorical and mythological representation of that trial of faith which this disciple, who imagined himself so strong, met so weakly, and which higher assistance alone enabled him to surmount.'

By the time of the twentieth century CE, empiricism and experimentation were the basis for rapid development of our understanding of nature and the universe. But significantly, it is not complete. The history of science, especially of the physical and biological sciences, is presented as a progressive accumulation of knowledge, in which true theories replaced false beliefs. But even advanced experiments using the most sophisticated measuring techniques and instruments have not delivered complete knowledge

---

211 Graham Twelftree, 2017, quoted in 'The Nature Miracles of Jesus' pp. 25, Cascade Books, Eugene, OR.
212 Graham Twelftree, 2017, quoted in 'The Nature Miracles of Jesus' pp. 26, Cascade Books, Eugene, OR.

to explain the factual base of 'miracles'. Eminent scientists have varying perspectives and interpretations of 'miracles', particularly those with associations to the Bible and ministry of Jesus.

There is anecdotal evidence that Albert Einstein asked—'Do you believe in miracles? Well, you should. In fact, life itself is a big miracle. There are so many things that are beyond our understanding. There are two ways to live: you can live as if nothing is a miracle; you can live as if everything is a miracle.'[213]

Richard Dawkins has made it his mission to destroy faith in the God of creation and the miracles of Jesus as not based on truth. He says, 'The truth is more magical—in the best and most exciting sense of the word - than any myth or made-up mystery or miracle. Science has its own magic: the magic of reality.'[214]

Colin Humphries, the author of *The Miracles of the Exodus*, established the truthfulness and historicity of these events around the Exodus of Moses and his people from Egypt. By examining the natural events surrounding the Exodus story, he is able to show that such 'miracles' can be explained. The real miracle is not in the explanation of nature but in the timing to suit the needs of the Jewish people to escape Egypt. Using scientific methodology, accepting the biblical text as written, examining historical documents and archaeological evidence, and mathematics to establish event times, he has provided both a rational and empirical understanding of the reality and truthfulness for such miracles.[215]

In the following discussion, the principles used by Humphreys will be used to explain a probable physical mechanism for Jesus

---

213 Albert Einstein, Quote, http://www.gurteen.com/gurteen/gurteen.nsf/id/X00405372/.

214 Richard Dawkins, 2011, 'The Magic of Reality: How We Know What's Really True', p.266, Simon and Schuster.

215 Colin Humphreys, 2003, 'The Miracles of the Exodus – A Scientists Discovery of the Extraordinary' Harper Collins, New York.

walking on water. More importantly, is the timing of the event and the resultant effect on the disciples' faith and appreciation that Jesus was the Son of God.

Text and Analysis:

Matthew 14:22-33	Mark 6:45-52	John 6:16-21
22. Then he made the disciples get into the boat and go before him to the other side, while he dismissed the crowds.	45. Immediately he made his disciples get into the boat and go before him to the other side, to Bethsaida, while he dismissed the crowd.	16. When evening came, his disciples went down to the sea,
23. And after he had dismissed the crowds, he went up on the mountain by himself to pray. When evening came, he was there alone,	46. And after he had taken leave of them, he went up on the mountain to pray.	17. got into a boat, and started across the sea to Capernaum. It was now dark, and Jesus had not yet come to them.
24. but the boat by this time was many furlongs distant from the land, beaten by the waves; for the wind was against them.	47. And when evening came, the boat was out on the sea, and he was alone on the land.	18. The sea rose because a strong wind was blowing.

25. And in the fourth watch of the night he came to them, walking on the sea.	48. And he saw that they were making headway painfully, for the wind was against them. And about the fourth watch of the night he came to them, walking on the sea. He meant to pass by them,	19. When they had rowed about three or four miles, they saw Jesus walking on the sea and drawing near to the boat. They were frightened,
26. But when the disciples saw him walking on the sea, they were terrified, saying, 'It is a ghost!' and they cried out for fear.	49. but when they saw him walking on the sea they thought it was a ghost, and cried out;	20. but he said to them, 'It is I; do not be afraid.'
27. But immediately he spoke to them, saying, 'Take heart, it is I; have no fear.'	50. for they all saw him, and were terrified. But immediately he spoke to them and said, 'Take heart, it is I; have no fear.'	21. Then they were glad to take him into the boat, and immediately the boat was at the land to which they were going.
28. And Peter answered him, 'Lord, if it is you, bid me come to you on the water.'	51. And he got into the boat with them and the wind ceased. And they were utterly astounded,	
29. He said, 'Come.' So Peter got out of the boat and walked on the water and came to Jesus;	52. for they did not understand about the loaves, but their hearts were hardened.	

30. but when he saw the wind, he was afraid, and beginning to sink he cried out, 'Lord, save me.'		
31. Jesus immediately reached out his hand and caught him, saying to him, 'O man of little faith, why did you doubt?'		
32. And when they got into the boat, the wind ceased.		
33. And those in the boat worshiped him, saying, 'Truly you are the Son of God.'		

The story unfolds at Lake Galilee, which lies in the lower portion of the Jordan Valley in a mountain range that rises to 1,200 metres (4,000 feet) above sea level. The lake itself is 215 metres (700 feet) below the Mediterranean Sea. One of the more noteworthy aspects of this body of water is that it is fresh water and is greatly susceptible to sudden and extremely violent storms. These storms are caused by the cold air rushing down from the mountains surrounding it and colliding with the warm, moist air rising off the surface of the water itself. The lake is about twenty-one kilometres (thirteen miles) long and thirteen kilometres (eight miles) wide.

Getting into a boat

As the leader of the mission, Jesus directed the disciples to 'get into the boat and go before him to the other side'—the text makes clear that this exit happened prior to Jesus dismissing the crowds attending His preaching and the subsequent 'feeding of the 5,000'. Israeli archaeologists have found a mosaic floor design depicting the feeding of the 5,000 in the remains of a church at Hippos, on the eastern side of Lake Galilee, and burned down during the Sasanian conquest of the city in 614 CE. Hippos is on the side of a hill close to the lake. Jesus specified they sail/row to Bethsaida on the north-west edge of the lake. The disciples were to 'go before Him', no doubt with the expectation they would all meet up in Bethsaida.

The text clearly states Jesus went back to dismiss the crowd after 'perceiving that they were about to come and take him by force, to make him king.' It is likely that by sending His disciples away, the people would accept the event was over and disperse. Significantly, Jesus 'withdrew again into the mountain himself alone'—no doubt to commune with the Holy Spirit and, we can assume, to recharge His energy and inner power.

In the middle of the lake

We note the text is very specific that, 'when evening came', and after Jesus had returned to the shore, He saw 'they were making headway painfully, for the wind was against them.' Not only have they been awake many hours, but also it is exhausting work to keep a small boat bailed and on course in the middle of the sea— in the midst of a storm. All the texts state the boat was close to the middle of the lake, some 6 kms (3.5 miles) off the shore. They were certainly not close to the shoreline.

Jesus walking on the sea

The text indicates this was 'in the fourth watch of the night', (3 to 6 am), and 'He came to them, walking on the sea. He meant to pass by them.' The common emphasis from each of the three Gospel accounts leaves no doubt that Jesus was out near the boat, some six kilometres off the shore and nowhere close to the water's edge. We, as readers, are left with no doubt that the passage means walking on deepwater and not paddling at the lake's edge.

Figure 10.1. Christ walking on the Sea of Galilee by Anonymous, twentieth century[216]

---

216 Anonymous, 'Christ walking on the Sea of Galilee'.

Importantly, there were twelve eyewitnesses and no doubt the disciples discussed the experience with the writers of the Gospels. Figure 10.1 depicts an artist's view of Jesus walking on water.

Disciples terrified—a ghost!

It is not surprising the disciples least expected to see Jesus on the water at four in the morning. It is natural they were terrified and expressed that terror: 'It is a ghost and they cried out for fear.' They clearly had not recognised it was Jesus as He approached them from the shore.

Be not afraid

Interestingly, Jesus had recognised their fear and immediately sought to reassure them by saying, 'Take heart, it is I; have no fear.' There was no mistaking that voice, and it brought great assurance. This experience is available to all followers of Jesus Christ.

Peter walks and sinks

This is, in part, the story of Peter, an impetuous man whose spontaneity is not matched by his stability. He needs personal assurance and calls out, 'Lord, if it is you, bid me come to you on the water.' Jesus, in full recognition of Peter's spontaneity, said, 'Come.' So Peter got out of the boat and walked on water and came to Jesus; but when he saw the wind, he was afraid, and, beginning to sink, he cried out, 'Lord, save me.' Jesus immediately reached out his hand and caught him, saying to him, 'O man of little faith, why did you doubt?' There is little doubt this example of walking on water when Peter's eyes stayed on Jesus and sinking when distracted would have been uppermost amongst the disciples after they reached the shore. It was after this exchange that the disciples welcomed Jesus into the boat and the wind ceased—another miracle where Jesus influences natural occurrences.

Truly the Son of God

In Mark's account, we read the disciples 'hardened their hearts' after the miracle of feeding the 5,000, whereas in Matthew, we read 'those in the boat worshipped him, saying, 'Truly you are the Son of God.'

The disciples showed the hardness of their hearts in that the working of one miracle did not prepare them either to expect or to comprehend any other miracle which followed. They ought to have worshipped Jesus as the Son of God when they saw the five thousand fed, but they did not. But when he had done that and had walked upon the water, and quieted the wind, and transported the boat to the land, they were overcome by the iteration of his miraculous power and confessed his divinity.

This was the first time Jesus was called the 'Son of God' by the disciples.

Miracle Elements and Scientific Explanation

The fundamental principle in scientific research is to continually test hypotheses in order to evolve more toward the 'truth' of the observed behaviours. Science is not about establishing what we should or should not believe, but in the words of the Royal Society of London—'it is to withstand the domination of authority and to verify all statements by an appeal to facts determined by experiment.' With this principle in mind, I again apply the words of Thomas Aquinas, 'describing a miracle as an exciting wonder, not because it is contrary to nature, but because it was beyond our knowledge of nature,' by examining current observations and experiments that describe human levitation.

As noted in the introduction, and during the eighteenth century, theologians and philosophers sought to use rationalism to explain Jesus walking on water rather than accept eyewitness accounts of the reality. In the twentieth century, Vincent Taylor commented, 'the hurried departure of the disciples under the constraint of Jesus, the reference to Bethsaida, the picture of the rowers buffeted by a contrary wind and their cry of fear on seeing Jesus suggested that the narrative had a factual base.'[217] Twelftree, in summing up theological and historical commentaries over the centuries, and approaching the story with the tools and skills of a historian, comments, 'As incredible as the story seems to modern minds, it cannot be ruled out of court as historically unreliable, for even the little information available points to the possibility of historicity.'[218]

Eyewitness Accounts of Consciousness-based Levitation

Besides the twelve disciples who witnessed Jesus' levitation above the water, many saints of the Catholic church are recorded as experiencing levitation. Such examples are important as their occurrence is not only recorded in the documents needed to achieve nomination to sainthood, but the witnesses were also examined, and their statements included in final documents, which exist today.

---

217 Vincent Taylor, 1981, 'The Gospel According to St Mark' pp 326, McMillan, UK.
218 Graham Twelftree, 1999, 'Jesus the Miracle Worker', pp 322, Intervarsity Press, London.

Saint Teresa of Avila (1515–1582)[219]

Her levitation incidents seem to have occurred spontaneously during states of spiritual rapture. Eyewitnesses claim to have seen her hovering a foot and a half above the ground for nearly a half-hour. According to the saint, she was not in control of these episodes, and because of this, they were a little frightening to her. 'It seemed to me when I tried to make some resistance as if a great force beneath my feet lifted me up.'

Saint Joseph of Cupertino (1603–1663)[220]

Saint Joseph was witnessed levitating in prayer so many times that he is regarded as the patron saint of aeroplane passengers. In the mid-1600s, Joseph was seen floating and even flying. His many specific accounts of levitation are affirmed by eyewitness accounts from fellow monks, the congregations he spoke in front of, and even Pope Urban VIII. He was canonised in 1767 by Clement XIII. It is important to note that everything that in any way had reference to God or holy things would bring on an ecstatic state in Cupertino: the sound of a bell or of church music, the mention of the name of God or of the Blessed Virgin or of a saint, any event in the life of Christ, the sacred Passion, a holy picture, the thought of the glory in heaven—all would put Joseph into contemplation. These conditions would occur at any time or place, especially at Mass or during Divine Service being indicative of his state of consciousness and spiritual oneness with the Holy Spirit. In this state, he was frequently observed to levitate, be raised from his feet and remain suspended in the air.

---

219 Saint Teresa, https://www.historydisclosure.com/teresa-de-avila-levitating-saint/.

220 Saint Joseph, http://www.religionfacts.com/library/catholic-encyclopedia/joseph-cupertino-saint.

Douglas D Home (1833–1886)[221]

In 1852, Home first demonstrated self-levitation. It is reported witnesses watched in astonishment as he rose a foot or more above the floor. When they tried to hold him down, they too were lifted off the ground. In a well-lit room before Professor David Wells of Harvard and three other spiritualist investigators, Home caused a table to move all about, even though he stood nowhere near it. It took all the strength of two of the witnesses to restrain the table. Upon its release, the table levitated completely off the floor for several seconds.

In 1871, Home was tested by William Crookes, a respected physicist and fellow of the Royal Society. With a contraption of weights he had devised, Crookes sought to measure the 'power, force or influence, proceeding from his hand.' Crookes measured a force equal to about three-quarters of a pound and was at a complete loss to explain it. Crookes also witnessed Home's levitation, which, he wrote, challenged his 'most firmly rooted articles of scientific belief.'

Buddhist monks[222]

Tibet is home to another mystic culture, with many cases of levitating Buddhist monks, including the great Milarepa. During the thirteenth century, Milarepa was noted as being able to perform many miracles, including the ability to both walk and sleep while levitating. Apparently, the Tibetans are capable of also causing the material surrounding them to float. There are modern accounts where massive blocks of stone were made to

---

221 Douglas D Home, https://www.liveabout.com/incredible-powers-of-daniel-dunglass-home-2596169.

222 https://subtle.energy/human-levitation-saints-yogis-citizens-and-science/.

gently drift in the air through sound vibration alone, utilising a technique called Tibetan Acoustic Levitation.

Laboratory Observation for consciousness-based levitation

In 1970, on a visit to a research laboratory in Moscow, William Tiller observed a demonstration of human activated levitation of a ping-pong ball (Figure 10.2). The experiment was repeated many times. In order to check for the presence of an electromagnetic field around the object, Tiller probed the area around the ball with a galvanometer. Significantly, he could not find any measurements to indicate emf fields. His conclusion was that the energy was being applied in the physical vacuum dimension and consisting of a plenum of negative energy states; i.e., the physical vacuum is not empty but consists of unknown 'stuff'. We will return to this explanation later in the discussion when considering consciousness powered levitation.

Figure 10.2 Nina Kulagina performing psychokinesis on a ping pong ball.[223]

Laboratory Observations for physical theories of levitation

Casimir Force

This energy, predicted seven decades ago by the Dutch scientist Hendrik Casimir, arises from quantum effects and can be seen experimentally by placing two opposing plates very close to each other in a vacuum. At close range, the plates repel each other, which could be useful to certain technologies. Only recently, in 2007, two theoretical physicists at St Andrews University in Scotland announced a major breakthrough which 'elevated levitation from being pure science fiction to science fact.' The scientists, Professor Ulf Leonhardt and Dr Thomas Philbin, were

---

223 James Conrad, 2016, The Ninel Kulagina Telekinesis Case: Rebuttals to Skeptical Arguments (jamesaconrad.com).

able to reverse the quantum mechanical Casimir Force: two atomic-sized objects could be made to repel each other rather than attract. The pair had worked out how to turn the normally 'sticky' quantum force of empty space from attraction to repulsion using a specially developed lens placed between two objects.[224] This experiment shows the possibility to use this 'frictionless' behaviour (levitation) in n micromachinery parts of the very small nanoworld. Experimental evidence for this effect was announced in 2017 when scientists from Princeton University and Hong Kong University of Science and Technology manufactured a clever assembly of micron-sized shapes etched into the plates, which then repelled each other as they are brought close together. However, such experiments are a long way from providing for human levitation but show the way to future possibilities.[225]

Acoustic Levitation

This is a method for suspending matter in air against gravity using acoustic radiation pressure from high-intensity sound waves. Two acoustic horns vibrate in the ultrasound region of 22,000 hertz, firing sound waves into a pocket of air between the two devices. 'When these two waves interact, you'll get what's called a standing wave, so they'll cancel in places and they'll reinforce in others to create nodes and antinodes.'[226] By spraying water into these nodes, one can watch the fluid coalesce into droplets along the string of nodes or point of a 'stationary' wave. In each of these 'pockets' the pull of gravity is cancelled, so achieving acoustic levitation. This has immediate application to the manufacture of specialist pharmaceutical drugs.

224 Scientist float levitation theory | University of St Andrews news (st-andrews.ac.uk).

225 https://phys.org/news/2017-04-harness-mysterious-casimir-tiny-devices.html.

226 https://www.wired.com/story/how-to-levitate-objects-with-sound/.

Although these examples explain how we may be able to design external levitation machines, it doesn't quite explain what is happening within a human body that could cause it to levitate.

Negative Energy Theory for Consciousness-based Levitation

Research shows that human consciousness is both continuous and discrete,[227] with both found to have credibility. This debate was started by Saint Augustine of Hippo (354–430 CE). He believed that humans had a perfect union of soul and body, and that consciousness permeated through us. Augustine said that 'the centre of consciousness, perception, and thought lies in our soul and we should learn to control sensory impulses.'

Augustine created the concept of a 'perception of knowledge' which he called 'Divine Enlightenment', where 'God is able to enlighten and bring knowledge to the human mind by giving it divine truths. Therefore, whoever knows God and is assured of his universal truth can reveal mysteries.' Augustine argued 'all souls occupy a middle position between God, the source of creation, and our bodies.' In other words, we exist somewhere between the unchangeable reality where existence stems from (continuous) and the ever-changing realm we live in (discrete). Expanding upon this knowledge, scientists believe that we are conscious at every single point in time (continuous), but also at specific moments in time (discrete). In other words, consciousness is both continuous and discrete. Reality for this existence is facilitated by interconnectivity with our spirit and the Holy Spirit.

---

227 Michael Herzog, Leila Drissi-Daoudi, and Adrien Doerig, 2020: 'All in good time: long-lasting postdictive effects reveal discrete perception', Trends in Cognitive Sciences, https://doi.org/10.1016/j.tics.2020.07.001.

Consciousness research, or neuroscience, and perhaps psychiatry, appear to be relevant to human levitation because trances and altered states of consciousness are so often mentioned.[228] This observation is consistent with the development of the entrepreneur mindset as displayed by Jesus during His ministry. The harmony between spiritual intelligence, emotional intelligence, intellectual intelligence, and our bodies facilitates access to information and energy from outside of our bodies and is relevant to our states of consciousness. However, it is difficult to define altered states satisfactorily, given that consciousness researchers are so sharply divided as to how normal consciousness works. Tiller says of consciousness:

> *The unconscious is gathering all the information and processing it, and in doing so generates small kernels of information, which it sends to your conscious mind so that the conscious will know it is alive [...] If you want to grow, give things meaning. Expand your consciousness bandwidth [...] Consciousness is not localised in your brain.[229]*

As for 'non-local' intuition, described in Chapter 3, the autonomic nervous system is attuned to receive information beyond our five senses through our network of energy points and, after processing the data in the heart, sends the information to the brain for a final decision on actions. Consciousness is continuous within our beings but can also inform our discrete actions. Entrepreneur mindset is part of this continuum.

---

228 Harvey-Wilson Simon, 2003 Human Levitation, http://levitation.greyfalcon.us/levitation.htm.

229 Nisha Manek, 2019, 'Bridging Science and Spirit', pp 101, Conscious Creations LLC.

Dr Dean Radin explains that,

> *when the evidence for an anomaly becomes overwhelming,*
> *and the anomaly cannot be easily accommodated by the*
> *existing scientific worldview, this is a very important sign*
> *that either our assumptions about reality are wrong or*
> *our assumptions about how we come to understand things*
> *are wrong.* [230]

In approaching our modern understanding of the science for the levitation of Jesus over the water of Lake Galilee, I propose to briefly review the application of Tiller's theories as included in appendix 7.1 and 7.3. In doing so, I am fully aware that the accounts of eyewitnesses to 'self-levitation' involves people who lived their life in devotion to the divine, and their consciousness may cause their inner vibratory state to become such that the atoms within their body are able to cross the light-speed boundary— literally making them enlightened!

Also, the Tiller observation of the Russian levitator showed no electromagnetic field around the levitated object, suggesting strongly that magnetic monopoles are present in the negative energy spectrum of reciprocal space.

Tiller points out that Dirac realised his equations for the electron's 'antiparticle', the positron, could be solved by using two equally viable answers: positive and negative. He envisioned the negative solution for an electron existed in a sea of negative energy, also known as the 'Dirac Sea' or 'physical vacuum,' due to the lack of charge-based 'stuff.' In a schematic energy spectrum associated with this Dirac model, the plenum of negative energy

---

230 Dean Radin, 1997, 'The Conscious Universe: The Scientific Truth of Psychic Phenomena', pp 250, Harper One.

states is separated from a plenum of positive energy states by a band gap of disallowed states. Dirac's key assumption was that the physical vacuum consisted of a plenum of negative energy states; i.e., the physical vacuum is not empty but consists of unknown 'stuff'.

In the Tiller concept of 'conditioned space', he proposed that this Dirac energy spectrum include the higher dimensional domains of emotion and mind which include consciousness. Such an expansion allows one to provide a possible explanation for why levitation of objects and humans might be possible.

Tiller uses the findings of astronomers that, when observing the movement of celestial bodies, spatial energy density variations locally alter the curvature of space and that this gives rise to gravitational forces, but in the past half-century, astronomers have also observed celestial body movements associated with 'unseen' attractors. To account for these observations, they have postulated the presence first of dark matter and later also of dark energy, with both of these having produced spatial curvature effects without any correlated electromagnetic instrument detection.

Traditional gravitational forces involve positive mass— positive mass interactions plus electromagnetic (EM) radiation acting as the communication vehicle between positive masses. Non-traditional gravitational forces (dark energy) involve negative mass and negative mass interactions plus a different type of radiation acting as the communication vehicle between this negative mass substance that this author has labelled 'magnetoelectric (ME) energy (moving magnetic charges inducing electric fields in the physical vacuum).

In the human body, just as in inanimate bodies, experimentally human intention has been shown to interact with this (wave faster than speed of sound) vacuum information wave substance. Thus, one should expect that sufficiently inner-self managed humans should, in principle, be capable of intentionally drawing into their body, from the outside environment, a sufficient amount of the negative energy substance so that the net gravitational force interaction between their body and the Earth shifts from a strongly attractive force to a neutral force and ultimately to a repulsive force. Then the human will be observed to be levitating relative to the Earth. One might also speculate that, when these new concepts are ultimately accepted by orthodox physics and understood in a quantitative way, technology will be developed to make the levitation of inanimate objects a practical industry[231]

Summary

By accepting the texts describing the eyewitness accounts of Jesus 'walking on water' and the scholarly summary of theological and historical commentaries over the centuries using the tools and skills of a historian, Twelftree comments, 'As incredible as the story seems to modern minds, it cannot be ruled out of court as historically unreliable, for even the little information available points to the possibility of historicity.'[218] Of particular note is the accepted eyewitness accounts of Catholic saints demonstrating levitation experiences and for which records of eyewitness testing and examination are held in Church documents. An important

---

231 William Tiller, 2009, 'What does the Dirac Negative Energy Sea Mean and Why Has Todays Orthodox Physics Neglected it?', White Paper 6, Tiller Foundation.

corollary to this record is that all the occurrences are associated with what can be called 'devotional, spiritual' behaviour both before and during the levitation events. This is the strongest indication that humans can self-levitate by linking into energy states from outside themselves.

From the observed experiments on human-powered levitation, it is found that such behaviour is not associated with electromagnetic energy levels, thus providing the possibility for the negative energies of reciprocal space to be functional.

Based on Tiller's theoretical description for the presence of negative energy in both 'conditioned' space and the power of human 'intention' to effect observed changes to natural behaviour not explained by conventional physics, it is reasonable to conclude that Jesus would have the inner power to 'walk on water.'

Although this conclusion may seem amazing, it is nowhere near as awesome as the reality that Jesus could effect this event at precisely the time when the disciples were in dire difficulties. This awesomeness is confirmed by the text reporting 'those in the boat worshipped him, saying, truly you are the Son of God.'

Chapter 11: Case #4—Jesus Stilling the Storm

If you want to see the sunshine,
you have to weather the storm.

—Frank Lane

One of the most common topics of conversation concerns the weather and its impact on our lives, travel, and the farming community. Indeed, the media—TV, radio, and newspapers—as well as governments and UN agencies devote significant resources to help in both informing and managing the weather cycle and its effects on the economy and our personal wellbeing.

Weather miracles are a common feature in both the Old and New Testaments of the Bible. Twelftree comments, 'many rain and analogous large-scale nature miracles resemble the accounts of "Jesus stilling the storm".' In the Old Testament, such accounts are associated with Noah, Moses, Elisha, and Elijah.[232]

In the nineteenth century, such evangelical luminaries as George Müller and J Hudson Taylor reported experiences that could be understood as weather miracles.[233] To better appreciate the prevalence of 'miraculous' accounts around weather change

---

232 Graham Twelftree, 2017, 'The Nature Miracles of Jesus' Cascade Books, Eugene OR, pp 57.

233 Paul King, 2001, 'Moving Mountains: Lessons in Bold Faith from Great Evangelical Leaders', Grand Rapids: Chosen. Pp 15–16, 20, 42.

by ordinary human beings in the twentieth century and support from eyewitnesses, I propose to quote Twelftree:

> *Others recount dramatic provisions of water. For example, an eyewitness recounts that during one of the worst droughts in Papua New Guinea, a dry well filled completely with clear water within hours after her ministry team leader publicly prayed for it. Normally the well was only clear during the rainy season, but there had been no rain in months. Others report that in Myanmar, the gathering of three thousand persons for a conference threatened to strain a village's water resources. Believers prayed, and 'miraculously', a spring broke out in the middle of the village on the day the conference began. This spring supplied enough water for the crowds and still exists today.*
>
> *When a raging wind and waters threatened to swamp an evangelism's team boat in Southern Nigeria, the leader commanded the storm to stop, and the sea became 'as placid as glass.*

When one of Twelftree's PhD students was an undergraduate, rain was pouring down on the day they had planned an outreach. After they prayed, the rain stopped precisely in their part of the city, allowing the outreach and astonishing a non-Christian witness. Twelftree himself claims he witnessed a group of college students pray for the stilling of a severe storm that was forecast to continue throughout the day. The storm stopped almost immediately and the sky quickly cleared for the rest of the day. Twelftree notes this was not a distant recollection, 'because I recorded it in my journal the day that it happened.'

Returning to the focus of this case study—Jesus stilling the water, and prior to the miracle, Jesus revealed His true humanity: He needed rest and time away from crowds, and He was so exhausted that even the battering of the boat did not awaken Him (Matthew 8:24) from a deep sleep. This experience helps us to realise that Jesus was genuinely human with the same basic needs we all have. In Chapter 5, we concluded Jesus exhibited a fully developed entrepreneur mindset. Yet it was this same Jesus and with an entrepreneur mindset, who, when wakened by the fearful disciples, could 'rebuke the wind, and say to the sea, "Peace! Be still!" And the wind ceased, and there was a great calm' (Mark 4:39).

Text and Analysis:

Matthew 8:23-27	Mark 4:35-41	Luke 8:22-25
23. And when he got into the boat, his disciples followed him.	35. On that day, when evening had come, he said to them, 'Let us go across to the other side.'	22. One *day he got into a boat with his disciples*, and he said to them, 'Let us go across to the other side of the lake.' So they set out,
24. And behold, there arose a great storm on the sea, so that the boat was being swamped by the waves; but he was asleep	36. And leaving the crowd, as he was. *And other they took him with them just as he was ,in the boat.* And other boats were with him.	23. and *as they sailed he fell asleep.* And a storm of wind came down on the lake, and they were filling with water, and were in danger.

347

25. And *they went and woke him*, saying, *'Save, Lord; we are perishing.'*	37. And a great storm of wind arose, and the waves beat into the boat, so that the boat was already filling.	24. And *they went and woke him,* saying, *'Master, Master, we are perishing!'* And he awoke and rebuked the wind and the raging waves; and they ceased, and there was a calm.*
26. And he said to them, 'Why are you afraid, O men of little faith?' Then he rose and rebuked the winds and the sea; and there was a great calm	38. But he was in the stern, asleep on the cushion; and they woke him and said to him, 'Teacher, do you not care if we perish?	25. He said to them, 'Where is your faith?' And they were afraid, and they marvelled, saying to one another, 'Who then is this, that he commands even wind and water, and they obey him?'
27. And the men marvelled, saying, 'What sort of man is this, that even winds and sea obey him?	39. And he awoke and rebuked the wind, and said to the sea, 'Peace! Be still!' And the wind ceased, and there was a great calm.	
	40. He said to them, 'Why are you afraid? Have you no faith?'	

| | 41. And wind they were filled with awe, and said to one another, 'Who then is this, that even winds and sea obey him?' | |

As in Chapter 10, Jesus is again in a boat, on Lake Galilee, in the midst of a storm. This story confirms that Jesus availed Himself of water travel many times to get to destinations around the lake rather than walking around the coast. Clearly, these experienced fishermen, as disciples, could provide the boat, rowing, and sailing experience for all weather and water conditions. Yet, for both Jesus walking on water in Chapter 10 and Jesus stilling the water in this chapter, His disciples demonstrated fear in the stormy conditions. We have learned that Lake Galilee was susceptible to sudden and extremely violent storms. These storms are caused by the cold air rushing down from the mountains surrounding it and colliding with the warm, moist air rising off the surface of the water itself.

The backdrop to this story commences early in the same day on the edge of Lake Galilee, with 'a very large crowd gathered about Him.' The crowd was so large he addressed them from a boat tethered near the lake's shoreline. Mark 4:2–34 describes the preaching as composed of many parables—parables He used to preach the principles of the Kingdom of God. For Jesus, this is a day of both significant teaching—including the seven parables of Matthew 13—and considerable testing. He is sought by concerned friends, His mother, and half-brothers, and is accused of being demon-possessed by some who think that He is not in His right mind. In verse 34, we read Jesus taught the people in parables but 'privately, to His disciples, He explained everything. So when evening came, He was exhausted and said, "Let us go across to the other side".'

With Jesus showing signs of fatigue from incessant interruptions and distractions by the large crowds pursuing Him, He tells His disciples to take Him in their small boat to the quieter region of Perea across Lake Galilee.

Once onboard, Jesus falls asleep on a pillow, an item normally found among the sparse furnishings of that type of boat.

A windstorm arose, beating waves into the boat (Mark 4:37)

A storm rose suddenly, an event frequently experienced on the lake, and we are told this one terrified the disciples. The storm must have been severe to frighten these experienced fishermen. Mark (v. 37) describes the waves as beating into the boat and filling it, thus requiring constant bailing of the water along with the need to keep the heaving boat pointing into the wind.

Jesus was sleeping, but was wakened by His disciples fearing for their lives (Mark 4:38).

Luke (v. 24) expresses the disciples' urgency by repeating the Greek word *epistates*, which means 'Master, master!' or 'Rabbi, rabbi!' It is clear that their faith that Jesus would keep them safe did not extend to being thrown about in a turbulent storm. By contrast, Jesus was completely relaxed, deep in sleep and secure in the providence of God at this time. The team certainly felt forsaken by their leader.

Twelftree identifies a parallel between that of Jesus asleep in the boat and that of Jonah being aroused by the fearful mariners with a cry 'arise, call upon thy God' (Jonah 1: 4). Indeed, the two outcomes were the same with the sea ceasing to 'rage'. But for Jonah, he accepted being tossed into the sea and saved by a great fish. Jonah completed the experience with fervent prayer and was delivered onto dry land.[234]

It is noted in Matthew 8:24, the word used for 'storm' is *seimos* (which normally means 'earthquake'), suggesting it was extremely severe. Some scholars see in the intensity of the storm a parallel associated with the testing of the disciples as part of team building and full commitment and passion to faith in Jesus, their leader.

Jesus rebuked the wind and calmed the seas (Mark 4:39) (as illustrated in Figure 11.1[235])

Jesus treats this storm and the sea as if they were antagonistic and rebelling forces under a dominating, unrestrained power, but His word is sufficient to calm them, just as He commands demons to leave those who are possessed. Conflicts and rebellions have their source in both the physical and spiritual worlds.

To the disciples' amazement, Jesus only had to speak a few words, and the storm became silent. The wind stopped and the water was still. He spoke and the sea obeyed.

When Jesus speaks to calm the storm, Mark indicates that He addresses more than a meteorological force but a being behind it. When He commands the sea, 'Peace, be still!' the Greek phrase means 'be muzzled or gagged,' as though the storm were a maniac that had to be bound and restrained.

---

234 Graham Twelftree, 1999, 'Jesus the Miracle Worker', pp. 71,Inter Varsity Press, Illinois.
235 James Tissot (1836–1902), 'Jesus tilling the Tempest'.

Figure 11.1, Jesus Stilling the Tempest, James Tissot (1836–1902)

He then reproached His disciples for their fear and lack of faith (Mark 4:40)

When the storm had been calmed, Jesus chastised the disciples for their lack of faith in a safe passage to the other side of the lake, a possible contrast to Jesus' serene faith and confidence. Perhaps the contrast here might indicate the behaviour of an entrepreneur mindset involving commitment, passion, and belief to leading a mission with the mindset of the team members involved in the mission providing quality support.

Filled with great fear, His disciples expressed their awe of Jesus to one another (Mark 4:41)

Following Jesus' demonstrated power over the material world, the awestruck disciples receive a newfound understanding of the power and glory of their Lord and Master. His power definitely impresses them, but His faithfulness, peace, and ability to 'make this happen' are what truly awed them. This miracle brings them in reverence, wonder, and godly fear before Him. This reveals the full measure of Jesus' interconnectivity with the Holy Spirit to accomplish the outcome through being a faithful human being. Jesus explains to His disciples in Mark 11:23–24:

> For assuredly, I say to you, whoever says to this mountain, 'Be removed and be cast into the sea,' and does not doubt in his heart, but believes that those things he says will be done, he will have whatever he says. Therefore I say to you, whatever things you ask when you pray, believe that you receive them, and you will have them.

As discussed in the next section, we will relate this assurance with an understanding of the reality and power of 'human intention.'

Miracle Elements and Scientific Explanation

As discussed in the previous three cases, the principles and experiments pertaining to explaining Jesus' use of the natural laws of physics are also fully relevant to this case of Jesus stilling the storm.

We should note from the introduction to this chapter, from the Gospel texts, and from eyewitness experiences that humans appear to have a capacity to influence weather behaviour. This does not easily fit with our linear view of the physical world. However, in every case, the initiator of the changed weather event was deeply involved in prayer and also in demonstrating an intimate/interconnected relationship with the Holy Spirit. It is worthy of note that Jesus exhibited true humanity in His exhaustion from the day of preaching with the need for sleep and renewal of energy. When awakened from sleep to the dangers to the boat, He first stilled the storm before addressing the fear and lack of faith amongst the disciples. This, too, was a demonstration of His human behaviour.

Science, as an activity, is also an enquiry into what it means to have an intention. As we have seen in appendix 7.1, consciousness is influenced by intention, and consciousness is the human connection to the Spirit. Exploring the eyewitness accounts provides a base to explore the consequences of their intention.

As seen in Tiller's experiment (appendix 7.2), his intention to change the pH of water by one full unit was achieved. This has shown the consequence of his intention-action. It is not unreasonable to conclude from the eyewitness accounts (introduction) and Jesus' 'intention' to still the storm that humans can invoke certain qualities from within to change or deform basic quantities of space and time. As Tiller comments,

> It isn't as if the old laws are wrong and need to be thrown out—no more than Newton was wrong when Einstein came along and showed that the laws of gravitation had to be altered when one adopted a frame of reference for observation that moved at velocities approaching the speed of light.[236]

From the Gospel text, we conclude the storm experienced by all on the boat was severe enough to cause the experienced fishermen-disciples to believe they were about to perish. Using some simple physics, it is possible to estimate a storm's strength. By considering the mass of the air passing over the water, it is

---

236 William Tiller, 2015, 'Bridging Science and Spirit', as quoted by N. Manek. Pp. 192.

possible to calculate the amount of energy in the mass flow of moist air, known as its kinetic energy. The kinetic energy of an object depends on the mass multiplied by the velocity squared.

For this example, moisture-laden air has a density of around one kilogram per cubic metre, so the mass of turbulent air is simply density multiplied by the volume of the storm. This volume will be a big number with the storm confronting the small fishing boat. If the storm is blowing at say 50 miles/hour or about 22 metres/second, then for every cubic metre of the storm space, the energy for this kinetic energy would be about 242 joules. But the storm will comprise thousands of cubic metres, so the kinetic energy of the storm will be a big number. This storm energy will be experienced by all on board in what is physical space.

In Chapter 9, we noted that Tiller identified the presence of an extremely high energy density in 'reciprocal' space, where the so-called vacuum is not 'empty' or void. Indeed, the available energy in this dimension of reality is staggering, of the order of 10^{94} grams per cubic centimetre which is equivalent to 10^{97} kilograms per cubic metre—a truly ginormous number. In the previous cases, it has been concluded that human consciousness (based on a developed intention), can interact with this parallel dimension of reciprocal space and tap into the awesome amount of energy quanta available within the vacuum. It is, therefore, reasonable to maintain that by accessing even a small amount of this real energy, an intention-guided human can change things in the physical world.

With this background, it is realistic to propose that Jesus, our primary subject of this case, but also considering the prayer experiences of those examples mentioned in the introduction, was using the power of intention to transfer the energy quanta from reciprocal space to change the turbulence of the storm to a quiet weather pattern.

As a fully developed social entrepreneur, Jesus can be seen as both conscious of and committed to the need to develop in His mission team total faith in whom their leader truly is, loyalty to Jesus, understanding of spiritual interconnection, and the practice of intention in the work of the mission.

Summary

In each of the last three cases, water has been an important element in the miracle. Fundamentally, we have seen in all the cases Jesus was called on to influence the specific circumstances of those present. First, by Mary requesting water be turned to wine, second, by Peter asking to be saved from sinking in the water, and thirdly, by the disciples calling out in fear to be saved. In every case, Jesus needed to influence the natural law of creation to facilitate the required outcome.

Using the demonstrated capacity of human spiritual inter-connectivity with the Spirit and the development of an 'intention-based' practice of prayer and meditation, an explanation for these behaviours has been provided using the natural law of creation.

What is an awesome reality is that these, and other events, were actioned at just the time the action was required. This is surely the real miracle.

Accompanying these miracles, the recipients of the action showed a true change in belief and practice. After the stilling of the storm, we note the disciples saying, 'Who then is this, that even winds and sea obey him?' (Mark 4:41), and also 'Who then is this, that he commands even wind and water, and they obey him?' (Luke 8:25)

Final Reflections

We commenced with the question as to whether the concept of Jesus as a social entrepreneur was compatible with His ministry from age thirty to His crucifixion.

The most significant aspect of being an entrepreneur—whether social or commercial—is to be 'opportunity focused' in terms of one's mindset, recognising that any potential output of product or services needs to be valued by the end user, and actually meeting the needs of the end user. If the user values and then exchanges value to gain the benefit, then innovation actually occurs. The specific opportunity identified as describing the ministry of Jesus is 'changing community values and behaviours through a new relationship with God.' Fundamentally, entrepreneurship behaviour is a truly human characteristic in seeking to meet the needs of potential users. Essential to this study is the assessment made as to the humanity of Jesus—was he 'fully man?' Based on the secular historical evidence for the presence of Jesus Christ in first century CE, the archaeological evidence of a Jewish 'worship-centred community' within Judea and the Galilee, and the clear interpretation from the biblical/theological record that Jesus was 'fully human' (and not a super-man) it seemed appropriate to examine the actions and practices of Jesus in terms of entrepreneurial behaviours.

From an understanding that man comprises a body, a soul, and a spirit, the behaviour of Jesus was assessed on all levels.

Essentially, and at the most obvious level, man is made up of physical material, the body (soma), that can be seen and touched as both flesh and bone and expressed in the five senses. The levels of soul (psyche), and spirit (pneuma) are often used interchangeably. I consider they are different expressions (dimensions) of the inner or immaterial aspects of man, which are intangible. We are not simply body and soul but persons who include the spirit of the creator. From the application of validated personality assessments, it was possible to assess Jesus' soul in terms of creativity and ingenuity, intuition, commitment, tenacity and determination, a passion for succeeding and excelling, emotions, leadership, and team-building skills. The spirit dimension comprised the holistic functions of awareness, insight, understanding, judgement, love, authenticity, and all aspects of spiritual intelligence. Assessment of the three intelligence dimensions of the human include intellectual intelligence (IQ), Emotional intelligence (EI), and spiritual intelligence (SI), and together provide the basis for understanding 'entrepreneur mindset' and answering the question of 'compatibility' between Jesus' ministry and social entrepreneurship.

As a successful social entrepreneur, Jesus built a mission/ organisation, opened a new relationship with God, established high personal values, made significant and passionate contributions to the mission and community outreach, and delivered real value to His followers and disciples. Significantly, as with current social entrepreneurs, He built an organisation where economic value and societal contribution are two sides of the same coin. Jesus, in 'making it happen', delivered on His opportunity to solve problems related to spiritual wellbeing, relationship values, education, health care, poverty, and the environment— to name a few. Jesus was a change agent using the fundamental principles of entrepreneurship to promote positive change and permanent impact. As a social entrepreneur, and with His team, they created the principles and mindset for the next 2,000 years of Christian mission and care through a living and practising social entrepreneur mindset.

There is little dispute today that the entrepreneurial team is a key ingredient in the development and growth of a higher-potential venture/mission. Clearly, the new mission to the Jews of Judea and Galilee in the first century CE required the lead social entrepreneur, Jesus, to demonstrate His physical, emotional, and spiritual characteristics (entrepreneur mindset) in presenting the message of a new relationship with God. In addition, His authority from God, including signs and wonders, was central to the mission, but without a loyal, committed, sacrificing, and entrepreneurial team of apostles and extended follower disciples -growth of the mission (locally and international) would have been severely limited.

This strongly expressed 'desire to serve' is at the core of Jesus' leadership in delivering and growing His mission and is also a major characteristic of leaders exhibiting an entrepreneur mindset in the society of today. 'Servant'-style leadership is a major component of current leadership teaching courses. Also, Jesus led His team of Apostles as both a player and a coach. It is important to note that Jesus, like all outstanding entrepreneurs, acted to some degree like a 'magnet' in attracting motivated, quality individuals who passionately desire to be associated with the leader and His mission as a team player. This ability and skill in attracting key apostles to the mission and building this group into an A-grade team of intensely loyal, committed 'followers', enabled the team to cope with any problems that may limit growth. These behaviours are synonymous with expressions from recent research on team cohesiveness in successful faith-based ventures—team members comment, 'I did not think first about the inconvenience', considered 'the opportunity was greater than the cost of personal inconvenience', and 'felt enthused by the opportunity to serve.' From the perspective of interconnectedness, 'a large or small team did not matter', 'Interconnectedness with others was satisfying', 'Interconnectedness with others who share values inspires me.' This comparison confirms the value of the close-knit team in achieving the desired and effective outcomes.

In reflecting on the ministry of Jesus, the impact on the lives of His followers, and the ongoing mission and practice of the Christian church, even after 2,000 years, it is appropriate to consider Jesus as the greatest and most effective social entrepreneur of all time. In terms of the benefits experienced and valued by followers (users), we have an outstanding example of the classic innovation, where an identified opportunity is transformed into valued and useful outcomes that have and continue to meet the need of millions of users worldwide.

In reflecting on this reality and noting the significance of Jesus' baptism of the Holy Spirit, and His wilderness experience of prayer, fasting, and meditation (Chapter 5) immediately prior to His ministry and effective social entrepreneurial behaviour, it is informative to review the transformative change at this time. Jesus entered this period of reflection as 'fully' human and commenced His ministry some forty days later, still 'fully' human, but with a deep understanding of what it meant to be 'made in the image of God', His ministry, and future death on a cross. Significantly, Jesus experienced the human potential to tap into the available spirit resources (awareness) and hence demonstrate the power and authority in 'human intention', 'quantum entanglement', 'quantum energy', and 'non-local intuition', and add 'authority' to His mission through 'signs and wonders.' Indeed, the Catholic catechism (1705) expresses this reality: 'By virtue of his soul and his spiritual powers of intellect and will, man is endowed with freedom, an 'outstanding manifestation of the divine image.'

It is this insight into accessing such spiritual resources that gives full meaning to the reality of the 'entrepreneur mindset' and our human potential. There is an umbilical link between our thoughts, beliefs, and actions leading to our expressed behaviour resulting in an inextricably linked mindset focused on developing recognised opportunities into growth-oriented and value-adding innovations that meet user needs. But a mission organisation, of itself, is not entrepreneurially minded—the behaviour that may be present within the mission organisation is driven by the human propensity, spirit, and energy to be entrepreneurial as expressed by leaders and staff identifying the opportunities with application to user need and perceived value. Importantly, no matter how entrepreneurial either an individual's mindset or an organisation's culture is— 'interdependencies exist between the manager's mindset and the disciples/organisation culture such that 'entrepreneurial culture and entrepreneur mindset are inextricably interwoven.'

As discussed in Chapter 7, under the section 'Bridging Science and Spirit', we noted that 'man' in his immaterial nature reflects his Creator. This is not saying that the physical body of man reflects the Creator, but in his immaterial nature through the dimensions of 'soul' and 'spirit' this immaterial part of man reflects God, yet it is housed in a material body that has to be the best possible expression of that which is the representative and the reflection of God. We are to represent God and reflect His character in ruling this creation. It is this perspective we see in Jesus post-forty days in the wilderness. Indeed, this reference to 'image' in Genesis 1:27 does not imply that God is in human form, but that humans are in the image of God in their moral, spiritual, and intellectual essence. Thus, humans have the potential to reflect God's divine nature in their ability to achieve the unique spiritual characteristics with which they have been endowed. Indeed, Jesus is the great exemplar of this relationship.

With this insight into human potential, it is appropriate to review the processes associated with Jesus' wilderness experience of prayer, fasting, and meditation with God the Holy Spirit. In Chapter 7, we explored the connectivity between our human spirit and a relationship with the Creator and the energy within the universe. Tapping into this channel through prayer, or 'talking with God', enables real communication through interaction (connectivity) between the two distant but connected 'objects'. Such connectivity is demonstrated by Jesus and countless followers down the centuries. The link between this amazing human capability, and the science of quantum mechanics, is fully understandable using the principles of quantum entanglement (appendix 7.4). Similarly, fasting is a way to grow in a deep appreciation of the 'spirit' by a reflected focus on a personal commitment to and recognition of one's dependence on God the Holy Spirit.

The 'process' of meditation is understood as the focusing of attention beyond thought and imagination and leading to a still, wakeful presence to the reality of God the Holy Spirit. Indeed Jesus used the stillness of the desert to become fully in touch with the Holy Spirit. Fundamental to our examination of the 'nature miracles' is the understanding of developed 'human intentions' from deep meditation that can influence material reality. We know Jesus practised meditation, often prior to or after performing 'miracles'. The disciples also demonstrated 'signs and wonders'. Theoretically and experimentally, William Tiller, in appendix

7.2, discovered that there are actually two levels of physical reality and not just the one with which we are all familiar. It is this new level of physical reality (described as the 'mirror image' or reciprocal space) that can be significantly influenced by human intention—not our familiar electric atom/molecule level. Tiller's research demonstrated that it is possible to make a significant change in the properties of a material substance by consciously holding a clear intention to do so. Details of these subtle energies and their relationship to the 'spirit' dimension of reality were described in appendix 7.3.

With the above reflection on accessing the 'spirit' dimension and influencing material reality, I return to our current understanding of the entrepreneur mindset (EM). From Chapter 5, we showed that an EM could be recognised by combining the four dimensions of leadership, decision-making, behaviour, and awareness and derived from the integration of the contributions of intellectual intelligence, emotional intelligence, and most importantly, spiritual intelligence. This holistic insight integrated what were traditionally considered narrow personality traits, personality dispositions, and cognitive processes with the spiritual aspects of human intention, decision-making, and proactive behaviours within the mission enterprise. Of significance to this reflection is the dimension of 'awareness'. Awareness is usually defined as 'knowledge that something exists; understanding of a situation at the present time based on information or experience'. Indeed, self-awareness is knowledge and awareness of one's own personality or character. Together cognition and spirituality form the natural characteristics for an aware person. Cognition is the mental process involved in knowing, learning, and understanding things. Spirituality is the quality of being concerned with the human spirit or soul as opposed to physical or material things. Jesus fully reflected this spiritual characteristic throughout His recorded ministry. Such aware behaviour is also associated with current-day, value-driven entrepreneurs. It has been demonstrated that successful social entrepreneurs have a very strong propensity for spiritual connectivity and action within the dimension of awareness. From Chapter 4, research shows high-EM entrepreneurs exercise freedom and act with responsibility, called an 'inner voice' and often referred to as spiritual intelligence (SI) and synonymous with accessing the reality of reciprocal space mentioned above. Significantly, all high-EM entrepreneurs are characterised by high energy levels of action. Jesus also fits this characteristic. They each draw down power from the spiritual dimension of the universe into the human being.

This spirituality in high-EM entrepreneurs, including Jesus, is reflected in their observed and measured propensity for intuitive decision-making and proactive behaviour. This non-local intuition or quantum coherence is expanded on in appendix 7.5.

The above reflections provide a classic backdrop to reflect on the findings from Chapters 8 to 11: can the 'nature miracles' be attributed to Jesus conforming with natural laws of physics and matter? Reflecting on the evidence from Chapters 2 to 6, it is clear that Jesus was both real and truly man, albeit with a deep and personal relationship with God the Father. He exhibited all the characteristics associated with the human body, including tiredness, thirst, emotions, anger, love and compassion, plus the added dimensions of soul and spirit. It was at age thirty, at His baptism, and during the solitude of the desert experience, that Jesus fully integrated the potential and energy available to man through the spirit dimension. He was now the full expression of 'man' in the 'image of God' with the consequential access to the power/energy of reciprocal space vested in the spirit dimension. It follows that Jesus could use these enhanced powers of human intention, interconnectedness, and close personal relationship with God the Holy Spirit to effect the observed 'miracles' that would confirm His authority. But the question still remains—did Jesus use the natural mechanisms of physics and science to effect a miracle?

In this reflection, I rely on the concept of a 'miracle' that concords with Augustine (Bishop of Hippo; 354-430 CE) who said, 'Miracles are not contrary to nature, but only contrary of what we know about nature.'

In this case, the 'new' knowledge is based on our current understanding of quantum particles as the building blocks of nature. Using the principles that govern the behaviour of these particles, both theoretical and experimental evidence shows that these particles can also behave as waves. Importantly, these quantum particles, considered as material objects, do not have two different components but are single objects that can manifest two different natures—particle and wave. Using this duality, first proposed by de Broglie, we have seen the theoretical and experimental research of Tiller show a relationship between 'direct space' or D-space (the familiar four-dimensional world of matter comprising all elementary particles, and associated governing forces such as electromagnetism and gravity), and a second dimension having magnetic wave information characteristics but not material stuff. Tiller identifies this as the physical vacuum which he calls 'reciprocal space' or R-space. This R-space is of a 'negative' energy state within the Dirac concept of the vacuum with waves being superluminal or faster than the speed of light and having a magnetic nature. This R-space is the mirror image of D-space. Tiller comments, as time (t) in D-space increases, then its inverse in R-space means the measure is 1/t (which increases hyperbolically), implying this space can reach infinity.[237]

237 Tiller William, 1997, Science and Human Transformation: Subtle Energies, Intentionality, and Consciousness, Walnut Creek, CA, Pavior.

Tiller has described this space as the 'spirit' dimension and experimentally demonstrated that human consciousness can interact with this information full and extreme energy space. His experiments show, unambiguously, that humans can tap into this field through prayer, fasting and meditation, and using 'human intention' can access available energy to produce physical change in the selected material objects in D-space.

Based then on the observed 'miracle' changes to physical reality discussed in Chapters 8 to 11, those witness examinations recorded for miracles by Christian saints, and the validated experiments of Tiller to change physical reality through human intention (Chapter 7), we can conclude the 'nature miracles' attributed to Jesus and observed by witnesses in D-space can be fully explained in accordance with the natural laws of physics and R-space. This conclusion conforms with the language of Aristotle to understand miracles by first identifying the efficient cause as 'a natural agent' (in this case 'human intention'); the final cause as 'the will of God' (Jesus demonstrated such authority), and the revelation of the miracle by the extraordinary timing of the event.

The emphasis in this review of the 'nature miracle' is focused on 'what is true'. The acts by Jesus, along with the experiments of Tiller, reinforce the principle that God works through natural resources to effect change. In no way does the scientific explanation destroy the wonder and awe of the observed event. Indeed, the wonder and awe experienced by witnesses of the events were substantial, just as we today can stand back in awe at the wonder of created man having the capacity to deliver change through spiritual means. Of particular significance is in the timing of the event so that the 'miraculous' observation occurs at exactly the time and place it is required.

Bibliography

1. Text and diagrams © Dr. William A. Tiller 2009. Used with permission throughout book.
2. C.W. Allinson & J. Hayes 1996. All rights reserved.
3. Donald Kuratko and David Audretsch 2009, 'Strategic Entrepreneurship: Exploring Different Perspectives of an Emerging Concept', Entrepreneurship Theory and Practice, Vol 33, Issue 1.
4. William A. Tiller and Walter E. Dibble, 2001, 'Conscious Acts of Creation: The Emergence of a New Physics' Walnut Creek, CA, Pavior.
5. Winston Churchill, 'Birth Throes of a Sublime Resolve,' broadcast 16 June 1941.
6. Jeff Conklin, 2005, 'Wicked Problems and Social Complexity' from Chapter 1 in the book 'Dialogue Mapping: Building Shared Understanding of Wicked Problems,' John Wiley & Sons.
7. Paul Kelly, 2020, 'Team Australia' our new normal, for now', The Weekend Australian 04/04/2020.
8. Hazelton and Gillin 2017, 'From Compliance Culture in Elder care to Resident Focus Innovation as Social Entrepreneurship – A Global Opportunity'. In Campbell C.L. (eds) The Customer is NOT Always Right? Marketing Orientations in a Dynamic Business World. Developments in Marketing Science: Proceedings of the Academy of Marketing Science. Springer.

9. Australian Institute of Health and Welfare, 2018, https://www.aihw.gov.au/reports/australias-health/australias-health-2018/.

10. Colin Humphreys, 1995, 'Star of Bethlehem' Science and Christian Belief, Vol 5, (October): 83–101.

11. Gillin, 1998, adapted from Howard Stevenson, 1983, 'A perspective on entrepreneurship', Harvard Business School Working Paper, 9-384-131.

12. Sakari Häkkinen, 2016, 'Poverty in the first-century Galilee', https://www.researchgate.net/publication/309254500_Poverty_in_the_first-century_Galilee.

13. Douglass E Oakman, 2008, 'Jesus and the Peasants', https://www.academia.edu/3079887/Oakman_D_E_2008_Jesus_and_the_peasants_Cascade_Books_Eugene_Matrix_The_Bible_in_Mediterranean_context_.

14. M. I. Finley, 1999 'Ancient History – Evidence and Models', https://www.amazon.com/Ancient-History-Evidence-M-Finley/dp/1597400432#reader_1597400432.

15. Ben Z Rosenfeld & Haim Perlmutter, 2020, 'Middle Groups in Jewish Roman Galilee and Jesus and his Disciples' Social Location: New Insights', https://bibleinterp.arizona.edu/articles/middle-groups-jewish-roman-galilee-and-jesus-and-his-disciples-social-location-new.

16. Cecelia Wasson, 2016, 'The Jewishness of Jesus and ritual purity' https://www.researchgate.net/publication/326888106_The_Jewishness_of_Jesus_and_ritual_purity.

17. E. P. Sanders 2016, 'Judaism: Practice and Belief, 63BCE-66 CE' https://www.amazon.com/Judaism-Practice-Belief-63BCE-66-CE/dp/1506406106.

18. Douglass E Oakman, 2008, 'Jesus and the Peasants', https://www.academia.edu/3079887/Oakman_D_E_2008_Jesus_and_the_peasants_Cascade_Books_Eugene_Matrix_The_Bible_in_Mediterranean_context_.

19. Ariel Sabar, 2016, 'Unearthing the World of Jesus', Smithsonian Magazine, January Washington, DC.

20. Megan Sauter, 2020, 'Excavating El-Araj—a Candidate for Biblical Bethsaida' Biblical Archaeology Society, https://www.baslibrary.org/biblical-archaeology-review/46/2/2.

21. K. C. Hanson & Douglas E Oakman, 1998, 'Palestine in the Time of Jesus: Social Structures and Social Conflicts'. Fortress Press, Minneapolis, MN:.

22. Richard, A, Horsley, 2008, 'Jesus in Context: Power, People, and Performance'. Fortress Press, Minneapolis:.

23. https://www.themaparchive.com/pompeys-campaign-against-jerusalem-63-bce.html.

24. John Riches, 1990, 'The World of Jesus First-Century Judaism in Crisis' See Chap 1 – 'The Political, Economic, Social, and Cultural Context of First-Century Palestinian Judaism' https://www.cambridge.org/core/books/world-of-jesus/political-economic-social-and-cultural-context-of-firstcentury-palestinian-judaism/78E9FC5FF52226BA04868426D9EDF481.

25. Morten Hørning Jensen, 2012, 'Rural Galilee and Rapid Changes: An Investigation of the Socio-Economic Dynamics and Developments in Roman Galilee, Biblica, Vol. 93, No. 1.

26. John S Kloppenborg, 2000, 'Excavating Q. The history and setting of the sayings gospel,' Fortress Press, Minneapolis, MN.

27. David Mathis, 2016, https://www.desiringgod.org/articles/jesus-is-fully-human.

28. Jeffry Timmons, Murray Gillin, Sam Burshtein and Stephen Spinelli, 2011, 'New Venture Creation: Entrepreneurship for the 21st Century', (Regional Edition) McGraw Hill (Australia).

29. Lawrence Mykytiuk, 2015, 'Did Jesus Exist? Searching for Evidence Beyond the Bible'. Biblical Archaeology Review article, January/February 2015.

30. Bart D Ehrman, 2013, 'Did Jesus Exist?: The Historical Argument for Jesus of Nazareth', Harper Collins USA.

31. Bruce A Ware, 2013, The Man Christ Jesus; Theological Reflections on the Humanity of Christ, Crossway.

32. Dale Fletcher https://www.faithandhealthconnection.org/the_connection/spirit-soul-and-body/.

33. Gayle Weinraub, 2016, https://www.truity.com/blog/what-was-jesus%27-personality-type.

34. Carlyle Fielding Stewart, III, 2011 'Creative Problem Solving: A Jesus Perspective', A sermon, https://www.carlylestewart.com/creative-solving-problem-a-jesus-perspective/.

35. Scott Shane and Sankaran Venkataraman 2000, 'The Promise of Entrepreneurship as a Field of Research,' Academy of Management Review, 25(1): 217–226.

36. Mark Conner, 2016, 'The Theology of Creativity' https://churchleaders.com/children/childrens-ministry-articles/280445-theology-creativity-mark-conner.html.

37. Ray Bradley, Murray Gillin, Rollin McCraty and Mike Atkinson, 2011, 'Nonlocal Intuition in Entrepreneurs and Nonentrepreneurs: Results of Two Experiments Using Electrophysiological Measures', International Journal of Entrepreneurship and Small Business. vol 12 (3): 343-372.

38. Daniel A. Helminiak, 2015, Brain, Consciousness, and God: A Lonerganian Integration, State University of New York; Daniel A. Helminiak, 2014, More than awareness: Bernard Lonergan's multi-faceted account of consciousness. Journal of Theoretical and Philosophical Psychology 34(2):116–132.

39. Darius Foroux https://dariusforoux.com/core-values/.

40. Victor E Frenkel, 1962, Man's Search for Meaning - An Introduction to Logotherapy – From Death Camp to Existentialism. New York: Touchstone Book.

41. Rollin McCraty, Mike Atkinson and Ray Bradley, 2004, 'Electrophysiological Evidence of Intuition: Part 1. The Surprising Role of the Heart'. Journal of Alternative and Complementary Medicine, 10(1): 133–143.

42. Danah Zohar and Ian Marshall, 2004, Spiritual Capital, Bloomsbury Publishing, London.

43. Kelly Monroe Kullberg, 2009, 'Finding God Beyond Harvard: The Quest for Veritas' Inter Varsity Press, Illinois.

44. Dean A Shepherd, Holger Patzelt and J. Michael Haynie, 2010. 'Entrepreneurial spirals: deviation-amplifying loops of an entrepreneurial mindset.' Entrepreneurship Theory and Practice, 34(1): 59–82.

45. Susan Calloway Knowles, 2013 https://www.crosswalk.com/family/career/jesus-a-social-entrepreneur.html.

46. William Clarke, 2017, https://www.tempstarstaffing.com/2017/05/11/passion-key-success/.

47. James Austin, Howard Stevenson and Jane Wei-Skillern, 2006, 'Social and Commercial Entrepreneurship: Same, Different, or Both?' Entrepreneurship Theory and Practice, Vol.30 issue: 1, page(s): 1–22.

48. Murray Gillin and Stephen Spring, 2016, 'Entrepreneurship'. In 'Innovation and Entrepreneurship', (eds. D Samson and M Gloet), Oxford Press, Melbourne, pp 215–247.

49. Bart D Ehrman, 2013, 'Did Jesus Exist?: The Historical Argument for Jesus of Nazareth', Harper Collins USA.

50. John Piper, 2001, Quoting from Roman Emperor Julian in the 4th Century CE, https://www.goodreads.com/quotes/342592-the-roman-emperor-julian-writing-in-the-fourth-century-regretted.

51. Donald Kuratko and David Audretsch 2009, 'Strategic Entrepreneurship: Exploring Different Perspectives of an Emerging Concept', Entrepreneurship Theory and Practice, Vol 33, Issue 1.

52. Fred Hollows quoted in Gillin And Spring (2016) - (http://www.hollows.org.au/Fred-Hollows).

53. Brotherhood of St Laurence https://www.bsl.org.au/about/our-history/.

54. Jeffrey Timmons, Murray Gillin, Sam Burshtein and Stephen Spinelli. 2011 'New Venture Creation – Entrepreneurship for the 21st Century, McGraw-Hill, Australia (Pacific Edition) PP 240.

55. Gregory Dees, 1998, 'The Meaning of Social Entrepreneurship', Kauffman Foundation and Stanford University, Kansas City and Pao Alto.

56. Loris Gillin, 'Social Value Creation: Core Determinant from the Impact of Social Entrepreneurship', PhD Thesis, Swinburne University of Technology, 2005.

57. Jeffry Timmons 1998, 'America's entrepreneurial revolution', Franklin Olin Graduate School of Busines, Babson College MA.

58. Princes Trust, https://www.princes-trust.org.uk/about-the-trust/news-views, June 2020.

59. HRH Prince Charles, June 2020, https://princestrustinternational.org/about-us/.

60. The Telegraph- September 15, 2014.

61. Penny Junor, 1998, 'Charles Victim or Villain', (pp.54).

62. http://www.muhammadyunus.org.

63. Muhammad Yunis, 2017, 'A World of Three Zeroes - The New Economics of Zero Poverty, Zero Unemployment, and Zero Carbon Emissions.' Hachette Books NY.

64. Barbara C. Phillips, www.NPBusiness.ORG/florence/.

65. https://vauxhallhistory.org/florence-nightingale-times-obituary/.

66. Rosie Batty with Bryce Corbett, A Mother's Story, 2015 Harper Collins.

67. Loris Gillin, 2006, 'A Model for Social Value Creation Within Social Entrepreneurship Ventures: Governance and Stakeholder Factors', AGSE Entrepreneurship Research Exchange, Auckland. NZ.l.

68. Roberto Parente, Ayman El Tarabishy, Massimiliano Vesci, Antonio Botti, 2018, 'The Epistemology of Humane Entrepreneurship: Theory and Proposal for Future Research Agenda', Journal of Small Business Management, Vol. 56.

69. Covin, J. G., and D. P. Slevin (1991). 'A Conceptual Model of Entrepreneurship as Firm Behavior,' Entrepreneurship Theory and Practice 16(1), 7–25.

70. White book (2016). Humane Entrepreneurship. Available https://docs.wixstatic.com/ugd/cc1725_c642180108094a59b-1c53bb81a8b6d2b.pdf.

71. Roberto Parente, Ayman El Tarabishy, Antonio Botti, Massimiliano Vesci & Rosangela Feola (2020): https://doi.org/10.1080/00472778.2020.1717292.

72. Tom Lumpkin, Todd Moss, David Gras, Shoko Kato, and Alejandro Amezcua, (2013), 'Entrepreneurial processes in social contexts: how are they different, if at all?', Small Business Economics 40(3):1–23.

73. Lois Hazelton, 2012, 'Governance and Stewardship in the Aged Care Industry: Evaluating a model for Corporate Social Entrepreneurship - The relationship of Board culture To entrepreneurial behaviour' Thesis, University of Adelaide.

74. Robert Ipasso, 2002, The strategic intent of entrepreneurs within entrepreneurially led companies and the preconditions for their success or failure, Thesis, Swinburne University of Technology, Australia.

75. Duane Ireland, Michael Hitt and David Sirmon, 2003, 'A Model of Strategic Entrepreneurship: The Construct and Its Dimensions', Journal of Management 29(6).

76. Pidduck Robert, Clark Daniel and Lumpkin Tom, 2021 Entrepreneurial mindset: Dispositional beliefs, opportunity beliefs, and entrepreneurial behavior, Journal of Small Business Management, DOI: 10.1080/00472778.2021.1907582.

77. Murray Gillin, 2020, 'Facilitating intuitive decision-making and an entrepreneurial mindset in corporate culture – a case study' - (Chapter 17) 3rd Handbook of Intuition Research Ed. Marta Sinclair, Handbook of Intuition as Practice, Edward Elgar Publishing, Cheltenham.

78. Murray Gillin and Lois Hazelton, 2020, 'Bringing an entrepreneurial mindset to health care: a new tool for better outcomes,' Journal of Business Strategy, https://doi.org/10.1108/JBS-03-2020-0049.

79. Dean Shepherd, H Patzelt, & J.M. Haynie, 2010. 'Entrepreneurial spirals: Deviation-amplifying loops of an entrepreneurial mindset.' Entrepreneurship Theory and Practice, 34(1): 59–82.

80. Jonathon Haidt, 2013. 'The righteous mind.' New York: Vintage Books.

81. Laurence Gillin & Lois Hazelton, 2020, "Bringing an entrepreneurial mindset to health-care: a new tool for better outcomes", Journal of Business Strategy, Vol. ahead-of-print No. ahead-of-print. https://doi.org/10.1108/JBS-03-2020-0049.

82. Haidt, J. 2013. The righteous mind. New York: Vintage Books.

83. Dana Zohar and Ian Marshall, 2004, 'Spiritual Capital - Wealth We Can Live By.' Bloomsbury Publishing, UK.

84. Kelly Shaver Jan Wegelin and Immanuel Commarmond, 2019, 'Assessing Entrepreneurial Mindset: Results for a New Measure,' Discourse and Communication for Sustainable Education 10(2):13–21.

85. Hazelton Lois, 2012, Thesis – 'Governance and Stewardship in the Aged Care Industry: Evaluating a model for Corporate Social Entrepreneurship - The relationship of Board culture to entrepreneurial behaviour', University of Adelaide.

86. Victor Hugo, 1964, The Future of Man. From the series Great Ideas of Western Man.

87. Donald F. Kuratko and Richard M. Hodgetts, 2003 'Entrepreneurship: Theory, Process, Practice.' South-Western College Pub, USA.

88. William Drayton, 2002, 'The Citizen Sector: Becoming as Entrepreneurial and Competitive as Business,'California Management Review. 44:120–133.

89. Ken Dark, 2020, https://www.livescience.com/jesus-home-nazareth-discoveries.html.

90. Laurie Beth Jones, 2002, Jesus Entrepreneur, Using Ancient Wisdom to Launch and Live Your Dreams, Crown ce.

91. Flavius Josepheus, Early 2nd Century, The Life. Against Apion (Book 1:60), Harvard University Press, 1926.

92. Tirri, Nokelainen (2011). Measuring Multiple Intelligences and Moral Sensitivities in Education. Moral Development and Citizenship Education. Springer.

93. Linda S. Gottfredson, 1994, The Wall Street Journal copyright, Dow Jones & Company, Inc.

94. Laan, Ray Vander, 2006. In the Dust of the Rabbi Discovery Guide (That the World May Know) (pp. 25–26). Zondervan. Quoting Rabbi Judah ben Tema in (Ethics of the Fathers 5:21).

95. Carolyn McCann, et al 2020, Emotional Intelligence Predicts Academic Performance: A Meta-Analysis,Psychological Bulletin, 2020, Vol. 146, No. 2, 150–186.

96. Peter Salovey, Lohn Mayer, and David Caruso, (2004), "Emotional Intelligence: Theory, Findings, and Implications", Psychological Inquiry, pp. 197–215.

97. Roy, M. Oswald and Arland Jacobson. 2015. The Emotional Intelligence of Jesus. Rowman & Littlefield Publishers.

98. Goleman, D. (1995). Emotional intelligence: Why it can matter more than IQ. London, UK: Bloomsbury.

99. Daniel Goleman, 2005, Emotional Intelligence: Why It Can Matter More Than IQ, Bloomsbury, London.

100. Cindy Wigglesworth, 2012 'SI21: The Twenty-One Skills of Spiritual intelligence.' New York: Select Books.

101. Danah Zohar and Ian Marshall (2004), Spiritual Capital – Wealth We Can Live By. Bloomsbury Publishing, London.

102. Ray Bradley, Murray Gillin, Rolin McCraty, and Mike Atkinson, 2011, 'Nonlocal Intuition in Entrepreneurs and Nonentrepreneurs: Results of Two Experiments Using Electrophysiological Measures,' International Journal of Entrepreneurship and Small Business. vol 12 (3): 343-372et al., 2011).

103. Allinson, W.C., & J. Hayes.1996. The Cognitive Style Index: A measure of intuition-analysis for organizational research. Journal of Management Studies, 1: 119–135.

104. Haidt, J. 2013. The righteous mind. New York: Vintage Books.

105. Kreuger, N.F. Jr. 2007. What lies beneath? The experiential essence of entrepreneurial thinking. Entrepreneurship Theory and Practice, 31(1): 123–138.

106. Frank LaPira and Murray Gillin, 2006, 'Non-local Intuition and the Performance of Serial Entrepreneurs,' , Journal of International Entrepreneurship and Small Business, Vol 3 #1, pp 17–35.

107. L Murray Gillin, 2020, 'Facilitating Intuitive Decision-making and an Entrepreneurial Mindset in Corporate Culture - A Case Study.' (Chapter 17) 3rd Handbook of Intuition Research Ed. Marta Sinclair, Handbook of Intuition as Practice, Edward Elgar Publishing, Cheltenham, UK/ Northampton, MA, USA.

108. William Drayton, 2002, California Management Review. 44:120–133.

109. Jeffrey Timmons, Murray Gillin, Sam Burshtein and Stephen Spinelli. 2011 'New Venture Creation – Entrepreneurship for the 21st Century, McGraw-Hill, Australia (Pacific Edition).

110. Rollin McCraty, Mike Atkinson and Raymond Trevor Bradley, 2004, 'Electrophysiological Evidence of Intuition: Part 1. The Surprising Role of the Heart,' Journal of Alternative and Complementary Medicine 2004; 10(1): 133–143.

111. Petitmengin-Peugeot C. 1999 The intuitive experience. In: The view from within. First-person approaches to the study of consciousness. Varela FJ, Shear J, editors. Imprint Academic: London; 43–77.

112. Ed Michaels, Helen Handfield-Jones, and Beth Axelrod, 2001, Harvard Business Press, ISBN 978-1-57851-459-5.

113. Jeffrey Timmons, 2011, New Venture Creation.

114. Loris Gillin, 2006, Social Value Creation – as a Core Determinant from the Impact of Social Entrepreneurship, Thesis, Swinburne University of Technology.

115. Duane Ireland, Michael Hitt and David Sirmon, 2003, 'A Model of Strategic Entrepreneurship: The Construct and Its Dimensions,' Journal of Management 29(6).

116. Dean Shepherd, H Patzelt, & J.M. Haynie, 2010. 'Entrepreneurial spirals: Deviation-amplifying loops of an entrepreneurial mindset.' Entrepreneurship Theory and Practice, 34(1): 59–82.

117. Jeffrey Timmons, Murray Gillin, Sam Burshtein and Stephen Spinelli. 2011 'New Venture Creation – Entrepreneurship for the 21st Century, McGraw-Hill, Australia (Pacific Edition).

118. C. Gene Wilkes, 1998, 'Jesus on Leadership – timeless wisdom of servant leadership' LifeWay Press.

119. Phillip Kingston, 2016, '7 Ways to Lead Successful Entrepreneurial Teams' Entrepreneur – Asia Pacific, https://www.entrepreneur.com/article/279438.

120. Ethan Lin, 2016, 'The Importance Of Leadership In Today's World', www.leadershipgeeks.com.

121. Alan Grant, 1992, 'The Development of an entrepreneurial Leadership Paradigm for Enhancing Venture Capital Success,' – as adapted by Jeffrey Timmons, Murray Gillin et al, 2011, 'New Venture Creation'.

122. Frank LaPira and Murray Gillin, 2006, 'Non-local Intuition and the Performance of Serial Entrepreneurs', Journal of International Entrepreneurship and Small Business, Vol 3 #1, pp 17–35.

123. Bill and Melinda Gates Foundation, https://www.gatesfoundation.org/.

124. J Kirby, 2004, 'Richard Pratt: Business Secrets of the Billionaire Behind Australia's Richest Private Company' Wiley & Sons.

125. Australian Financial Review, 15 February 2000.

126. Thorsten Grahn, Blog, 'Jesus: The Role Model for Christian Leadership', http://christian-leadership.org/jesus-the-role-model-for-christian-leaders/.

127. General Georges Doriot's dictum – quoted in Jeffrey Timmons, Murray Gillin, Sam Burshtein and Stephen Spinelli. 2011 'New Venture Creation – Entrepreneurship for the 21st Century, McGraw-Hill, Australia (Pacific Edition.

128. Robert Hisrich, Michael Peters and Dean Shepherd, 2020, 'Entrepreneurship', McGraw Hill Education, New York.

129. https://www.gotquestions.org/70-or-72-disciples.html.

130. Robert R. McLaughlin, 'The Twelve Apostles', https://gbible.org/doctrines-post/the-12-apostles/.

131. Loris Gillin, 2006, 'Social Value Creation as a Core Determinant from the Impact of Social Entrepreneurship', Thesis, Swinburne University of Technology, Hawthorn, Australia.

132. Robert R. McLaughlin, 'The Twelve Apostles', https://gbible.org/doctrines-post/the-12-apostles/.

133. Ranjit A. Thuraisingham, 2019, 'Prayer and Entangled Quantum States' http://iscast.org/articles/Thuraisingham_Prayer_and_Entanglement_Opinion_Published_Jan_2019.pdf.

134. Ralph Wilson, 2020- http://www.jesuswalk.com/lessons/4_1-13.htm.

135. William Tiller, 2019, Quoted in Nisha Manek, Bridging Science and Spirit, pp.63.

136. Robert L. Dean, Jr, 2003, http://www.divineviewpoint.com/sane/dbm/setup/Genesis/Gen022.html.

137. Editorial staff, Christianity Today 2019, www.christianity.com/wiki/bible/image-of-god-meaning-imago-dei-in-the-bible.html.

138. Catechism of the Catholic Church, (1705) https://www.vatican.va/archive/ccc_css/archive/catechism/p3s1c1a1.htm.

139. John Main, 1987, The Inner Christ. (London: Darton, Longman & Todd, 1987), 15.).

140. Ray Bradley, Murray Gillin, Rolin McCraty, and Mike Atkinson, 2011, 'Nonlocal Intuition in Entrepreneurs and Nonentrepreneurs: Results of Two Experiments Using Electrophysiological Measures,' International Journal of Entrepreneurship and Small Business. vol 12 (3): 343–372et al., 2011).

141. William Tiller, William Dibble and Michael Kohane, 2001, 'Conscious Acts of Creation : The Emergence of a New Physics,' Pavior Publishing.

142. William Tiller, 2007, Psychoenergetic Science: A Second Copernican-Scale Revolution, Pavior Publishers, ISBN 978-1-4243-3863-4.

143. Kinney Douglas, 2014, Framework of Reality: Understanding Our Subtle Spiritual Nature, Mira Digital Publishing.

144. Collins Francis, 2006, The Language of God, Free Press, New York, NY.

145. Pepperell Robert, 2018, Consciousness as a Physical Process Caused by the Organization of Energy in the Brain, Fronter Psychology, 9: 2091.

146. Graziano Michael and Kastner Sabine, 2011, Human consciousness and its relationship to social neuroscience: A novel hypothesis, Cognitive Neuroscience, Jan 1; 2(2): 98–113.

147. Walach Harald, 2020, Inner Experience – Direct Access to Reality: A Complementarist Ontology and Dual Aspect Monism Support a Broader Epistemology, Frontier Psychology, 11: 640.

148. Ray Bradley, Murray Gillin, Rolin McCraty, and Mike Atkinson, 2011, 'Nonlocal Intuition in Entrepreneurs and Nonentrepreneurs: Results of Two Experiments Using Electrophysiological Measures,' International Journal of Entrepreneurship and Small Business. vol 12 (3): 343–372et al., 2011).

149. Hope Umansky, Academic Dean of the California Institute for Human Science.

150. Manek Nisha, 2019, Bridging Science and Spirit, Coscious Creation LLC, USA.

151. Van der Kolk Bessel, McFarlane Alexander and Weiseth, 1996, Traumatic Stress – The Effects of Overwhelming Experiences on Mind, Body and Society, The Guilford Press, New York. NY.

152. Gillin Murray and Gillin Loris, 2003, , Subtle Energies, Intentionality and the Healing of Traumatically Abused Persons September, International Conference on Trauma, Attachment and Dissociation, Melbourne, Australia.

153. Ray Bradley, Murray Gillin, Rollin McCraty, and Mike Atkinson, 2011, 'Nonlocal Intuition in Entrepreneurs and Nonentrepreneurs: Results of Two Experiments Using Electrophysiological Measures,' International Journal of Entrepreneurship and Small Business. vol 12 (3): 343–372.

154. Nisha Manek, 2019 'Bridging Science and Spirit' Conscious Creation LLC.

155. Robert Kanigel. 1991, 'The Man who Knew Infinity', illustrated. 438 pp. New York: Charles Scribner's Sons.

156. Tiller William, 1997, Science and Human Transformation: Subtle Energies, Intentionality, and Consciousness. Walnut Creek, CA, Pavior.

157. Bradley, R. T. (2007). The psychophysiology of intuition: A quantum-holographic theory of nonlocal communication. World Futures: The Journal of General Evolution, 63: 61–97.

158. William Tiller, 2009, 'It Is Time for a Consciousness-Inclusive Science' White Paper #4, The William A Tiller Foundation.

159. William Tiller, 2009, 'A Brief Introduction to Intention-Host Device Research', White Paper #1, The William A Tiller Foundation.

160. R. Gerber, 2001, Vibrational Medicine, Bear & Coy., Rochester, Vermont.

161. William Tiller, 1997, Science and Human Transformation, Pavior, California.

162. D. Chalmers, 1996, The Conscious Mind, Oxford University Press, New York.

163. T. W. Barrett, 1988, Comments in the Harmuth Ansatz, IEEE Transactions of Electromagnetic Capability, 30, 419.

164. D. Deutsch, 1997, The Fabric of Reality, Penguin Books, New York.

165. D. Bohm, 1980 Wholeness and the Implicate Order, Routledge & Kegan Paul. London.

166. William Tiller, W.E. Dibble and M. J. Kohane, 2001, Conscious Acts of Creation, Pavior, California.

167. William Tiller, 1999, 'Towards a Predictive Model of Subtle Domain Connections to the Physical Domain Aspect of Reality: The Origins of Wave-Particle Duality, Electric-Magnetic Monopoles and the Mirror Principle' Journal of Scientific Exploration, Vol 13 No 1, pp41–67.

168. Murray Gillin & Loris Gillin, 2003, 'Subtle Energies, Intentionality and the Healing of Traumatically Abused Persons,' International Conference on Trauma, Attachment and Dissociation. Melbourne, Australia.

169. R. C. Broderick, Catholic Encyclopedia (New York: Thomas Nelson Publishers, 1976), 485–487.

170. The quotes from the Bible were taken from the New American Standard Bible, Reference Edition (1973), Foundation Press, CA, USA.

171. A. Einstein, B. Podolsky, and N. Rosen, 'Can Quantum–Mechanical Description of Physical Reality Be Considered Complete? Phys. Rev. 47 (1935): 777.

172. E. Schrödinger, 'Discussion of Probability Relations Between Separated Systems.' Proceedings of the Cambridge Philosophical Society 31 (1935): 555–563.

173. 5 Bub, Jeffrey, 'Quantum Entanglement and Information,' The Stanford Encyclopedia of Philosophy (Spring 2017 Edition), Edward N. Zalta (ed.), https://plato.stanford.edu/archives/spr2017/entries/qt-entangle/.

174. Ranjit A. Thuraisingham, 2019, 'Prayer and Entangled Quantum States' http://iscast.org/articles/Thuraisingham_Prayer_and_Entanglement_Opinion_Published_Jan_2019.pdf.

175. Bradley, R. T. (2007). The psychophysiology of intuition: A quantum-holographic theory of nonlocal communication. World Futures: The Journal of General Evolution, 63: 61–97.

176. Gabor, D. (1946). Theory of communication, J. of Inst. Electrical Engineers, 93: 439–457.

177. Schempp, W. (1992). Quantum holography and neurocomputer architectures, J. of Mathematical Imaging and Vision, 2: 109–164.

178. Pribram, K. H. (1991). Brain and Perception: Holonomy and Structure in Figural Processing, Lawrence Erlbaum Associates, Hillsdale, NJ.

179. Bradley, R. T., & K. H. Pribram (1998). Communication and stability in social collectives, J. of Social and Evolutionary Systems, Vol. 21, 1: 29–81.

180. Bradley, R. T. (2006). The psychophysiology of entrepreneurial intuition: A quantum-holographic theory. 3rd AGSERE, UNITEC, Auckland, NZ.

181. Marcer, P., & W. Schempp (1998). The brain as a conscious system, Int. J. General Systems, 27: 231–248.

182. Raymond Bradley, Murray Gillin, Mike Atkinson, Frank LaPira, and Rollin McCraty, 'Intuitive perception: As measured on repeat entrepreneurs in the Cambridge

Technopol using electrophysiological instrumentation'; 2007, Frontiers of Entrepreneurship Research, Babson College, Boston.

183. William Tiller, 2009, 'A Brief Introduction to Intention-Host Device Research', White Paper #1, The William A Tiller Foundation.

184. William Tiller, 2009, 'A Brief Introduction to Intention-Host Device Research', White Paper #1, The William A Tiller Foundation.

185. Daniel A. Helminiak, 2014, More than awareness: Bernard Lonergan's multi-faceted account of consciousness. Journal of Theoretical and Philosophical Psychology 34(2):116–132.

186. Colin Humphreys, 2016, https://www.cis.org.uk/ireland/walton/documents/Colin-Humphreys-3-Nov-2016-slides.pdf.

187. Colin Humphreys, 2018, https://www.premierchristian-radio.com/Shows/Saturday/Unbelievable/Episodes/Unbelievable-Is-there-scientific-evidence-for-Old-Testament-miracles-Colin-Humphreys-Bob-Price.

188. Alexander Ivanov, 1824, http://nnm.ru/blogs/hhnu/ivanov_aleksandr_andreevich_1806_1858/, Public Domain, https://commons.wikimedia.org/w/index.php?curid=9086637.

189. Ranjit A. Thuraisingham, 2019, 'Prayer and Entangled Quantum States' http://iscast.org/articles/Thuraisingham_Prayer_and_Entanglement_Opinion_Published_Jan_2019.pdf.

190. Bradley, R. T. (2007). The psychophysiology of intuition: A quantum-holographic theory of nonlocal communication. World Futures: The Journal of General Evolution, 63: 61–97.

191. William Tiller, 2009, 'A Brief Introduction to Intention-Host Device Research', White Paper #1, The William A Tiller Foundation.

192. Bradley, R. T. (2006). The psychophysiology of entrepreneurial intuition: A quantum-holographic theory. 3rd AGSERE, UNITEC, Auckland, NZ.

193. Schempp, W. (1992). Quantum holography and neurocomputer architectures, J. of Mathematical Imaging and Vision, 2: 109–164.

194. Fernando Ortega-Ojeda, Matías Calcerrada, Alejandro Ferrero, Joaquín Campos, and Carmen Garcia-Ruiz1, 2018, https://www.ncbi.nlm.nih.gov/pmc/articles/PMC5948505/.

195. Kobayashi, M., Kikuchi, D., & Okamura, H. (2009). Imaging of Ultraweak Spontaneous Photon Emission from Human Body Displaying Diurnal Rhythm PLoS ONE, 4 (7) DOI: 10.1371/journal.pone.0006256.

196. Rachael Towne, 2020, 'What is Kirlian Photography? Aura Photography Revealed', https://www.lightstalking.com/what-is-kirlian-photography-the-science-and-the-myth-revealed/.

197. A Einstein, The World As I See It, translated from Mein Weldbilt by Alan Harris, Philosophical Library, 2011 (originally published 1934).

198. C. S. Lewis, 1970, 'God in the Dock', William B Eerdmans Publishing, Cambridge., UK.

199. Chris Kidd, 2015, 'The True Meaning of Turning Water into Wine', http://madeworthy.com/jesus-turns-water-into-wine/.

200. Robin Ngo, 2020, 'Where Did Jesus Turn Water into Wine?', https://www.biblicalarchaeology.org/daily/biblical-sites-places/biblical-archaeology-places/where-did-jesus-turn-water-into-wine/.

201. Edward W. Klink III, 2017, 'An Exegetical Reading of the Wedding at Cana (John 2:1-11)', https://zondervanacademic.com/blog/an-exegetical-reading-of-the-wedding-at-cana-john-21-11-an-excerpt-from-john.

202. Giotto di Bondone, 14th Century, Marriage at Cana - Wikipedia.

203. Graham Twelftree, 1999, 'Jesus the Miracle Worker' pp 196. Intervarsity Press, IL. USA.

204. Graham Twelftree, 2017, 'The Nature Miracles of Jesus', Cascade Books, Wipf and stock Publishers, Eugene, Oregon, USA.

205. William Tiller, Walter Dibble, and Michael Kohane, 2001, 'Conscious Acts of Creation: The Emergence of a New Physics', Pavior.

206. Nisha Manek, 2019, 'Bridging Science and Spirit' pp. 211 Conscious Creation LLC.

207. C. S. Lewis, 2001, 'Miracles' Zondervan.

208. Graham Twelftree, 2017, quoted in 'The Nature Miracles of Jesus' pp. 15, Cascade Books, Eugene, OR.

209. Graham Twelftree, 2017, quoted in 'The Nature Miracles of Jesus' pp. 20-21, Cascade Books, Eugene, OR.

210. Graham Twelftree, 2017, quoted in 'The Nature Miracles of Jesus' pp. 23, Cascade Books, Eugene, OR.

211. Graham Twelftree, 2017, quoted in 'The Nature Miracles of Jesus' pp. 25, Cascade Books, Eugene, OR.

212. Graham Twelftree, 2017, quoted in 'The Nature Miracles of Jesus' pp. 26, Cascade Books, Eugene, OR.

213. Albert Einstein, Quote, http://www.gurteen.com/gurteen/gurteen.nsf/id/X00405372/.

214. Richard Dawkins, 2011, 'The Magic of Reality: How We Know What's Really True', p.266, Simon and Schuster.

215. Colin Humphreys, 2003, 'The Miracles of the Exodus – A Scientists Discovery of the Extraordinary' Harper Collins, New York.

216. Anonymous, 'Christ walking on the Sea of Galilee'.

217. Vincent Taylor, 1981, 'The Gospel According to St Mark' pp 326, McMillan, UK.

218. Graham Twelftree, 1999, 'Jesus the Miracle Worker', pp 322, Intervarsity Press, London.

219. Saint Teresa, https://www.historydisclosure.com/teresa-de-avila-levitating-saint/.

220. Saint Joseph, http://www.religionfacts.com/library/catholic-encyclopedia/joseph-cupertino-saint.

221. Douglas D Home, https://www.liveabout.com/incredible-powers-of-daniel-dunglass-home-2596169.

222. https://subtle.energy/human-levitation-saints-yogis-citizens-and-science/.

223. James Conrad, 2016, The Ninel Kulagina Telekinesis Case: Rebuttals to Skeptical Arguments (jamesaconrad.com).

224. Scientist float levitation theory | University of St Andrews news (st-andrews.ac.uk).

225. https://phys.org/news/2017-04-harness-mysterious-casimir-tiny-devices.html.

226. https://www.wired.com/story/how-to-levitate-objects-with-sound/.

227. Michael Herzog, Leila Drissi-Daoudi, and Adrien Doerig, 2020: 'All in good time: long-lasting postdictive effects reveal discrete perception', Trends in Cognitive Sciences, https://doi.org/10.1016/j.tics.2020.07.001.

228. Harvey-Wilson Simon, 2003 Human Levitation, http://levitation.greyfalcon.us/levitation.htm.

229. Nisha Manek, 2019, 'Bridging Science and Spirit', pp 101, Conscious Creations LLC.

230. Dean Radin, 1997, 'The Conscious Universe: The Scientific Truth of Psychic Phenomena', pp 250, Harper One.

231. William Tiller, 2009, 'What does the Dirac Negative Energy Sea Mean and Why Has Todays Orthodox Physics Neglected it?', White Paper 6, Tiller Foundation.

232. Graham Twelftree, 2017, 'The Nature Miracles of Jesus' Cascade Books, Eugene OR, pp 57.

233. Paul King, 2001, 'Moving Mountains: Lessons in Bold Faith from Great Evangelical Leaders', Grand Rapids: Chosen. Pp 15–16, 20, 42.

234. Graham Twelftree, 1999, 'Jesus the Miracle Worker', pp. 71,Inter Varsity Press, Illinois.

235. James Tissot (1836-1902), 'Jesus tilling the Tempest'.

236. William Tiller, 2015, 'Bridging Science and Spirit', as quoted by N. Manek. Pp. 192.

237. Tiller William, 1997, Science and Human Transformation: Subtle Energies, Intentionality, and Consciousness, Walnut Creek, CA, Pavior.

Index